really small gardens

The Royal Horticultural Society

a practical guide to gardening in a truly small space

really small gardens

Jill Billington

Quadrille

First published in 1998 by Quadrille Publishing Limited
Alhambra House, 27–31 Charing Cross Road, London WC2H 0LS

Cataloguing-in-Publication Data: a catalogue record of this book is available from the British Library.

ISBN 1 902757 06 8
Printed by Star Standard Industries (Pte) Ltd, Singapore

contents

To my husband Bill, with much love and appreciation.

previous page **The terracotta head emerging from the green flowers and foliage of the pineapple lily (Eucomis bicolor) is an integral part of this plant group at the foot of a tree.**

left **Timber trellis echoing the wooden decking allows climbers to festoon the boundaries, creating a pleasingly intimate green enclosure.**

choice

In very small gardens everything counts. Meticulous planning is therefore essential, involving clear-sighted decisions about how you intend to use the garden and what you wish to have in it. The owners of large gardens often cannot resist acquiring too many plants and garden features and, in cramming them all in, they make places which lack balance and unity. The really small garden, on the other hand, lends itself to being planned as a simplified whole and becomes an intimate expression of the owner.

A tiny, internal patio is disturbed by neither wind nor weather, making the enclosed space still, tranquil, and contemplative.

Symmetry rules in this brick-paved garden, the planting retained within geometric beds edged by dwarf hedges of box.

Parallel lines of timber decking are juxtaposed with rounded pebbles to create textures that enhance the diminutive courtyard all year.

In a tiny city garden the essential storage shed has been made into an attractive feature with a coat of glossy cream paint.

Green textures fill the space while false perspectives, created through the skillful use of trellis, suggest there is more to see beyond.

The usable area of this small garden has been extended by reaching up toward the light, to create a multilevel space for children. The water feature of rippling steel rivets our attention.

thinking small

Planning your small space is all about making fundamental choices and deciding what you will have to sacrifice to achieve your aims. Having to make choices leads to decisiveness: functions have to be ruthlessly selected and you must get rid of any superfluous objects, features, or plants, otherwise you will find that the site becomes depressingly overcrowded and confused.

Which is more important to you—*al fresco* living or an intense love of plants? Many people today want to use their gardens as an extension of indoor living, yet the great pleasure of dining outdoors requires space—which cuts down planting opportunities. If you are passionate about plants, you may wish to plan your garden so that it is possible to have a short stroll around it, with different planting groups to see along the way. Must you have a lawn? Grass is soft and welcoming, but needs looking after and will not do well in small dark yards; you may simply have no space to store a lawn mower.

Some practical needs have to be balanced with the other requirements for your tiny space, depending on your lifestyle and interests. If you have a great love of plants, how important to you is a paved area? Must you have a shed or can you dispense with storage in favor of a tiny lean-to greenhouse or a cold frame? If indoor storage is available for garden tools, this will leave space outdoors for more pleasurable items. Do you really need a barbecue if the garden leads off the kitchen? Make all such decisions at the very start of the planning stage.

coming to terms with scale
Scale must be the first concern of the small-garden owner. This is the relationship between ourselves and the space in

which we move. In the limitless horizons of prairie or desert, with large skies overhead, it is we who are small and vulnerable. As the landscape becomes confined by hills or woodland, we relate more comfortably to the altered scale. Within very small, intimate units we assume large proportions, like Alice when she accepted the instruction "Drink me" and grew to ceiling height.

more influential than anything else. But the challenge is to turn constraints into creative assets. Light levels, climate, soil, and boundaries are fixed conditions (see Down to Earth, page 54): you may work with them or around them, but you cannot change them. In resolving the problems they create, however, you may well hit upon solutions that are ingenious and original, even if elegant proportion sometimes has to be sacrificed for convenience. Certain problems are common to

So just how small is your space? Is it as big as 20 feet (6 meters) square or not much wider than a passage, about 5 feet (1.5 meters) deep? The scale of the first allows for people to eat outdoors, whereas the scale of the latter is so intimate that the garden becomes a virtual stage set, best suited to being viewed from a

above left *Also intended for outdoor living, the simple concrete bench seat behind a granite refectory table doubles as a raised bed for plants.*
above right *Carefully selected, comfortable furniture takes little space, but the inclusion of the huge clay pot is a bold decision.*

right *Although it is as narrow as a passage, this garden is conceived as a space for plants. The timber path, fringed with irises, gently climbs toward an implied, hidden distance.*

window. To enjoy any small space to the full, you need to make the reduced scale work for you. This does not mean that everything in the garden has to be miniature: a tiny space, crammed with bijou furniture, Lilliputian pots, and dwarf plants is uncomfortable. People using the garden should be at ease, whether moving or resting, and, even if the small space is intended to be viewed rather than entered, it should not be necessary to use a magnifying glass to appreciate the planting. Some well-chosen, larger plant forms will balance smaller ones and, at the same time, bring us into the picture.

advantages and constraints

Apart from the dimensions themselves, certain other features of the small plot will be immutable, so these may become the majority of small plots. Since many really small gardens are in cities, bounded by high walls or sunk among surrounding tall buildings, they are overlooked and have problems of shade cast by either buildings, boundary walls, or neighboring trees. But there are ways of screening your garden and, by planting suitably shade-tolerant plants, of making it look verdant and attractive. Advice on suitable plants is given in the following chapter (see page 27).

Access is another potential problem in small city gardens. If there is no side passage, all the hard materials, compost, and plants will have to be carried through the house; if the plot is attached to a basement floor, there may be the extra hazard of carpeted stairs. Provided you take this into consideration early on, solutions can be found, even if it means taking some specimens through a window or, *in extremis* and if cost is no object, the use of a crane to hoist a mature tree over row houses, as happened in one urban garden I designed. Remember that a reverse journey may also be necessary for plant waste: if you choose not to reserve some of your precious space for a compost heap, prunings, grass clippings, weeds, and dead leaves will have to be bagged up and taken through the house. It pays to be tidy in a small garden and to remove waste promptly, as you go along.

left Creamy limestone suits this elegant, sunny courtyard where warm sunlight is reflected from the walls. Caught in the light, a classical sculpture suits the mood, as well as balancing the detail of the steps. The only other decoration is green foliage.

far left The decking garden seen on the previous page is reached by steep steps from a deep and narrow basement. The tiny space is well used, providing a sitting area, a closet, even a drying rack. White paints reflect light.

dealing with shade

The first impressions of a small garden can be of a dark, gloomy site, but no space is beyond improvement, so enjoy the challenge to your imagination. Nature provides vegetation for all situations, except dry, sterile sand, and plenty of attractive plants thrive in dark areas. Even a dark "well" can be transformed by using pale colors, luminous in darkness, such as white-flowered honesty (*Lunaria annua* "Variegata") or the white-variegated form of the evergreen euonymus (*E. fortunei* "Silver Queen"). Have fun with trickery and mirror effects, to bring illusions and light down into the garden (see Trickery, page 80).

Open to the sky, this beautiful roof garden is exposed to all weathers and to blazing sunlight. It has been enclosed by a protective boundary of slatted trellis which filters both wind and heat on all sides, as well as overhead.

exposed gardens

Being exposed to relentless sun and heat can be just as damaging to plants as wind or frost. If you garden in a hot climate, where an enclosed courtyard concentrates reflected heat, you will need to choose plants which are adapted for these conditions. Small slim leaves covered with fine hairs, like those of many artemisias, will not lose moisture through evaporation so choose plants like these, as well as lavenders, santolinas and *Cistus* "Silver Pink."

Roof gardens present a different set of problems. Nearly always small, they have to contend with exposure to wind as well as to sun. Wind is not only physically destructive but also dries out soil extremely fast in a process known as desiccation. Since the beds on roof gardens are usually raised, the soil is already less deep than in ground-level beds and a system of drip irrigation may be essential. Some form of boundary will be necessary for protection from wind, as well as for safety; tall buildings tend to funnel the wind so it has even greater force at rooftop level. Solid boundaries like walls may simply create eddies but a semipermeable form of screening, such as pierced walls or panels of trellis, slatted timber, bamboo or wattle fencing, would be more effective, filtering the wind and reducing its force. Hold the panels in place with strong supports of timber or scaffolding. Heat too is more concentrated higher up, so a light canopy of slatted

Privacy has been achieved in a small roof garden surrounded by housing, yet light pours through the opaque rigid plastic boundary panels. Overhead, screening creates dappled shade, making the area attractive for both plants and people.

timber may be needed to give shade and protect those plants which will bleach out in strong sunlight. Select plants, such as sea buckthorn and pyracantha, to cope with the extremes which occur on rooftops. Despite all their drawbacks, there are some wonderful small gardens in the sky.

creating privacy

In contemporary living, privacy is a quality that is highly prized. In a tiny, enclosed city yard you may well feel exposed to all—but solutions can be found. If you are overlooked from above, erect slim wires above head height to support climbers like wisteria or vines, which are not so heavily foliaged that they will block light: lightly foliaged plants screen effectively the same way that net curtains do, allowing one-way vision. Alternatively, if you have room for it, a small tree like *Betula pendula* "Tristis", which will filter light without creating dense shade, could be used to provide a canopy that gives privacy. This way you can ignore the world beyond and enjoy the benefits of your inward-looking space.

the positive aspects

There are some real advantages in owning a small garden. For a start, it is much cheaper to run. Cost is a factor not often referred to in garden books but, when you are faced with buying plants and maintaining a garden, expenses escalate very fast. Having a really small garden means that you can contemplate using more expensive paving materials, like real flagstones rather than simulated concrete pavers, or making solid boundaries from the best materials, such as a robust, carpenter-crafted fence. You can also buy a few more costly mature plant specimens to start the garden off.

In small, enclosed plots, boundary walls and fences protect the garden from wind and foster a microclimate several degrees warmer than the surrounding locality. This would enable you to grow wall shrubs and climbers which benefit from such protection. In full sun try bignonia (*Campsis radicans*) or the fragrant, slightly tender *Trachelospermum jasminoides* "Madison;" on a wall in part-shade you might grow an abelia. You could even try some exotic, albeit usually more expensive, subjects (see page 50).

Small spaces can also offer real benefits in terms of their care: they are easily managed by people with very full lives. Hours of turning the soil in the fall are reduced to possibly one. Pruning and heavy, back-aching jobs like dividing plants can be accomplished quickly and deadheading will take only a matter of minutes each day to keep your plants looking their best. Since the workload will not be onerous, you will have more time to stand and stare, and to enjoy your garden, which the managers of large gardens rarely do.

planning your small space

In assessing what you have, you must decide what can be discarded and what is an asset. Since everything counts in the small space, anything which does not fulfill its purpose, whether functional or aesthetic, should be discarded—and this may mean removing some much-loved baggage. But do not be too hasty about getting rid of what could turn out to be an asset. If your first visit to the site is in winter, when most gardens look their worst, be especially careful: you may not appreciate the value of dormant plants. By spring, your site may benefit from the green overflow of neighboring gardens or you may find some good, established plants which add maturity.

what is already there?
What have you inherited? Exactly how small is your space and how many square feet of floor do you have? Is it big enough to

accommodate a small seat or allow for an extending deck chair? Could you fit in a small fold-up table? Is it shady, exposed, or overlooked? Write lists of pros and cons: you may be surprised to find the first list longer than the second.

Do not remove any existing plants before you have assessed their worth: some, like the slow-growing Japanese acer (palmatum), may have taken years to become a tree. On the other hand, you should think twice about keeping dwarf conifers which are no longer miniature or a youthful magnolia which will eventually dominate not only your space but the neighboring yards too, reducing the light on both sides of the fence. Magnolias usually flower only once, as well as limiting the planting prospects beneath them, and they do not take kindly to being hacked. Since every feature and plant needs to earn its space, large plants should be kept only if they are easy to control by pruning or other means.

Check the orientation of the site to see where the sunny side is. Warm, protected walls provide a sheltered place to sit as well as an opportunity to grow fragrant climbers: scent is all the more concentrated in a small space. Is the garden surrounded by tall buildings which exclude light? If so, make your planned features particularly eye-catching so that the garden becomes entirely inward-looking. Sculpture or dramatic planting will provide an internal focal point, distracting the eye from the boundaries and beyond.

If close inspection of a neighboring property reveals back walls covered with drainpipes, windowless tall edifices, or an unrelieved factory wall, you can erect screening above the existing wall height, such as timber trellis festooned with magnificent climbers like wisteria or *Actinidia kolomikta*; these will come to dominate the view, replacing the ugly surroundings. Looking around beyond the small plot, you may find exciting views. There might be an elegant church spire or, in a city apartment, you may catch a glimpse of the Empire State Building or some other spectacular manmade structure. Perhaps you overlook a river. If such attractions are part of the view they may be "borrowed" and incorporated into the garden. Plants can be chosen to frame the view or the view could become the focus of the whole garden, no other distracting features being allowed.

If your yard is so small that you can barely move within it, think of the garden as a living, framed picture and design it with the house windows in mind. Create a dominant focus which is attractive in all seasons, perhaps a large urn or pot, and restrict the planting to a minimum, possibly a specimen ornamental grass like purple maiden grass (*Miscanthus sinensis* var. *purpurascens*) with a trailing small-leaved ivy, such as *Hedera helix* "Sagittifolia Variegata", at its foot.

what would you like to see there?

Having objectively assessed the existing space, you can realistically tackle your ambitions for it. You will be deciding on the overall style of the garden as well as how you intend to use it and, even if your priorities have to be made on practical grounds, this does not exclude the possibility of the garden having an atmosphere all its own. What style of garden do you dream of? We all have a vision of how we would like to see our own space and these ideas differ widely—which is what makes each garden personal. To some a scramble of plants clinging to one another in sweetly scented disarray is pure sensual heaven. To others, of the view that plants should have their required space to display themselves at their best, this would be merely a mess. Formal order can be elegantly seductive in a small space, so you may choose the simple art of symmetry, using axes to lead the eye in lines toward focal points. Or you may reduce these ideas to minimalism, in which the essence of a plant's structure with a contrasting single rock can express the exquisite harmony inspired by classical Japanese courtyards. Think your scheme through before committing plants to the soil. If you feel unsure about what style to choose, let the photographs in this and later chapters inspire you.

Family life obviously makes more demands on a small plot than that of a single person: multi-use means a hard-working site which probably has to allow for some storage

opposite **Concentric circles of granite setts, echoed by a round table and seats, make a feature of this well-established apple tree. The terrace overlooks the city.**

left above **On a small rooftop the view of a church spire is "borrowed" to become the focus of the garden. Trees frame the view to either side, while green boundaries are maintained at a lower level too.**

left below **Even very small city gardens can provide vertical play space for children, leaving room to accommodate an area of lawn for family use.**

below **An informal family garden with rough-cut grass is divided by open, but sturdy trellis that also screens the children's "den." Framed glimpses, echoed by reflections in old mirrors, show collections of personal ephemera.**

space. For some people, being able to dine outdoors will be an absolute must in summer, while all that others require is the space to savor a glass of wine beneath an arbor. Even if you do not have space for a table, try to make room for at least one chair; you may be able to create a postage-stamp-sized paved area for such a purpose. And in summer you will be eternally thankful that you did: sitting out is simply not the same as sitting in.

On the other hand, even the owner of a small courtyard may be a serious plantperson, in which case the only paving required will be for dry-footed access to the plants. If you are passionate about plants, a variety of growing conditions will extend the range you can grow. Even if the land is flat, many small gardens are roomy enough to contemplate a change of level in order to create exciting effects, as well as to increase the growing space. A tiered system of raised beds allows some plants to scramble upward toward the light and others to trail over the retaining walls which, if they are made of timber or brick, will double as seating. Containers further extend the range of plants you can grow by enabling you to provide different soil conditions for them so that, for example, acid-loving plants like small azaleas may be grown even in areas of alkaline soil.

In spite of the small scale of this site, the selected plants and materials are not miniaturized. Substantial rounded boulders, timber, and dressed stone create an imaginative hard surface. Bold choice of plants includes a larch and a large phormium. The larch is container-grown, restricting its roots and curbing its growth.

choosing materials

It is crucial not to pander to the small scale of your garden in terms of miniaturization, which only draws attention to the compactness of the space. It is equally important to avoid a cluttered look, which can arise from using too many different materials. On the other hand, do not rule out juxtaposing two materials just because the yard is small. Stepping from a timber deck to a brick path works well, and setting flagstones in gravel is pleasing both to use and to look at. But if you have a contrast in texture, be sure that you do not contrast the colors as well: too many changes will make the space look fussy and restive.

the floor

There are many arguments against the use of lawns in small spaces. Grass does not support furniture; it needs cutting—and where will you keep the lawn mower? But if you really

"Crazy" paving can be stylishly handled to create a pleasing surface. As its successful use in this formal, small garden shows, it is important to pay as much attention to the jointing pattern as to the size and placement of the slabs themselves.

want the softness of grass and the sensual pleasure of feeling it underfoot and you are prepared to keep a lawn mower somewhere, do not give up: you certainly cannot lie on gravel. Your "lawn" does not have to be as smooth as a billiard table so choose the right seed for wear and tear, or even for shade, and you will succeed.

If you are prepared to forgo a lawn, or wish to create a courtyard style, you could pave your garden with either large or small paving slabs. It is important that all hard surfaces are laid correctly on a rolled-hardcore base. A few very large natural flagstones, laid in a random, non-grid fashion, would be stylishly effective in a small space, whereas smaller slabs of different sizes (available in both real and quality-simulated stone) would look fussy laid in a random style, even where the floor area is tiny: the result would be to reduce the apparent area. However, if identically sized small slabs were laid in a geometric grid, this would create an all-over pattern which carpets the ground in a unifying manner. The pattern does not then diminish the space because it is the whole area, not the individual units, which becomes significant.

Brick or concrete paths, tiles and granite setts, which are all usually standard sizes, can also be used to create unifying bonds or patterns. The basketweave or "chevron" pattern (where bricks are laid at 45 degrees to each other) is traditionally rural in feel. A running bond of bricks indicates direction and is therefore well suited to paths. Think twice before using natural materials, such as bricks or stone, in damp shade, as they attract slippery algae and moss, making constant cleaning necessary. "Crazy paving" also creates patterns. Do not ignore this economic material: in the hands of Japanese experts, randomly shaped stone can be very beautiful in their tiny courtyards, so why not in yours too?

Concrete is a wrongly maligned material, which is both economic and convenient. Concrete paving can be made on site so that only the dry materials, in bags, need be brought through the house. This durable and fluid medium can be poured to fill exactly the shape and space you require. Its surface texture may be enhanced by incorporating small stones or grit, described as "aggregate"; coarse textures are less slippery than smooth ones in wet weather. Some people have fun setting in personal mementos, such as broken china, children's marbles, foot and even paw prints; such detail can be attractive and amusing in small spaces. Concrete can also be laid with a ridged or grooved texture, made when wet, which is advisable for a shady garden prone to damp weather. If the climate is dry, the concrete can be laid smoothly and either sealed with a proprietary sealer or painted with bright colors.

Pebbles may be either set in cement or laid loosely on gravel; they look attractive in association with alpine shrubs, Japanese acers, or small pines like *Pinus mugo*. Although you cannot walk upon them with any comfort, rocks provide interest and are a real asset in an inward-looking, tiny space. A few rocks used with pebbles and gravel can be associated with one or two small shrubs to create year-round effect,

particularly suitable for a small courtyard or a little garden that is mostly viewed from a window.

Gravel, on the other hand, is well suited for walking upon. There are different types of gravel, from coarse grit to rounded, rolling pea shingle. Choose those which relate to local building materials or the house masonry. White is very glaring and chippings of quartz resemble gardens of rest, so look for granite, sandstone, limestone, dolomite, porphyry, and slate gravels. All offer color and texture choices: warm pinky-brown, ambers and mixed browns with grays are subtle foils for plants. Large-scale gravel is unattractive in association with delicately structured plants, as well as being unpleasant to walk on, as we have experienced on a beach.

One advantage of gravel for small spaces is that it may also act as a mulch, flowing over the whole courtyard so that the walking area is indistinct from the planted area. If you put a layer of ground cover matting beneath the walking area, it

below **Sandstone and old stock bricks, both originally honey-colored, have weathered together. Since sandstone can be very slippery when wet, choose slabs with a riven surface and keep brickwork clear of moss.**

left **Mixed materials work well together in a small space where one dominates, as here. The parallel flagstones are laid as "rafts" in a sea of pebbles.**

Decking lends itself to geometric designs. Level changes are easily made and can provide built-in seating. Separate areas may be identified by laying the deck in different directions. The addition of a traditional "deck" chair suits the sophisticated style of this modern garden.

for some of the year. However, timber dries quickly, which makes it a good choice if your small yard serves as living space. Always use pressure-treated timber and decide whether you prefer a weathered finish or a stained surface. Ready-made decking modules are available, but these tend to create a "paved" look, which spoils the visual potential of continuous linear patterns.

If there is room for a small path from the access door of the house, use the same paving material as that chosen for the garden to avoid a cluttered look. Bear in mind that a path less than 3 feet (90cm) wide will not allow for plants to spill over, but in a tiny space you may need a width of only 2 feet 6 inches (75cm) to step into the garden and tend the plants.

will prevent the growth of plants there, but elsewhere plants will thrive under the protection of a layer of gravel. First remove perennial weeds from the soil, then spread a gravel layer of approximately 2 inches (5 cm), which will suppress annual weeds and conserve moisture. If you wish to let plants like valerian self-seed informally, leave out the ground cover matting and allow creative weeding to come into play.

Timber decking suits small spaces, especially roof gardens where weight is a factor. It is best built on cross-beams which are supported by solid posts, 4 inches by 4 inches (100mm by 100mm). Cover the soil below these beams with either a 3-inch (8-cm) layer of stone chippings or heavy-duty plastic sheet covered with sand, to prevent weed growth beneath. Plants can lap over onto the slats at the edges, and gaps can be made in the timbers above planting pockets to allow stemmed shrubs or very small trees to grow through.

Timber decks are best suited to warm, sunny sites where they may be enhanced in association with gray-foliaged small shrubs. Timber is unsuitable for dark areas of high rainfall, frost, or snow, when it would become dank and unappealing

the walls

Boundaries can be evident to the point of being oppressive in very small gardens. But they may be clad with climbing plants or the boundary itself can become a design feature, attractive in its own right. Brick or dry stone walling may be the vernacular style, and if the brick is old and mellow in coloring or the stone wall blends with the stone of the house, you are fortunate indeed. Cheap, new brick, often a harsh red in color, makes an unflattering backing for plants. It is rarely a good idea to paint a brick wall, even if you feel that this will bring light into the courtyard, because climbers or shrubs will have to be pulled away from the wall for repainting every three or four years, when the paint becomes dirty and covered with green algae. Outdoors, most paints eventually peel off anyway, so the continual repainting means that your garden will never attain the desirable mature look. It is far better to let brick or stone mature into natural hues that blend into the background, allowing the plants to reveal themselves at their best. If you inherit an ugly wall, robust wooden trellis will camouflage it very effectively and the growing plants will do the rest.

Timber fencing takes little planting space from the garden and creates an instant effect. An open-slatted fence also reduces the strength of the wind, allowing it to filter through, whereas a solid fence does not effectively block the wind, but instead creates turbulence inside the boundary. Wind is the leading enemy of gardeners, since it browns foliage or kills whole plants. A sturdy fence made of vertical planks, which are staggered and overlapping on either side of the bearing rails, allows air to flow through while giving complete privacy, rather like the two-way value of louvers. On roof gardens, where privacy is less of an issue, a lighter structure of latticed wood screening is effective. Use pressure-treated softwood or hardwood from a renewable source.

casual rustic effect, choose wattle or half-round poles laid diagonally. Knotted split bamboo canes or supported mats of woven reeds provide additional texture and have a slightly oriental feel, albeit they are short-lived.

The effect of boundaries becomes less oppressive once light and views are allowed through; picket fences do this effectively in rural gardens although in cities you may not want the exposure. On roof gardens, fully transparent panels of reinforced glass or rigid plastic sheet, fixed to secure posts, will allow views but reduce wind; these could be textured or opaque, letting in light but providing seclusion. Iron railings are a traditional and ornamental way of providing a

below and below left **These pictures illustrate the diversity of trellis. Three different decorative effects are shown: a transparent, close-meshed, open grid (below left) to raise the height of the wall; slimline, vertical screening for privacy, emphasized by the perpendicular grooves in the posts (below); and solidly made, diamond-pattern trellis battened to the wall to give it an all-over textural embellishment.**

Softwood can be sealed, emphasizing the natural color of the wood, or stained to bring out the grain of the timber. The tones which blend best with plant coloring are soft greeny-blues or gray-browns. Unless your budget is very restricted, do not choose ready-made, woven wooden fence panels as they are flimsy, often garishly stained orange-brown, and the cheaper ones can warp to the point where they are no longer held in place and fall upon plants. For a

boundary definition at ground level, or a safe edging to a balcony, but they provide little privacy or security.

The best way to reduce the impact of dominant boundaries that are very close to the house is to clothe them with plants. Living boundaries are best for noise baffle, but you should bear in mind that hedging takes a lot from the soil—nutrients as well as water—making underplanting difficult. Hedges

Hedges are living boundaries which may be tightly clipped for architectural effect. Other features of this elegant, square enclosure include a central square pool, fringed with Pachysandra terminalis, and an unexpected corner-sited "grotto" containing a small figurative sculpture.

also take up at least 2 feet (60cm) in depth, so they are not ideal for a small courtyard. To cover a wall or fence, choose climbers like clematis to save planting space or plant a wall shrub such as pyracantha that can be clipped flat to the wall, taking up only about 9 inches (23cm) of depth. If you have more space than this, you can consider bulkier climbers, such as jasmine or the shrub escallonia. Once you regard every boundary as a surface to drape with evergreen or flower-covered plants, you will realize that vertical gardening is a significant element of very small, enclosed spaces.

choosing plants

In its protected environment, a magnificent variegated Cordyline australis "Albertii" *thrives in an enclosed small garden where the emphasis is on foliage plants.*

In small gardens, where there is room to grow only a few plants, your selection should be meticulous. You must be confident that the plants you select are both reliable and appropriate for their environment, as well as giving good value in terms of their sustained interest.

The first criterion for your choice of plants has to be that, horticulturally, they suit the conditions of the site, since you cannot change these. This means, in the first place, finding out what type of soil you have, acid or alkaline, whether it is dry or moist, and what condition it is in. Tiny gardens supporting many plants make great demands on the soil, so it is always worth adding plenty of well-rotted, organic

compost or manure to improve its structure and enrich its quality (see page 57). The hardiness of plants is another vital consideration, and you should look at this in the context of your small garden. Small city gardens, which are often enclosed, tend to be significantly milder than rural gardens, allowing you to include less hardy subjects.

Secondly, you must assess how well each plant fills the bill, in terms of your plans for the garden and its structure. It is obviously important to choose plants that do not become too large. The framework of a garden is usually made by shrubs and, in tiny sites, these must be amenable to pruning so that they may be flattened against a wall or maintained as freestanding specimens; they should always include some evergreens. The framework really counts in winter, when permanent greenness or beautiful habit sustains the scene.

The third criterion is that each plant must justify its inclusion in terms of its performance. Since the whole of the small garden is on show all year round, there is no point giving room to a shrub that flowers for two weeks, then looks boring for the rest of the year. The mainstay will generally be plants with good foliage because even deciduous leaves offer long-lasting and varied effects: look, if possible, for

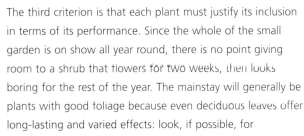

attractive, year-round foliage or for more than one season of interest, such as spring blossom and glowing fall leaf color. The next priority is a long flowering period or repeat-flowering, as with some roses and clematis. Bearing in mind the value of seasonal change, make sure you include plants for every season. After a crisp winter, spring bulbs hold the stage early in the year, gracefully retiring behind the wings to make way for brilliant summer color without leaving ugly gaps. From late summer, the shape and fall color of plants like Japanese acers assume prominence, to be replaced by the elegant, skeletal winter structure of perennials like *Sedum spectabile* and some ornamental grasses.

Choosing from the superabundance of plants now available is a challenge in itself, so it is important to be clear what your aims are. Visits to the garden center or nursery are always tempting, but in a small plot you will have to forgo self-indulgence in favor of a thoughtful selection. In terms of the style of garden you want, your first thoughts about

plants will be a good guide, so note them down, but better the well-judged few than a confused excess. In small spaces, quality is far more relevant than quantity, and happily settled plants will flourish and fulfill the role you planned for them.

do they suit the conditions?

In making your choices, ask yourself pertinent questions about each plant's horticultural needs. You will glean a wealth of information from the plant Directory in this book (see page 130), as well as in garden reference books about a plant's height and spread, its habit, and its preferences for

soil and for sun or shade, and must use this when deciding on its suitability for your small space. Height and spread are usually given after five years in the case of perennials and shrubs, ten years in the case of trees. Buy your plants from a reliable nursery, which will advise you on a plant's ultimate size, as well as its speed of growth. Like all living things, plants grow irregularly and it is not possible to be exact, but you need to have a rough idea of how much space your plants will fill and how long this will take.

Armed with this information, resist the temptation to plant too close together. When planning your planting, work to a scaled drawing where plants are centered a measured distance apart. Allow them enough space to develop to their full diameter and, for the first year or two, fill in any gaps with summer bedding or annual seeds.

In the natural world, plants rarely occur singly. They nearly always grow in a mass, having spread by seed, runner, or underground roots. This "natural" look can be a valuable guide when designing with bulbs and perennial plants, even in very small spaces. Groups of odd numbers please the eye because they look more naturalistic, so plant in groups of three or five, depending on their ultimate size and on how significant the plant is in the overall planting scheme. Sometimes a singleton can be very effective, however, leading the eye across a space. For example, a group of three small blue phlox (P. divaricata subsp. laphamii "Chattahoochee") beside paving may be subtly echoed by placing a single one further along, among other edging plants. This happens in nature, when a seed gets dispersed a little further from the parent, and can look charming.

do you have room for them?
Every plant has its own natural spread and not all take happily to being confined; it is therefore essential to avoid

left *Leafy canopies offer an oasis of cool shade in sunny climes. Beneath this one, clipped spheres of box contrast with the tender, glossy-leaved holly fern (Cyrtomium falcatum), below which grow evergreen winter-flowering* Sarcococca confusa *and grassy lilyturf (*Liriope spicata*).*

overcrowding. Be careful of plants which appear to be low-growing, but which extend widthwise, like witchhazel (*Hamamelis*). If the growth habit of a plant is spoiled by pruning, it is not for you. Even some large shrubs, like the

twiggy bush 4 feet by 6 feet (1.2 meters by 2 meters), covered in mauve flowers in spring, while the taller and narrower *S. puberscens* subsp.*microphylla* "Superba" blooms later in spring, as well as repeat-flowering in late summer.

right **Very narrow sites present a great opportunity for growing upward. Here, climbing roses and jasmine festoon the walls and below them are shade-tolerant plants, including hydrangeas, box, hostas, and small rhododendrons.**

far right **This group of shade-loving evergreens will need to be kept to manageable proportions by pruning. Mahonia, variegated Portuguese laurel, aucuba, and elaeagnus are massed closely with the large-leaved loquat (Eriobotrya japonica).**

floriferous buddlejas, which benefit from being cut back severely, will still manage to grow tall again by summer, which rules them out in diminutive spaces. So look out for smaller versions of the plants you admire, like *Buddleja davidii* "Nanho Blue," which is at most 5 feet (1.5 meters) tall and wide. There are also some small, but very fragrant lilacs: **Syringa meyeri** var. *spontanea* "Palibin" is a rounded,

Very small spaces generally mean very small shrubs. If you have acid soil, these must include azaleas and dwarf rhododendrons (see Down to Earth, page 56, for more information on these). Otherwise, there are many other dwarf shrubs that are valued for their flowers, foliage, and scents. Daphnes are both fragrant and compact. The deciduous *D. mezereum* has welcome, pink-purple, strongly

scented flowers in late winter. The much smaller, evergreen *D. sericea* Collina Group likes peaty soil and is fragrantly flowered in late spring. By summer the choice of small flowering shrubs increases to include potentillas, santolinas, helianthemums, cistus, hebes, rosemary, rue, and lavender.

Cotoneasters come in small forms like the mounding *C. salicifolius* "Gnom" and the creeping *C. congestus*, both of which have white flowers and small red fruits. Or you may prefer small willows like woolly-leaved *Salix lanata*, which has catkins in spring, or a low broom (*Chamaecytisus purpureus*). The golden-flowering *Hypericum* x *moserianum* blooms all summer, and later there are many blue-flowered, small shrubs to provide interest into the fall, such as *Ceratostigma willmottianum,* at about 2 feet 6 inches (75cm) tall and wide, and *Caryopteris* x *clandonensis* "Kew Blue." Both associate well with hydrangeas and fall reds.

When considering size and habit, bear in mind that some shrubs, such as *Mahonia* x *media* "Winter Sun," arch over others, leaving planting space beneath. Others grow so slowly that they may be regarded as dwarf, like *Acer shirasawanum* f. *aureum* and some evergreens such as hollies (*Ilex*), whereas several so-called "dwarf" conifers are very

slow-growing, like the rich deep velvet-green *Chamaecyparis obtusa* "Nana Gracilis." All make suitable candidates for small plots.

can they be cut down to size?

The ultimate height and spread of a shrub need not necessarily put you off, provided its vigor is manageable. Many shrubs are amenable to pruning, among them forsythia, deutzia, and kolkwitzia—indeed, they must be cut back immediately after flowering because they flower on the previous year's growth. Other flowering shrubs, like the ornamental quince (*Chaenomeles*) and smaller hydrangeas, may be kept to size by sensitive pruning, working with their natural growth pattern. Some shrubs are better left alone and merely tidied once a year, so their proportions should be critically assessed from the start: *Viburnum davidii*, hebes, daphnes, and the compact, acid-loving skimmias all grow with a naturally neat habit, requiring only an occasional trim for tidiness. In the case of shrubs like box (*Buxus*), yew (*Taxus*), and privet (*Ligustrum*), careful pruning gives way to sculpting with shears. These are ideal for low hedging and topiary and therefore invaluable in small spaces, where they can be clipped to almost any size.

the influence of microclimate

It is quite possible for two gardens to be in the same climatic zone and only half an hour's drive apart, yet one may be in the city, enclosed by buildings and protected by walls and the other in the countryside, open to the sky and without any protection from the wind. The first will be several degrees warmer than the second because it is sheltered and because being "wrapped in" among buildings makes the temperature changes less extreme. Having a small city garden with its own protected microclimate expands your choice of plants considerably. In a temperate locality it will allow you to grow some frost-tender plants, including Mediterranean species, and even cacti if the garden is truly frost-free; you might also try a few "exotics" such as *Dicksonia* or *Monstera*. On a warm, sunny wall climbers like *Eccremocarpus scaber* may be encouraged in place of a hardier wisteria. A wall on the shaded side may still be warm enough for the evergreen coral plant (*Berberidopsis corallina*), provided this is in well-drained, alkaline soil. Never let the ground become waterlogged, however, as these plants will then rot.

coping with shade

It is crucial to establish first whether the shade is damp or dry. In dark, dry conditions you can introduce color in spring with good-natured perennials like spreading *Euphorbia robbiae* with its lime-green flowers, blended with fresh green shield ferns, such as *Polystichum aculeatum,* and some decorative ground cover in the form of dead-nettles (*Lamium*), ivies, purple-leaved bugle (*Ajuga reptans*), periwinkles like *Vinca minor* "Variegata," and the trailer *Waldsteinia ternata*, with small yellow flowers. Early spring is also the time for elegant, mounding epimediums to show their tiny flowers suspended on wire-thin stems. The perennial honesty (*Lunaria rediviva*) produces mutations of purple and white spring flowers and transparent, elliptical seedheads in the fall. All bergenias are valued for their boldly

glossy leaves and pink or cerise-purple flowers, but there is a particularly outstanding small form, *B.* "Morgenrote" that is only 15 inches (38cm) tall and has cherry-pink flowers. As summer progresses, *Alchemilla mollis* bursts into foaming pale yellow flowers over frilled leaves, and you can enliven the area with a butter-yellow grass, *Milium effusum*

A lightly shaded tunnel leads through to the compact, enclosed sitting area where the superb ship's figurehead holds attention. Summer-flowering annuals and tender perennials provide color.

"Aureum," which seeds generously, but is easily weeded out. In the fall the spikes of purple-flowering lilyturf (*Liriope spicata*) appear; this suits small spaces well because its grassy foliage is evergreen and only 1 foot (30cm) high.

If the soil does not dry out completely, you can expand the range of plants. For evergreen backing, *Viburnum tinus* has the bonus of being winter-flowering: look for the neat form, *V. tinus* "Gwenllian," which is 4 feet by 4 feet (1.2 meters by 1.2 meters). *Aucuba japonica* "Rozannie" has brilliant red berries and will do well with the small, slim-leaved *Prunus laurocerasus* "Grünerteppich." Deciduous shrubs like *Hydrangea* "Blue Deckle" are compact and massed with flowers in late summer; *H.* "Preziosa" has the bonus of bronzed fall foliage surrounding the pink mophead flowers.

Below these shrubs, choose low-growing perennials, preferably those which have a long flowering period. Several hellebores, such as *H. argutifolius* and *H. foetidus,* cover themselves with pale green flowers for about four months from early spring. *Brunnera macrophylla* provides sprays of blue or white flowers and large rounded leaves; *Omphalodes cappadocica* has more delicate leaves with sprays of "forget-me-not" flowers in spring. Solomon's seal (*Polygonatum* x *hybridum*) arches over these low-growing plants, dangling

creamy bell-flowers in late spring, while bleeding heart (*Dicentra spectabilis*), columbines (*Aquilegia*), and foxgloves (*Digitalis*) will add seasonal flower color. *Viola cornuta* "Alba" is successful in lighter shade, working its way around the vigorous buckler ferns (forms of *Dryopteris filix-mas*). All of these do well in low light and normal soil.

choosing for hot and exposed sites

If your garden is surrounded by buildings, the heat from all the walls, particularly brick, may rebound into the airless site, intensifying the heat and creating a hotter microclimate. Intense sunlight can be just as difficult for plants to tolerate as deep shade. Nature has resolved the problems to some extent by reducing the size of leaf or covering some plants with a mat of fine hairs, preventing rapid evaporation and deflecting the heat from the leaf surface. This is why so many sun-loving plants look gray and silvery. Your choice of plants for dry, sunny conditions will be those that come from the Mediterranean, or from arid regions like deserts, or even from some sub-tropical sources. In all cases, they will prefer the dry conditions to be constant, so if you have high rainfall in winter, you need to make sure that the drainage is really good; these plants will fail if standing miserably in cold, soggy soil. Bear in mind that mulching is crucial for moisture-retention and that a covering of gravel has a cooling effect.

In an exposed site, such as a roof garden, group together compatible plants which will withstand long periods of drought and exposure to heat. Small shrubs provide a foundation, like forms of the long-flowering *Potentilla fruticosa*. Many are less than 3 feet (91cm) high and, although the leaves are very small, they have masses of flowers, mostly yellow; the small, trailing *P. fruticosa* "Manchu", which has pure white flowers among grayish leaves, is almost prostrate. The smaller members of the cistus family are perfect shrubs for compact sunny sites, having

*left **Although the wall, with a superbly designed copper fountain mounted on it, gets little sun, the border to the left of it receives plenty and is therefore an ideal site for gray-leaved Mediterranean plants, like lavender and** Stachys lanata.*

right *An exposed roof terrace in Paris basks in the heat of the midday sun as its boundaries give no protection overhead. But the silver-leaved santolinas and artemisias thrive in the heat.*

above *The vertical spikes of Kniphofia "Little Maid" and the fleshy-leaved Sedum spectabile "Brilliant" make a good contrast in form, but they share a need for hot, well-drained conditions.*

flowers for a month as well as some interesting evergreen leaves. Look for mounding *Cistus* x *hybridus* or *C.* "Silver Pink," with gray leaves and pink flowers. When crossed with halimium, the result became the beautiful x *Halimiocistus sahucii,* which is low at 1 foot (30cm), but widely spreading and covered with white flowers.

Hebes are ideal for small, all-year-round sunny gardens; they include many dwarf forms, like pewter-gray *H.* "Carl Teschner," which has deep purple flowers, glaucous *H. pinguifolia* "Pagei," and the textured, silver *H. pimeleoides* "Quicksilver." Santolinas and lavenders are also ideal for sunny spaces. These small shrubs have to be clipped in spring, like lavender, to keep them in neat form. The reliable, ever-gray cotton lavender (*S. chamaecyparissus*) usually has

mimosa-colored flowers, but there is a smaller, lemon-colored variant, *S. pinnata neapolitana* "Edward Bowles," whose foliage is slightly greener-gray. For a fresh, moss-like green, *S. rosmarinifolia* "Primrose Gem" is charming. Lavenders deserve a place in the sun for their scent, shape, and versatility. *Lavandula angustifolia* "Hidcote" is a dwarf form of the species that is dense and well suited to hedging, with its deep lilac flowers. White-flowered *Anthemis punctata* subsp. *cupaniana,* another evergreen silver plant, is good company for lavenders. Add deep maroon spots of color with *Allium sphaerocephalon,* with its purple-crimson drumstick flowers and, later in summer, with *Knautia macedonica,* a scabious-like flower, and edge the lot with one of the smaller geraniums, such as *G. renardii,* a small, slightly furry, sage-green plant with purple-veined china-white flowers.

do they fill the bill?

Plants can be seen as structural material, to be used as the building blocks of a garden or the means of sub-dividing the space. In a small area all plants have a crucial role to play, whether they are creating the framework, clothing the walls, or simply providing colorful highlights.

the bones of the garden

The framework of a small garden is generally maintained by evergreens, as they keep their leaves all year round and create a permanent structure against which plants included for seasonal interest can ring the changes. Their constancy is as valuable to an intimate space as are the paving, the boundaries, and the hard landscaping in general.

Those evergreen shrubs particularly suited to small spaces include the laurels, whose polished leaves will, in the dark recesses of a yard, reflect light. *Prunus laurocerasus* "Mischeana," which is smaller than the type, performs even in deep shade as a freestanding, strong-growing foundation plant with its long, smooth leaves and flat-topped habit. The fragrant Mexican orange blossom, *Choisya ternata* also has shiny foliage and could be kept small by formative pruning. The aromatic foliage is cheerful in sun or light shade and

can flower twice, once in late spring and again in late summer; protect it against harsh weather with a fleece if necessary. For deep shade, nothing beats pyracantha, which can be manipulated to fit snugly against your wall. At the foot of the foundation shrubs, try a dwarf variegated euonymus (*E. fortunei*) to add color and light: "Emerald Gaiety" has white and green variegated leaves, while those of 'Emerald 'n' Gold' are yellow and green.

Evergreen ceanothus are lovely in sunny West Coast gardens and there are many rich blues to choose from, although you will have to keep them under control by removing a few shoots annually to encourage young growth; seek out one of the toughest forms, like **C**. "Autumnal Blue," and plant it against a warm wall. Or try the tiny *Escallonia* "Red Elf," which is generally evergreen but may lose its leaves in exceptionally cold weather. The planting framework would be dull if it consisted of nothing but evergreen wall shrubs. Some dramatic forms will add style; although the lethally spiked yuccas are too aggressively rigid in tiny spaces, you can achieve the same sword-like vertical look with evergreen phormiums. *Phormium tenax* "Maori Sunrise" is relatively small and has purple-crimson leaves; *P. cookianum* subsp. *hookeri* "Cream Delight," also small, has elegantly recurved foliage around the central base of sword-shaped leaves.

divide and control

A very small space can quickly become an overgrown mess if you do not take account of the wayward nature of many plants. Containing them within neatly clipped dwarf hedges can make the whole garden look presentable and dividing even a small area can be an effective way of preserving order. The most immaculate space divider, clippable to suit any space, is box and there are many different forms. *Buxus sempervirens*, the species, is hardy; "Suffruticosa" is the traditional dwarf form and "Rotundifolia" is well suited

left *The "bones" of this garden are provided by evergreen, colorful conifers. Other foliage plants, like the red-leaved maple and variegated cornus, provide extra color for half the year, while the planting of tender perennials in containers adds summer interest.*

pyracantha, the sun-loving, evergreen ceanothus, or, in a slightly more protected site, flowering escallonia take up less space than many wall shrubs and can all be clipped to lie flat against the boundary. The soil at the foot of a wall will need to be enriched with plenty of well-rotted, fibrous compost to help it retain moisture.

Early-flowering ornamental quince (*Chaenomeles speciosa*) is a deciduous alternative that has an elegant habit, so it should be carefully pruned. There are many hybrids with red, pink, and white flowers: one unusual beauty is *C. speciosa* "Moerloosei," which has appleblossom flowers; *C.* x *superba* "Pink Lady" has a low, wider habit, so looks good beneath windows. In the same position the low-fanning form of *Cotoneaster horizontalis* will fringe window sills attractively and sweep over paving; it is easily cut back.

*above **The use of clipped box to outline herbaceous areas lends itself to symmetrically designed formal city gardens like this one. The enclosures contain changeable seasonal planting; in summer the squares are filled with pinks (Dianthus).***

*right **Quite different in feel, this garden is awash with mingling foliage plants, among which a single clipped form—a conifer trained as a standard—stems the romantic, free-flowing disarray.***

to sculpting into dome shapes, while silver-variegated "Elegantissima" or yellow-variegated "Aureovariegata" provide color. Lavenders and santolinas make equally compact, gray-leaved hedging, ideal for sectioning off areas for decorative infilling. In warm areas, myrtle makes a scented alternative; it likes a mild climate and a well-drained soil. Germander (*Teucrium chamaedrys*), an aromatic, mid-green plant with pink flowers in late summer, will grow with rather less precision to a height of 1 foot (30cm). If you want to separate seating from planting or to screen a barbecue, a fragrant hedge of lavender or the more informal *Caryopteris* x *clandonensis* "Kew Blue'"will fill the bill.

clothing the walls

To create a green oasis, cover the boundaries with wall shrubs and climbers to hide all masonry and fences: select those plants which do not spread too widely or which respond well to training. The reliable, shade-tolerant

Climbers take up less room in the ground than wall shrubs, so may be a better choice in squashed spaces. Few are evergreen, however, but a small-leaved ivy, such as *Hedera helix* "Oro di Bogliasco," is indispensable for full shade, where its yellow leaves brighten the darkness; in its mature state it will become top-heavy, so keep cutting it back. There are many clematis which adapt well to being confined. Of the two evergreen species, *C. cirrhosa* var. *balearica* has ferny foliage and pretty, nodding cream bells in winter, but it must be cut down by a third each spring, while *C. armandii* is of generous proportions with long, glossy leaves and sprays of white or pink flowers in early spring. *C. alpina* and

C. macropetala are both small-scale and hardy, with tiny lantern flowers in spring and fluffy whorled seedheads in the fall. The viticellas flower later in summer with small purple or white flowers; "Polish Spirit" is one of the best, with rich blue flowers. There are also many huge-flowered cultivars that still take up little ground space.

Climbing roses have a place even in the tiniest gardens. Look for disease-resistance as a priority because airless, enclosed sites foster fungal growth, such as mildew, as well as insects like aphids. Some climbing roses, like red "Guinée" and free-flowering "Mme. Alfred Carrière," will grow on shady walls, while in sun the white noisette "Aimée Vibert" is vigorous and early flowering, and "Adelaïde d'Orléans" has massed clusters of small, powder-pink flowers. There are many more: look for scent, habit, and controlled vigor. The pillar roses suit very restricted spaces: consider "Casino", a scented rose with clusters of globular, double, yellow flowers, and the fragrant "Dublin Bay," red cluster-flowered. Other suitable flowering climbers

could include the white Chilean potato vine (*Solanum jasminoides*), which has a long flowering period and likes a sunny wall, and the passion flower (*Passiflora caerulea*), which will do well, provided your garden is truly frost-free and enjoys hot summers. For foliage, choose the self-clinging vines, such as the neat *Parthenocissus henryana* with its white-veined, dark green, five-lobed leaves; it flames into life in the fall, bringing vibrant color to the small garden.

trees for small spaces

Small trees can fulfill several roles in a compact garden. They will give dappled shade and a certain amount of screening from above, or they may be used as the garden's focal point. Trees suitable to become a focus include the fastigiate *Malus* "Brandywine" or the much smaller, weeping *Cotoneaster salicifolius* "Pendulus," which is grown as a standard grafted on to a 6 foot (2 meter) stem. The grafting technique is used for other ground-covering plants like variegated euonymus and some of the alpine willows, such as *Salix helvetica*. *Caragana arborescens* "Walker" is a prostrate shrub which can be top-grafted to make a very small flowering tree with its trailing, yellow, pea-like flowers and ferny foliage. The diminutive, tree-like forms made by these shrubs are dwarf enough for the tiniest site yet, as trees, they still command attention.

There is rarely enough space in our truly small garden for real trees unless you choose very slim ones like *Prunus* "Amanogawa," which grows with a sentinel habit; its shape makes it too dominant to site centrally and it is best placed to the side of your view. For a softer effect, the weeping pear (*Pyrus salicifolia* "Pendula") is quite small, with trailing branches and silvery foliage, charming for most of the year. In a small site a tree must offer more than a few weeks of pleasure, so do your homework and discover those that offer value; always beware of instant appeal at the garden center.

opposite above **Grown as a specimen tree, Acer japonicum "Vitifolium" provides a central focal point in this small garden. The rounded pebbles at its foot, with the intentionally sparse planting, reinforce its role.**

opposite below **The horizontal layering of the elegantly tiered Cornus controversa "Variegata" is unmistakable. Wherever it appears, it focuses attention like a leading opera star.**

left **Climbers decorate the walls without taking up too much ground space. Clematis jackmanii "Superba" and C. macropetala "Markham's Pink" interweave their way through the beautiful purple-gray foliage of Vitis vinifera "Purpurea."**

opposite far right **Lightly sugared by frost, the reddened leaves of Nandina domestica 'Nana' stand out in front of a carpet of blue Juniperus squamata 'Blue Star', bringing interest to the small plot in winter.**

For sheer elegance, Japanese acers are the front runners for small spaces. They associate superbly in simple gardens with minimalist intentions. Acers are very slow growing, so they are often planted as shrubs, but they will make height eventually and their canopy spreads with an arching or horizontal form. Seen from beneath, with sunlight filtering through, they look magnificent. Some, like *A. palmatum*

"Osakazuki," have outstanding fall color and others, such as *A. palmatum* "Dissectum Atropurpureum," are primarily grown for their finely dissected foliage.

In sun-filled sites, treasure those small trees which give flickering shade. Silver birches like *Betula pendula* "Fastigiata" filter sunlight effectively, as do some of the rowans which offer flowers and fruit as well. The openly branched *Sorbus cashmiriana* has pale pink flower clusters and pure white fruits; *S. vilmorinii*, even smaller, has pretty, ferny foliage and pink-flushed white fruits. Some of the thorn family (*Crataegus)* are relatively small, but densely solid, making deep shade beneath. The slow-growing *C. laciniata* has white flowers and yellowish fruits; *C. mollis,* the downy hawthorn, has downy leaves in the early season and good yellow to red fall color. Early white flowers are followed by attractive red fruits.

planting for all seasons

The whole of the tiny space is usually on view from the house, so making it attractive all year round has to be a priority; we still look out of our windows in winter. Several small shrubs blossom in spring and many carry either fruits or foliage color in the fall; include these in the foundation planting of the garden. Herbaceous perennials and bulbs reflect seasonal change very effectively, so choose those plants which pop up and fade with no fuss and require little tidying up afterwards.

Many spring bulbs can be fitted in at the base of shrubs. Include the early winter aconites (*Eranthis hyemalis*) and wood anemones (*A. blanda*) in shaded corners, and follow them with early small daffodils, like *Narcissus* "February Gold," or the really miniature ones like *N.* "Minnow." Small spaces are the place to fully appreciate the delicate beauty of *Cyclamen coum*, with its pink and white flowers above silver-patterned, dark green leaves. The small *Iris reticulata* hybrids also become more important in intimate spaces. Crocus species

like *C. tommasinianus* are more delicately built than their progeny; when open to the sun, they are a welcome sight after the dark and cold of winter; *Scilla sibirica* can be massed without taking over. For formal scenes, tall tulips provide repeating vertical forms with a vast range of flower color and shape, and some smaller species, like *Tulipa tarda*, open like crocus in sunlight. By summer alliums will merge with most schemes: there are tall, slim drumsticks like *A. sphaerocephalon* and *A. hollandicum,* plus many smaller ones like yellow *A. moly.*

If you want to indulge in masses of herbaceous flowers, start early with doronicums and feast on old-fashioned pinks

(*Dianthus*), chrysanthemum hybrids, *Leucanthemum maximum, Campanula lactiflora* "Pouffe" and, later on, rudbeckias, phlox, Japanese anemones (*A.* x *hybrida*), and asters, followed by nerines and kaffir lilies (*Schizostylis coccinea*). Infilling with annuals, such as cornflowers, poppies, linaria, limnanthes, nigella, nicotiana, flax, and cosmos, will produce flashes of summer color in the places where you need it.

Bedding out with tender perennials, such as verbena, impatiens, tagetes, and the tender sub-shrub *Senecio cineraria* will fill any remaining gaps and bulk up a young garden before it matures.

By the end of the year the cotoneasters, roses, pyracanthas, and skimmias will be carrying red, orange, yellow, or white berries. Seedheads, like the fluffy ones of clematis, the papery ones of honesty (*Lunaria annua*), dead agapanthus flowers, and superb allium globes carried on tall stems, enhance the garden for months from fall until they are battered by adverse winter weather. Fall is also the time of brilliance, when the foliage of acers and many azaleas takes on fiery hues and vines flare into scarlet and crimson reds.

including food plants

Producing food from your small plot is a challenge because the dimensions of your garden will dictate the possibilities. But there are growing techniques, like training fruit trees as espaliers, which economize on space, and several crops which can be combined decoratively with more ornamental plants. And never forget the possibilities of growing herbs, as well as some fruit and vegetables, in containers.

Apples, pears or plums can be trained as single-stem espaliers against a warm wall and peaches and cherries as

*left **A deep purple variant of Helleborus orientalis, with cream stamens, is an exquisite sight in spring, here associated with golden celandines and small-flowered narcissi.***

*opposite **Majestically tall, Angelica archangelica is a bold centerpiece for a "mini potager," with herbs, salad greens, and small tomatoes inside a boundary created by fanned fruit trees. French marigolds (Tagetes) emphasize the geometry and vibrate with color.***

fans, their branches radiating out. If your site is shady, grow a morello cherry, which is decorative and produces bitter, black fruit for cooking. Creating such forms by pruning is discussed in Down to Earth, page 63. Some fruiting shrubs like gooseberries can be trained as half-standard trees, which look stylish in all seasons. Alternatively, you could grow one of the single-stem "ballerina" fruit trees like "Waltz", which has apple blossom along its column in spring and dessert apples in the fall.

Grape vines take up little space in the ground. *Vitis vinifera* "Brant," a hardy grape for temperate areas, can be grown on overhead wires in hot summers, as can the tenurier grape (*V. vinifera* "Purpurea") which is particularly beautiful in the fall. Along the walls a thorn-covered blackberry, like "Black satin," will deter unwelcome visitors, or you could try the friendlier parsley-leaved "Thornless." Making the most of

the vertical space, string beans may scramble up parallel canes on a wall or up conical cane wigwams, alongside small cucumbers, tomatoes, annual ornamental gourds, or even chillies. Some supports can be decorative in their own right: choose trellis with care or consider buying ready-made trellis obelisks, which can be either quite elaborate or very simple structures.

At ground level, there is probably no space for anything but salad crops and herbs, many of which are decorative in their own right. You could contemplate a few ornamental lettuces like "Brunia" or "Nesclun," as well as "Dwarf Blue Curled" kale, some "Red Ace" beet and ruby chard. Dwarf beans and peas, like "Sugar Daddy," can be grown in large pots or, if the seeds are sown indoors, can be planted out in a sunny part of the garden in light, rich soil. There are many dwarf cultivars which are ideal for the very small plot and even for window boxes.

Herbs are traditionally associated with small gardens. Thymes, sages, and rosemary will form the shrubby framework among which more tender herbs, such as basil, can be grown in summer. Plant chives (*Allium schoenoprasum*) as an edging in rich, moist soil where they will get sun, or fennel among herbaceous schemes, as it is attractive in both its green and bronze feathery forms. The sages, too, are ornamental: there are purple, yellow, variegated, and narrow-leaved gray forms. Red orach, golden marjoram, blue rue and flowering thymes add lots of color. You can enclose herb beds formally by dwarf hedges of lavender or santolina, or more informally with chives or small dianthus, or let them all flow together with some tall, slim alliums, swaying blue flax, and colorful flashes of marigolds and nasturtiums. Containers are the best method for growing invasive herbs, such as mint and tarragon; in fact, a whole herb garden can be contained in a clay sink or a window box.

plants for containers

In very small gardens, whether they be courtyards, roofs, balconies, or little more than a narrow passage, containers are invaluable. In areas where there can never be any soil-filled planting beds, they enable you to grow almost anything that can cope with restricted roots. And many small plots are primarily foliage gardens, relying on flowering plants in pots, boxes, and troughs for spring and summer color. Containers help you to ring the changes as the seasons progress or from one year to the next.

Small containers look much better if grouped, but those with high impact may stand alone as features in their own right, sometimes more striking than the plants. Indeed, huge Mediterranean terracotta "Ali Baba" pots or oil jars look best without any plants at all. Simulated lead tanks, made from fiberglass filled with lead powder, are large and stylish, ideal for simple feature planting like oleander in warm climates or a Japanese acer or massed white lilies for summer in temperate climes. Stone urns are dignified, so the plants contained within them need to be of similar status—handsome cordylines, elegant ornamental grasses, and trained bay trees all have commensurate presence. Masses of regal pelargoniums, trailing fuchsias, and silver ballota are more traditional and charming.

Timber containers are usually rectangular and therefore waste no space, using every corner of a site. Traditional square Versailles tubs are ideal for single specimen plants like summer-flowering standard marguerites, clipped narrow cones of bay, formally clipped hollies, or domes of box. Large and narrow rectangular troughs can be used to grow bamboos, which are normally rapacious rooters, yet great performers when contained. To provide privacy in the small yard, you could lay several of these end to end for effective

left *Matching plants of* Parahebe lyallii, *a semi-evergreen low-growing perennial, provide sprays of white flowers in early summer, bringing life to a flight of steps on a roof garden. If deadheaded regularly, they will sometimes flower again.*

screening. Wooden troughs give you a real chance to mass summer annuals, mixing pelargoniums, daisy flowers, blue lobelias, silver-leaved *Senecio cineraria* and verbenas, or rusty orange, mahogany red, and golden tagetes. This abundant planting compensates for any restraint in the main garden. Window boxes are usually made from fiberglass or timber. Include some plants, like the upright *Iris unguicularis* or

Sisyrinchium striatum, which edge your view from indoors, as well as those which trail down to be viewed from outside and below, like ivy-leaved pelargoniums, *Vinca minor*, *Helichrysum petiolare,* and trailing fuchsias.

You can achieve tiered planting effects if some pots are raised on plinths to elevate the planting, even above head height. This increases the number of plants you can use, as well as introducing those which like to trail and tumble down to lower levels, like attractive ivies with a small clematis, slow-growing honeysuckle (*Lonicera syringantha*) with trailing nasturtiums, or lobelias with verbena. It is also effective to have one tall plant in a large container "grounded" by lower-growing ones in smaller pots at its foot, for example

Phormium "Bronze Baby" surrounded by mahogany-colored *Tagetes* "Paprika." If you plant up some bulbs and follow them with seasonal plants during the year, the look of your containers will constantly change.

For summer color the range is huge and tempting and a small courtyard bursting with annual flower color is many people's summer dream. Marguerites, petunias, verbena, begonias, lobelia, osteospermums, French marigolds, mallow, salvias, cosmos, and mesembryanthemums, plus nicotianas large and small, offer all hues and shapes. It helps to color-theme the planting in some way so that your small space does not look too hectic. You might condense the color by planting, for example, mounds of heliotrope with trailing violet-flowered verbena or, in a quieter scheme, planting tall white *Nicotiana sylvestris* with trailing white *Campanula isophylla* and a small-leaved green ivy.

For brilliant summer effects, plant up some flame-orange *Dimorphotheca sinuata* with other vivid South African plants, such as gazanias and nemesias. For shade, there is nothing to beat the delightful *Impatiens* in cool white or vivid pinks and red. *Arctotis,* with its silvery foliage and rich bronze or deep orange flowers, is a particular favorite of mine. For best

value, choose plants that provide color right through into the fall, like petunias, pelargoniums, and lobelias. And tender shrubs, like the unusual *Fuchsia* "Thalia," can be grown in a container for summer; its long, slim flowers, like orange-red tubes, show up well against the maroon foliage.

Permanent planting, such as small rhododendrons, can be a means of growing some impressive plants which do not like your soil. So small azaleas, dwarf rhododendrons, and

skimmias become an option even in areas of alkalinity, and camellias, grown away from morning sunlight, have great *gravitas*. Or you may fill pots with evergreen topiary shapes and stroll them around the site in continuous changing relationships. Euphorbias like *E. characias* and tall grasses like *Miscanthus sinensis* look distinguished in large pots, as do acers and dwarf shrubs like the flowery potentillas.

For shallow, sink-like containers in full sun, there are very small plants which originate at high altitudes where they sit among bare rock or gravel, exposed to midday heat. Many

are very small shrubs that grow with a naturally charming habit, low or crawling along contours avoiding wind. In winter the trailing alpine shrub *Daphne cneorum* "Eximia" grows to about 6 inches (15cm) high, spreading to twice that; for damper soils there are some alpine willows like the rare *Salix* "Boydii" and the silver-leaved *S. repens* "Argentea." Dwarf *Cotoneaster congestus* and *C. astrophoros* are two charmers which, with little crassulas, all provide dwarf structure. Some rocks may be partly submerged in the gravel mulch among them, reinforcing the notion of a mini alpine landscape and adding to the growing possibilities with tiny plants like sempervivums, small sedums and rosettes of encrusted saxifrage which can be grown on them.

If you decide to go the alpine way by planting in sinks or small clay pots, choose easily grown plants, such as dwarf dianthus, campanulas, armeria, phlox, violas, saxifrage, sempervivum, and sedum. Back these with *Thymus minima, Helichrysum bellidioides, Limonium minutum, Raoulia australis,* and add tiny cyclamen bulbs and pygmy narcissi like *N.* "Little Beauty" and "Minnow;" *Scilla sibirica*, only 4 inches (10cm) tall, flowers deep blue in spring. Good drainage is essential; a top-dressing of small-scale gravel will cool the roots of alpine plants effectively.

The many uses of versatile containers demonstrate the range of opportunities available to the small-space gardener. Size inevitably controls much of your plant selection but, once you understand the limiting factors, you can explore your small garden's potential. A knowledge of plants and a fertile imagination are the route to a successful garden and in the next chapter we explore the different styles that can be created, no matter how small your plot.

above **Massed small terracotta pots are a chance to grow tiny, mat-like alpines which share specific needs for free-draining, gritty soil.**

left **Brightly painted in carnival colors, clay pots are mounted in special holders and filled with apple-blossom pink begonias which thrive together in sun.**

A tiny garden belonging to a true "plantaholic" shows how the use of containers allows even such a limited space to support a great range of plants from around the world. Containers of all shapes and sizes, on tables and in tiers as well as on the ground, are sensitively and knowledgeably grouped; the plants include Euphorbia mellifera, Ophiopogon nigrescens, hostas, hellebores, heucheras, dicentras, ivies and a small purple-bronze phormium.

planting for effect

Setting a scene and creating atmosphere are, ultimately, what gardens of any size are all about. Neither the details of planting nor sensible decisions of a practical nature will satisfy your inner self if the garden has no personal meaning. Your outdoor oasis should give you pleasure at all times: a garden fails if it is merely adequate and does not stir your emotions and restore your well-being at the end of a working day. In the last chapter we looked at the criteria on which to select plants for a very small garden; we concentrate here on using and combining them in such a way that they create the atmosphere you want. This involves being sensitive to the aesthetic qualities of plants and it is worth taking a closer look at these inherent qualities first. Plants are, after all, the living part of the equation: they turn an outdoor space into a garden.

the aesthetics of a garden

The essence of a garden, its pervasive ambience, is created by selecting plants and putting them together as an artist uses materials. As the artist's "tools of the trade," the aesthetic properties of plants—their form, their texture, and their color—make a significant contribution to the overall look of the garden space.

plant form

Every plant has a natural habit which, in two-dimensional terms, can be described as a silhouette. Some plants are tall and narrow, others have a wide horizontal spread; some trail or "weep," others hug the ground, following its contours as if draped like fabric. Each plays a part in the overall scheme.

Vertical forms are always eye-catching; they act as full stops to the movement. Sometimes a plant's distinctive form is used to provide a focus, rather than bringing in a more obvious hard feature like an urn. On an intimate scale the slimline *Juniperus scopulorum* "Skyrocket" or *Chamaecyparis lawsoniana* "Little Spire" are more relevant than the familiar Italian cypress or fastigiate yew. In tiny spaces, you could plant one of two erect ivies—*Hedera helix* "Congesta" or *H. helix* "Erecta"—to bring order to the scene.

You might look to the herbaceous perennials to achieve the same dominating effect. Phormiums are stiffly sword-like and both the smallish *P. tenax* "Maori Sunrise" and *P.* "Bronze Baby" are vertically eye-catching and strongly colored. Foliage color is also found in the spreading stiff blue lyme grass (*Helictotrichon sempervirens*) and the silver shafts of the glamorous *Astelia nervosa*. Deciduous *Crocosmia* "Lucifer" has the same sword-like form, but it is taller and less sharply V-shaped in profile, so it blends easily into a scheme, provided the intense red flower color suits your plan.

In this effectively designed paved yard, the rounded stones and containers set a static, sculptural theme in which the strongly vertical forms of ornamental grasses are dramatically displayed.

If the effect of a solitary spire is too strong, you can reduce the impact by grouping; a group of three will integrate more comfortably with the whole picture. A single *Iris germanica*, for example, looks very unhappy, whereas a group, with their sharply erect leaves, are effective without being dominating. Duplication elsewhere has the same unifying effect, so that once a dramatic upright is imitated in another part of the garden, it loses the power of a solitary dictator. Even if the second is a totally different plant, it forms a "connecting" line with another area. So if the irises were to be emulated

elsewhere by a few *Sisyrinchium striatum*, the visual link becomes part of the scheme. Narrowly upright flowers draw the eye in the same way. Giants like verbascums and delphiniums can be copied on a smaller scale by the spiky effects of *Veronica gentianoides*, followed later on by the upright rhythms of the compact, purple-blue *Salvia nemorosa* "Ostfriesland" and shorter kniphofias like *K. uvaria* or *K.* "Little Maid". Later in the year the pink-, red-, or white-flowered *Schizostylis coccinea* could be edged by evergreen *Liriope muscari*, with its violet-blue pokers.

left *Associating in form and texture with the rounded flowerheads* of Euphorbia characias *subsp.* wulfenii *is* Tellima grandiflora, *with its lengthy sprays of creamy-pink bell-flowers.*

Dense shapes, such as the rounded mounds of hebes, always enforce a sense of stillness and tranquillity: these inert forms never move with the wind. Lavenders are usually clipped into dome shapes from which the spiked flowers will echo other vertical forms in a planting. Some small evergreen conifers, like *Picea pungens* "Globosa" or the golden *Pinus mugo* "Winter Gold," grow in a naturally dense, rounded form; they work better among low-growing alpines or Japanese acers than with floriferous herbaceous plants. Weeping and arching plant forms are, on the contrary, suggestive of movement and bring an element of vitality to the small garden. These include the ornamental grasses, which sway and rustle with every breath of wind, and perennials with nodding, pendulous flowers, such as the wand-flower (*Dierama pulcherrimum*).

plant texture

Texture, like decorative detail, provokes an immediate reaction in small gardens because the plants are close enough to enjoy. We can trail our fingers along grassy seedheads, stroke the furry, silver lamb's ears of *Stachys byzantina*, the smoothly honed fine kid of pale gray *Artemisia ludoviciana* var. *latiloba* or the gleaming, satin-supple leaves of *Convolvulus cneorum*. Some of the alpine willows that are well suited to tiny spaces are particularly tactile: the dwarf *Salix helvetica* has silver-silk catkins, while the slightly larger *S. repens* "Argentina" is more densely structured, with silvered woolly foliage. Both would be especially attractive in an intimate gravel garden alongside rocks, small acers, tiny ferns, and alpine plants including dwarf spring bulbs, for example.

Not all textures are tactile; some are predominantly visual. The eye sees the differences between hazy *Gypsophila paniculata* (Baby's Breath) and the massed patterns of daisy-flowered *Anthemis punctata* subsp. *cupaniana*. Ferny-leaved artemisias like *A. schmidtiana* "Nana" make a striking juxtaposition with the leathery foliage of *Heuchera* "Pewter Moon." In a very small garden such contrasts add piquancy among close concentrations of plants.

Some textures give particular pleasure because they are a surprise, like that of the sun-loving, prickly eryngiums. *Eryngium giganteum* (Silver Ghost), which grows no taller than 2 feet 6 inches (75cm), has metallic silvery bracts surrounding its central cone-shaped flowers; *E. alpinum* has larger blue flowers and a finer-laced ruff at the neck. Contrast these with the haze of fennel (*Foeniculum vulgare*) or the trembling pincushion flowers held amid the encircling bracts of astrantias. Ornamental grasses provide a variety of textures, their soft, hazy flowers and reed-thin foliage looking particularly wonderful in midsummer. Upright *Calamagrostis* x *acutiflora* "Karl Foerster" contrasts in form as well as texture with the shining fragility of *Stipa tenuifolia* and the late-summer fluffy flowers of *Pennisetum orientale*. Allowed to remain after fall, these and the flowing miscanthus grasses offer pale parchment textures in winter; outlined in hoarfrost, they provide a breathtaking sight from a window.

plant color

Color is exciting, refreshing and emotive; it powerfully affects mood, calming the mind or lifting the spirits, and can effectively warm a place up or cool it down. The light in the garden will influence your selection of colors to a degree. Notice how pale colors are luminous in shadow but bleach out in brilliant sunlight: use them to bring life to a dark courtyard. Your color selection should be a personal one: your special, intimate space must please you at all times.

If you are passionate about strong colors, you need not rule out the hot reds, oranges, and yellows in a small space, but it is a good idea to make one color dominant rather than letting them all fight it out in a true "riot" of color. If scarlet is the dominant color, choose ocher-yellow or pale cream rather than the pure primary "golden" yellow. In a red and blue scheme, if crimson-red is the leader, then any blues should be either deeper and purplish or paler and subservient. The small, rich red *Astilbe* x *arendsii* "Fanal" could be grown in damp shade beside the glaucous *Hosta* "Halcyon" for contrast or try deep orange kniphofias and satin-orange tiger lilies with pale yellow herbaceous potentillas. Strong yellows can be stunning with pale blues or intensified by association with deep purples. So *Inula ensifolia*, which flowers for a long time in summer, would create an exciting combination with *Salvia* x *sylvestris* "Mainacht."

Cooler pastels are wonderfully responsive to low light, gleaming in the evening when working owners of city gardens are most likely to enjoy them. As the day draws to a close, ultraviolet light finds out the pale blue and lavender hues of, for example, *Geranium himalayense*, making them almost fluorescent. White is the coolest color of all and will glow in the dark recesses of a small garden. All-white gardens have became fashionable, but you need to be careful when planting such a monochrome scheme since most "whites" are really pale tints of other colors, like cream, powder blue, soft lilac, and pale pink. Whites are often set with silver foliage, which has a restful quality: for small gardens, make the most of the artemisias, including the strikingly beautiful *A. ludoviciana* "Silver Queen," with long, slim silver leaves, or the much smaller, finely textured filigree soft mass of *A. schmidtiana* "Nana."

Traditionally, soft colors like pinks and pastel blues also associate with silver leaves. Tones like these can be found among small plants such as the alpine dianthus and dwarf irises like *I.* "Tinkerbell" or *I.* "Eyebright," as well as the little blue-hued *Sisyrinchium idahoense* var. *bellum*. Small lavenders, cushions of campanulas, and soft, sprawling

anthemis work together well within this color scheme and are easily managed in very small spaces if tidied occasionally. Distribute pale blue flax (*Linum narbonense*) to sway softly above these lower-growing mounds throughout summer.

Green, which most refreshes the spirit, is the mainstay of compact gardens, where its tranquil qualities are best appreciated. In small, shady places, fresh green ferns grown with green-flowered hellebores and epimediums will provide a refreshing scene in spring and early summer. In furnishing the bones of the garden, evergreens become the foil for seasonal changes. Choose from blue-greens, like grassy *Festuca glauca*, lime-greens like that of *Milium effusum* "Aureum," apple-green as found in the foliage of the shrub *Griselinia littoralis*, or the dark green of the laurel (*Prunus laurocerasus* "Grünerteppich"). Each will create a slightly different effect, providing a dark foil for pale flowers or for setting off a brilliant color theme, such as yellows, oranges, and purples. Powder-blue scabious and the small-flowered wine-red *Astrantia major rosea* would create subtle color effects against deep greens. In full sun, ornamental grasses can be mixed with feathery light green fennel and green *Artemisia lactiflora*, mingled with summer flower color.

planting styles

In gardens, as in all things, style is a very personal matter. Many people look for tranquillity and peace in their gardens, others need to be excited and enthusiastic about them. Just as gardens can fulfill quite different individual needs, there are ways of planting which can create varied effects. Planting styles can vary from calm, classical formality to the fragrant overspill of the English flower-garden tradition. Always bear in mind the role of nature: however you design your small outdoor space, it will never have the static perfection of an interior. Seasonal fluctuations cause small gardens to mutate all the time, making them continually engrossing. So, choosing plants means selecting those which suit your space while using them means co-directing with nature to achieve the effects that you wish to create.

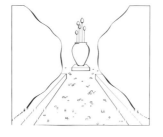

above **A planted urn provides a suitable focus, leading the eye down the length of a vista. Even in a small space, this technique can be most effective.**

right **Beneath Acer japonicum a low, brilliant-flowered Rhododendron Blue Tit Group, and a carpet of green helxine (Soleirolia soleirolii) are planted with sensitive restraint in gravel. The green velvet of real moss spreads into the crevices between the granite setts.**

restrained simplicity

Using a very restricted number of plant varieties can be a way to create a minimalist courtyard or a geometrically ordered formal garden: "Elegant sufficiency, where any more would be needless superfluity," to quote Oscar Wilde. Such gardens are orderly and peaceful; since nothing surprises and nothing challenges, they relax the spirit. The formal approach applies strongly to the pocket-handkerchief gardens of today because order works well in a small space and symmetry always satisfies because it has balance.

Once you create an axis along which the eye can be led, you need a focus. This could be an urn of generous proportions, but it may work better in a small garden to use a plant: choose something of interest like a striking *Yucca gloriosa* "Variegata" in semi shade or a phormium in sun. On a very intimate scale you might have a container-grown, evergreen bay tree (*Laurus nobilis*) clipped in a neat "Popsicle" shape or a grafted standard marguerite with gray foliage and white daisies, attractive through summer. Follow through the restrained planting against the walls, by training pyracantha into tightly clipped horizontal parallel lines (see Practicalities,

page 166) or growing small-leaved ivy on large diamond-shaped trellis.

Well-regulated planting styles are usually laid out geometrically. Elegant restraint can be achieved by using compact hedging to make tiny enclosures of box or the dwarf *Lavandula angustifolia* "Nana Alba" or *Santolina chamaecyparissus* var. *nana*. Frothy annuals and flowering perennials can be contained in beds edged by such neat plants or framing can give significance to some distinguished specials, like spring regiments of tulips followed by glamorous cannas or brilliant alstroemerias. For a strictly formal effect without using enclosed beds, include the tidy domes of dwarf hebes and mounds of *Sedum spectabile*, static forms which anchor firmly to the ground; the low, flattened flowers of *Achillea* x *lewisii* "King Edward" or the erect spikes of *Salvia nemorosa* "Ostfriesland" also have a formal stillness.

planting in tiers

Many small gardens are attached to a house and viewed from the back of it, so the garden is nearly always seen frontally, like a stage set. If the space is shallow, it is logical to plant in tiers, so that taller subjects at the back of the border do not conceal smaller ones in front. Layering can be a useful design principle in an intimate space, with trees or large shrubs as the top story, medium-size shrubs and herbaceous perennials as the middle one, and creeping or ground cover plants as the carpeting layer. Wall shrubs create the backcloth which, if plain, will be a foil for the action or, if highly textured and colorful, becomes part of the drama.

If the boundary faces full sun, espaliered or radially fanned fruit trees would make an elegant backdrop, or you can seek out manageable climbers (see page 31). *Actinidia kolomikta* and some vines, such as *Parthenocissus henryana*, are well behaved and unchallenging in both leaf and habit, making them ideal as a backing for intimate spaces. The former has green leaves which become blushingly pink as it twines its way upward in sun, while the self-clinging velvet green foliage of the latter is fetchingly veined for summer, turning claret-colored in the fall.

The middle tier could be created with tall artemisias, irises, and leucanthemum, enlivened with spikes of veronicastrum and, at their foot, small *Heuchera* "Red Spangles" or *H.* "Snow Storm" with alpine geraniums, such as

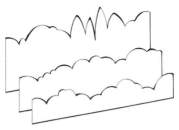

left ***Espaliered fruit trees line the walls of this formal front garden. Domed box sentinels flank the steps and a double row of hedging, sinuous and straight, separates house from street.***

below ***Tiered planting, with*** Miscanthus sinensis "Variegatus" ***at the back and low coreopsis and hemerocallis at the front, is enlivened by*** Pancratium maritima, ***a mid-height, white-flowered bulb.***

G. cinereum var. *subcaulescens*. Low planting can include the versatile *Alchemilla mollis* and the mounding mass made by *Anthemis punctata* subsp. *cupaniana*. Truly ground-hugging plants include many small-leaved cotoneasters, like *C. dammeri*, and some almost-flat conifers like *Juniperus communis* "Repanda."

Bulbs are invaluable for layering, providing interest at several different heights. Medium-height tulips are rhythmical in formal situations and there are some striking forms, like the dark maroon "Queen of Night," lily-flowered "White Triumphator," and pastel-pink "Elegant Lady." As regards narcissi, seek out the cool, sophisticated beauty of pristine white poeticus types, like *N. actaea*, as well as the alluring yellows of *N.* "February Gold." Alliums have class without taking up much space: you may like the purple drumsticks of *A. hollandicum* or the smaller, cornflower-blue *A. caeruleum*. In summer the statuesque, fragrant *Lilium regale* will grace formal gardens with style.

In shade, use the dependable variegated euonymus (*E. fortunei* "Silver Queen") or a cheerful ivy such as *Hedera helix* "Oro di Bogliasco" against the wall. Front these with a lower layer of shapely perennials, such as ferns, forms of *Helleborus orientalis* that do not flop, and some neat pulmonarias like *P. angustifolia* "Munstead Blue," spiced up

with foxgloves and martagon lilies. Intersperse runs of lily-of-the-valley (*Convallaria majalis*), and comely green-ruffed *Galium odoratum*, with its tiny white summer flowers. In fall *Cyclamen hederifolium* can be followed by thick carpets of winter aconites (*Eranthis hyemalis*) or *Anemone blanda*.

right *Golden-leaved* **Robinia pseudoacacia** *"Frisia" towers over the middle tier of variegated* **Kerria japonica** *and tender, white-flowered* **Nicotiana sylvestris**. *Edging at ground level includes hostas, yellow-variegated* **Lamium maculatum** *"Aureum," and purple-leaved* **Heuchera micrantha** *var. diversifolia "Palace Purple."*

raising the eye

If you do not have the space to spread widely, you must look upward for expansion. Arches and pergolas are the traditional frames for overhead planting. Provided these have sturdy timber or metal uprights, set firmly in concrete, cross-beams will carry plants like roses or vines across the garden, to be viewed from below. The cross-beams may be made either of the same material as the uprights or from rigidly stretched stainless steel yachting wire or heavy rope swags. In the smallest space, you can use a tall, upright timber post

1 foot 6 inches –2 feet 6 inches (45–75cm) square, can rise to considerable heights if properly anchored and strongly made. They may be filled with a columnar yew in the traditional seventeenth-century manner or climbers can weave in and out of the center.

Traditional wigwams of canes offer freestanding support for climbing vegetables, such as string beans, or annuals like climbing nasturtiums, and lightweight metal supports can now be found with the same purpose in mind. Made from aluminum in a stretched, open, silver spiral, they are decoratively sculptural in winter and can be clothed with climbers in summer. They are very versatile, they look attractive standing singly or may be used as paired flanking sentinels, grouped in threes, or in a marching row of verticals which doubles as screening.

left Twinned wooden obelisks tower above marguerites and petunias. They are unadorned for the first year, before the climbing roses are established enough to take over.

weaving plants

Planting in tiers is not the only solution for small gardens. If the space is very shallow, you may be able to make more of the depth by weaving plants in and out in a more informal way. Some plants with a slim habit, even though they are tall, are almost "transparent" and can be placed in front of other smaller or denser plants so that you look through them, as if through a screen. At the end of summer a group of tall, 5-foot (1.5-meter) *Verbena bonariensis* will make a tall, fragile screen of mauve flower clusters above branching, wire-thin stems. Heucheras are "transparent" in the same way: *H. cylindrica* "Greenfinch" has a rosette of leaves near the ground, but the flower spikes are tall and delicate. Many thalictrums have a similarly light structure, such as *T. delavayi* "Hewitt's Double," with airy sprays of pinkish-lilac flowers in late summer above gray-green leaves. *Campanula persicifolia* is another slimline plant whose basal rosette of leaves throws up a wand bearing nodding, blue or white bell-flowers.

to support clematis like *C.* "Polish Spirit" and pillar roses, such as "Zéphirine Drouhin," or it can become a living green column covered all year round with variegated ivy. There are now elegant metal obelisks available which can stride a base as small as 1 foot (30cm); these are ornamental in their own right, whether clad with flowers or not, and can make the perfect focal point. And freestanding piers made from narrow sections of wooden trellis, approximately

right *Holding the planting scheme together, aquilegias weave among a mélange of ferns, foxgloves, lamb's ears (Stachys lanata), and Welsh poppies (Meconopsis cambrica).*

The choice of plants will be founded upon qualities of scent, sound, color, and drama. Sensual delights are an important part of the garden experience and one which appeals to romantics. Color has a considerable effect upon mood (see page 43) and textures may be either tactile or visual (see page 42), or both. Scents are evocative, while the sounds in a garden full of movement give subtle pleasure.

fragrance

Scents are distilled in enclosed small spaces, putting fragrance high on our list of priorities. Shrubs like choisya, daphnes, the small *Philadelphus* "Snowflake" and the smaller lilacs such as *Syringa meyeri* var. *spontanea* "Palibin," contribute their perfumes in early summer. Protected in the microclimate of the enclosed city garden, myrtles like the compact *Myrtus communis* subsp. *tarentina* "Variegata" are very fragrant in summer; planted with scented roses and lavender, the combination is

positively indulgent. Summer evenings can be a heady experience too: nicotianas and lilies will perfume the air, reinforced by long-flowering *Cestrum parqui*. Artemisias, thymes, and rosemary will contribute their aromatic foliage.

"Transparent" plants such as these may be put in as curving meanders with smaller subjects in front and behind them. Rounder masses like *Coreopsis verticillata* "Moonbeam," rush-leaved day lilies (*Hemerocallis*), or dense mounds of astrantia can follow the flow. Other dense plants which grow well in sweeping curves include *Aster* x *frikartii* "Mönch," medium-height astilbes like the white *A. thunbergii* "Professor van der Wielen," and geraniums such as blue *G. malviflorum* and *G. clarkei* "Kashmir White." Tall alliums may also be used in such planting schemes, weaving in among the plant mass for summer, while aquilegias fit into an early-flowering scheme.

sensual indulgence

In contrast to the elegantly restrained, tiered, and woven planting styles we have looked at, you may like to consider the generously self-indulgent, free-flowing planting style which appears to be anything but ordered. For this to work in a small space, it is essential to know the plants used, so that you can subtly manage and retain the sensuality of the scheme, without its getting out of control. Understanding the habit of plants and why you have selected them is essential in deciding which you will allow to mingle together.

far right *Varieties of* Nicotiana alata *are grown as annuals and planted with perennial lavender and the golden-leaved* Choisya ternata "Sundance" *to perfume the air of this enclosed courtyard.*

Planted against a warm wall, the slightly tender wall shrub *Itea ilicifolia* is fragrant in summer; it may be echoed by the scents of the hardier wisteria or jasmine grown on walls or over arbors. For the dark months the winter-flowering shrub honeysuckle (*Lonicera* x *purpusii*) and winter sweet (*Chimonanthus praecox*) are invaluable. Mahonias will also stir the senses; choose the smaller ones, such as the 5-foot (1.5-meter) high *M.* x *wagneri* "Kings Ransom."

movement

Movement gives small gardens their vitality. Even if you have chosen a "settled," formal look, using static plant forms like the inert hebes, you could animate the garden scene with

the drifting light foliage of ornamental grasses which are responsive to any breath of wind. A sowing of pale yellow, fluttering *Milium effusum* "Aureum" will provide the undulating grassy image from late spring followed, later on, by *Miscanthus sinensis* "Ferne Osten" and *M. sinensis*

"Undine" which rustle delightfully with the breeze; both are about 4 feet (1.2 meters) tall. The tufted hair grass (*Deschampsia cespitosa*) has a lovely floating haze of feather-fine flowers and *D. flexuosa* is never still when its light, airy flowers drift above its reflexed fine leaves. Pennisetums, such as the fountain grass (*P. setaceum*), have slim, arching leaves which are joined by swaying, furry flowers in late summer.

While arching forms are seldom static, plants with a weeping habit are reminiscent of cascading water. The leaves of many Japanese maples, in particular *Acer palmatum* "Dissectum Viride Group," float with an almost balletic elegance, as do small fuchsias, such as the arching *F. magellanica* var. *gracilis* "Tricolor," which carry pendulous flowers. The wand-flower (*Dierama pulcherrimum*), alternatively named angel's fishing rods, is never still: its slim, arching stems ending in pink bell-flowers sway restlessly in every breeze, yet they are as strongly constructed as fine, whippy steel. To best appreciate this very special plant and display it with the panache it deserves, place it where the space around it is flat, whether it is paved or covered with the lowest of carpet plants.

using exotics

If you can create a frost-free microclimate in a sunny yard, you could consider creating a jungle effect with exotic foliaged plants and even some of the hardier subtropical species. Many such plants are large and wide-spreading so you should always have in mind their eventual size and know whether you can successfully interfere with this by pruning or restricting their root growth—by growing them in containers, for example. Exotic plants are challenging, so if you want an exciting garden environment in which large leaves abound and the flowers are unusual or dramatic, ignore scale and be bold.

left **This pampas grass (Cortaderia selloana "Pumila") is a small cultivar, 5 feet (1.5 meters) high, which grows stiff wands with fluffy, white flowers above tumbled slim leaves. It sways in the wind, like the grassy foliage of Pennisetum alopecuroides. The stabilizing foliage plants below include Aster amellus "Rosa Erfüllung," Artemisia "Powis Castle," and Heuchera micrantha var. diversifolia "Palace Purple."**

left *A square, deep-water pool, set in decking, is surrounded by exotic silver- and green-leaved feather palms, creating a jungle-like, but restful setting.*

left *A mass of exciting planting in this inspirational Californian garden contains a fan palm (Chamaerops humilis), green- and bronze-leaved phormiums and, arching over all, Cantua buxifolia.*

A suitable foundation planting of hardy, distinctive, large leaves might include those of the good-natured *Fatsia japonica* because they are tough and evergreen, yet will suggest a subtropical scene. Further into the light, the hardy loquat (*Eriobotrya japonica*), with its long, leathery-textured leaves, makes a striking sight if grown as a dense, almost mop-headed small tree. Smaller still—growing to no more than 3 feet (1 meter)—the tender, evergreen *Cuphea cyanea* from South America is covered with brilliant orange, tubular bell-flowers for weeks through summer. Small bamboos create an oriental look, but they are invasive and difficult to remove, so it is best to restrain them in containers. A magnificent small, shiny fan-palm from southern Europe, *Chamaerops humilis*, will instantly light up the yard but, being tender, will need to be wrapped in a horticultural fleece before the onset of winter. The knife-like foliage of yuccas and the neat *Cordyline australis* "Torbay Dazzler" all live up to the exotic aim; the easily grown phormiums or the reliable *Acanthus spinosus*, with its distinctive, sharply incized foliage, make extremely suitable companions.

For a truly dramatic look you could grow an Australian tree fern such as *Dicksonia antarctica*. This will unfurl in summer to canopy the whole garden, allowing through only green-tinged light; the drawback is that in winter you will have a thick, roughly textured brown stump, resembling a minimalist sculpture. In damp shade large, stylish ferns like the royal fern (*Osmunda regalis*) will grow as tall as 6 feet (2 meters); in drier conditions you could choose the relatively humble but shapely *Dryopteris filix-mas*. For really tiny spaces in damp shade the same exotic feeling can still be achieved with glossy-leaved ferns like varieties of *Phyllitis scolopendrium*.

If flowers are your priority, consider the hardier hibiscus, like *H. syriacus* "Oiseau Bleu" and, for acidic soils only, bottlebrush callistemon and red crinodendrons. In full sun,

include slightly tender plants which will benefit from the local microclimate, like the Californian poppy (*Romneya coulteri*) which, with its pewter-gray incized leaves and large, white, crinkled poppies, looks exotic. From the window these large-leaved flowering plants will readily suggest a jungle, excluding from view everything beyond your boundaries. *Euphorbia characias* subsp. *wulfenii*, a characterful evergreen perennial from the western Mediterranean, is something of a soloist, with its glaucous foliage and lime-green flowers. The red-leaved tender castor oil plant (*Ricinus communis* "Impala") would make a good foil for the ginger lily (*Hedychium coccineum*) which produces highly unusual, fragrant orange flower-spikes in late summer among broad lance-shaped leaves. If you have any space left, hardy plants such as agapanthus, nerines, cleome, and lilies will mix in well with their more exotic cousins.

On a warm wall you could grow parrot's bill (*Clianthus puniceus*), a scrambling semi-evergreen climber with brilliant scarlet, claw-like flowers in spring. For summer try the glowing, orange-flowered *Lapageria rosea* from Chile or the tender *Abutilon megapotamicum* in whose unusual dangling flowers the dark red calyx hangs from deep apricot petals.

Both the tropical and hardy passion flowers, like *Passiflora caerulea*, are exotic in appearance and the detail of their flowers, with their purple-ringed patterning and central corona of filaments, can really be appreciated in the intimacy of the tiny garden.

giant plants

The style of garden will, to some extent, be influenced by design within the house. Contemporary spareness indoors lends itself to fostering the extraordinary contrast of lush foliage outdoors. But this need not be exotic—many plants from temperate climates have giant proportions. This bold style of planting is both a denial of the garden's dimensions and a celebration of large foliage in diminutive surroundings. The use of deliberately over-large plants is theatrical and exciting, so choose the plants as you would sculpture, to dominate or create the drama.

Some large tree-shrubs need not be ruled out in mini-gardens—and some form of pollarding is the secret (see Practicalities, page 166). The tree of heaven (*Ailanthus altissima*) will produce massive pinnate leaves up to nearly 3 feet (90cm) long if it is pollarded each winter to 6 inches (15cm) of the ground. The white variegated form of the Japanese angelica tree (*Aralia elata* "Variegata"), which grows from a root-suckering forest of spiny stems, also makes large, pinnate leaves which will dramatically dominate a small space. Beneath these tree-like plants you might plant a clump of *Bergenia ciliata*, a frost-tender plant whose broad, mounding leaves are 1 foot (30cm) across, and which grows in light shade; *B. cordifolia* "Purpurea" is hardier and the diameter of its foliage even wider. Or cover the soil with really huge-leaved hostas, like *H. sieboldiana* var. *elegans* whose overlapping glaucous foliage brings drama to shady places. In theory the really huge bog plants like the American skunk cabbage (*Lysichiton americanum*), *Gunnera manicata*,

top left **In a sheltered city courtyard exotic planting of the huge-leaved banana (Musa basjoo), lengthy fronds of the tree fern (Dicksonia antarctica), and an elegantly pinnate-leaved acacia mix with dramatic foliage plants like fan palms. The banana should be well wrapped with horticultural fleece for winter protection in temperate climates.**

bottom left **The tall, large-leaved plume poppy (Macleaya cordata) has imposing lobed, dove-gray foliage from ground level to a height of over 6 feet (2 meters). At its top, buff-pink, feathery flowers emerge in summer, so that this giant plant completely dominates the sunny garden.**

right **Between the huge silver-leaved Verbascum bombyciferum and a spiky cordyline, another erect form—that of a slim metal obelisk—fits in stylishly.**

and the umbrella plant (*Darmera peltata*) would be impossible to grow in a small back yard, but to a plant enthusiast all things are feasible, even if their stature will be stunted. For sun, look at the elegant *Melianthus major*: this tall, sage-gray foliage plant has deeply serrated, softly silvered leaves and, although tender, will survive if cut down in the fall each year. The plume poppy (*Macleaya cordata*) is another tall perennial grown for its large-lobed, pewter-gray leaves and its haze of bronze flowers; it is hardy but invasive.

The flowering herbaceous perennials which, in large gardens, you would see planted in groups or massed together, can be grown as single specimens in the diminutive garden. Huge plants like white rosebay (*Epilobium angustifolium*) and the tall Canadian burnet (*Sanguisorba canadensis*) will lord it over other plants, even if grown in solitary splendor; both do well in lightly shaded areas. In a sunnier place, coneflowers (*Rudbeckia* "Herbstonne") would look startling grown with giant foxtail lilies (*Eremurus*). All these subjects grow to around 7 feet 6 inches (2.3 meters).

If you are planning to use giants, be daring and choose some really challenging candidates. The huge American cow parsley (*Heracleum lanatum*) reaches a height of 8–10 feet (2.4–3 meters) and a width of 3–4 feet (0.9–1.2 meters), so would inevitably become the dominating focus of a small garden, to be enjoyed from beneath. It bears very large heads of white flowers in summer. As it is biennial you would also have to be patient. The yucca look-alike, *Beschorneria yuccoides,* may survive in your yard; it is very tall at 8 feet (2.4 meters) but, for dramatic effect, scale gets ignored anyway. Rigidly knife-edged, its coral-pink flower sprays arch over its sword-like, gray leaves. Putting giants together means that the accompanying plants should be lower, even mat-like, to act as a foil for the prima donnas. Massed small grasses like green *Festuca gautieri* or golden *Hakonechloa macra* "Alboaurea," which turns rust colored in fall, will fulfill this role, or consider the neat rosettes of heuchera which send up their slim, non-competitive flowers.

As this wide variation of planting styles shows, plants help to create the spirit of a place and even small gardens can set a very particular scene. As the seasons and the years progress, your planting scheme will evolve, creating ever-changing relationships; some plants will inevitably become more dominant than others and every year you will need to reduce the height of some plants by pruning, remove a few others altogether, and add new discoveries. The practical tasks that constitute the management of a small garden are all covered in the next chapter. Not only do all gardens fluctuate with time but, since you are controlling it, your small space will become more intimately personal over the years.

down to earth

This chapter is concerned with the practical side of making a garden for a very small space. Although small gardens are less time-consuming than large plots, they still need managing to preserve their special intimate charm. Learning to anticipate problems and taking steps to circumvent them will help you to avoid expensive mistakes.

Small formal gardens can be kept under control easily, especially if clipped box is an important part of the design. Timely pruning keeps this beautiful and tranquil small space immaculately maintained.

In terms of the space available, you will already have resolved what you cannot do without in your small garden, bearing in mind that the more furniture and equipment you have, the greater your need for storage will be. You will have decided whether to lay a lawn or hard paving: since grass needs high maintenance and adds to the equipment load, you may feel that decking would be just as soft to sit on for summer. The amount of spare time you have for gardening will affect the

number and type of plants you can cope with. How much work are you prepared to put into pruning or clipping? Even in very small gardens time is well spent if you are able to keep shrubs and trees in check as they grow, preventing them from getting out of hand.

To ensure that your small space is an asset and not a drain on your energy and resources, think ahead about ways you can make the garden simpler to look after. Well-laid, quality paving and sturdy walls or fences will look good at all times and help keep maintenance to a minimum. Do not be tempted to put in more plants than you can manage, unless you particularly enjoy puttering around doing garden tasks. Think about the possible provision of an automatic watering system, which is both time- and labor-saving, and of lighting to expand the use of your outdoor haven. Once the paving has settled and the plants have made themselves at home, you will not want to disturb either. So plan ahead and enjoy the ease of a well-run little garden.

the soil

Soil is the most precious ingredient of your garden. Many demands will be made on it, so keeping it fertile and in good condition pays dividends. If you are gardening in a well-established plot, the ground may be compacted and the soil airless but, as long as it is not polluted, there is no need to change it. Instead, aim to improve its structure and fertility—good cultivation will pay dividends over the years. Soil originates from eroded rock which has been worn away gradually, over thousands of years, through the natural action of water, wind, frost, and ice, to produce the fine fragments which form your soil's mineral content. This will vary depending on the parent rock—whether, for example, it is granite, limestone, or sandstone. The progressive addition of organic materials, principally from the decomposition of dead plants and small animals, and the action of earthworms, usually over very many centuries, produces fertile soil. The gardener's aim is to have a well-balanced, fertile soil, often described as a good loam, but few of us inherit such perfection and will have to work hard to achieve it.

soil types

Understanding what you have will help you to make the right decisions about plants, so it is worth taking time to investigate your soil. The first characteristic—and the gardener's first priority—is texture. The proportion of sand to clay determines whether the soil is light and easy to work, very heavy to turn over, or something in between the two. If your soil is gritty to the touch and does not stick together when pressed or rolled between the fingers, then you have sandy soil, which is lightweight, easily dug, and well aerated. It also warms up early after winter, making it easier for growing plants from seed, and it drains easily. But its composition also means that the valuable nutrients of the soil are quickly leached out.

right **The rhododendron family must have acidic soil. This ruby-pink azalea is thriving beneath the feathery leaves of Acer palmatum var. dissectum, which will tolerate acid soil.**

Clay soil is entirely different: it is made from very fine particles and when compressed between the fingers it feels sticky. Clay compacts into smooth, dense, airless soil which is heavy to work, but it holds water and therefore remains rich in nutrients. Staying cold for longer, it also gets waterlogged easily and the roots of young plants can be drowned. If a clay soil dries out in summer, the dense mass shrinks, cracking like concrete. Many plants grow well in rich clay soils, however. A third type, alluvial soil, is from silt washed out, carried, and deposited by rivers or floods. It is usually fine, very fertile, and easy to work, but few of us are likely to benefit from a natural silt soil today.

Fortunately, extremes of soil type are rare and most people find they have a crumbly mix somewhere between clay and sand. All soils are improved by mixing in some form of organic material, such as compost. Clay soils benefit because they are lightened and able to contain more air, which makes them far easier to work. Adding compost to sandy soils helps them to retain water and therefore minerals as well.

organic content

The second characteristic of soil is how much organic material it contains. Humus occurs naturally in soils, enriching their growing potential and making them the living medium they are. Decomposed organic material, such as plants, produces chemical nutrients as it rots down, owing to the action of bacteria. Inorganic soils, which are basically minerals, are not fertile, so humus is literally the lifeline for your plants. Gardeners can add organic material in the form of compost; some choose to use it before it has completely rotted down so that it is bulky and lets more air in, rather than waiting for the very fine black tilth which takes longer. For tiny gardens, where there is no room for a compost heap, compost can be purchased in bags in various forms (see page 57): be sure it is clean and thoroughly rotted, without containing live seeds. Buy as you need it as there will be no room to store the bags.

acidity and alkalinity

Soils are either acidic or alkaline, with gradations in between. The pH of a soil indicates how alkaline or acidic it is and you can easily check this by using a soil test kit bought from a garden center. The scale reads from 4.5, confirming extreme acidity (often described as sour, such as that found in a natural peat bog), moving up to 6.5, which is still slightly acid. From 6.6 to 7.3, you have an evenly balanced, neutral

left *The distinct layers in the soil's profile are revealed where a rainstorm swept the bank away. Fine root trails hang down beneath the surface, the image resembling an abstract painting.*

soil, while a reading of 7.4 to 8.0 indicates mildly to strongly alkaline soil, say in a limestone area. It is always advisable to take a few tests in several different areas of the garden because even in small plots some soil may have been brought in from elsewhere at one point and a single reading could easily mislead you.

Most plants will cope with some acidity, even if they really prefer a limy soil. But there are some plants which will die in alkaline conditions: these are called calcifuges—literally "fleeing from calcium"—meaning that they cannot live in limestone or chalky soils where calcium is a major element. Rhododendrons, camellias, skimmias, pieris, heaths, and some heathers will gradually become yellow-leaved as they fail to absorb iron and other minerals which they are unable to get from alkaline soils. So you can only grow these plants if you have acid soil or plant them in ericaceous compost in a container. In the case of very small plots, you could consider making the soil acidic in a small raised bed, for instance. This would enable you to grow dwarf evergreen Japanese azaleas such as pink "Hinode-Giri," purple "Blue Danube," and white "Everest," although not in very dense shade. Ground-covering *Pachysandra terminalis* and the lacy fronds of the deciduous fern, *Adiantum venustum*, would cope with shaded areas. If, on the other hand, your soil is alkaline, small plants which flourish will include shrubby potentillas, cistus, irises and scabious, as well as many alpines.

soil profile

The characteristics of soil change vertically. Topsoil is the very fertile top layer that should be darkly rich with humus; it varies in depth from (2 inches) (5cm) to 1 foot 6 inches (45cm); in a small city garden, with centuries of cultivation, you may rarely get down to the subsoil. In gardens the topsoil often lies over a hard, impermeable "pan," which has built up over the years at the bottom of the level at which continuous cultivation takes place; this may need breaking up by digging deeply or by piercing with a fork. Below it is the subsoil, greatly affected by the base rock upon which it lies, so it tends to be mineral-rich but lacking organic matter. Because it contains less humus it is paler, so in turning deep soil you will see the difference. When digging a planting hole, lay the topsoil to one side and, without bringing the subsoil to the top, aerate it with a garden fork, adding bulky organic matter to improve its structure as well as its fertility. Although double digging is not really feasible in tiny gardens, always keep the topsoil separate, so that you leave the natural layers as they were before you started.

soil improvement and feeding

In your small garden you are likely to want to fit in as many plants as you can, making many demands on the soil. In these unnatural circumstances you will need to aid plant growth by improving the soil. There are two schools of thought about soil care: the "green" route means using natural organic composts and fertilizers, while the other involves the use of synthetic agrochemicals to compensate directly for deficiencies. Many gardeners, in fact, use a combination of the two approaches.

*below **Trilliums are one of the most beautiful ground covers for shade. This deep red form, flowering over a collar of three-lobed, marbled leaves, enjoys the acidic conditions created by the leaf litter at the base of a tree.***

Organic soil improvement means following a regime of good husbandry to create an ecologically well-balanced and ordered garden, with nothing "unnatural" added to the soil. This involves regularly working in decomposed organic material to improve the soil's structure, aerate it, conserve moisture, and break up solid clods of earth. Suitable additives include your own compost, if you have been able to make sufficient space for it, otherwise rotted manure, spent mushroom compost, leafmold, or cow dung, all of which can be bought, rotted-down, in bags from the garden center.

In addition to this, you may choose to use organic fertilizers in spring, to top up the soil's nutrients as a way of feeding your plants. Fertilizers, such as bonemeal, blood, and fish meal are readily available in powder or granular form. They add the main plant foods in a balanced proportion: nitrogen (N), which encourages the growth of foliage and stems, phosphates (P), which are the source of a healthy root system, and potash (K) for healthy fruiting and flower. The chemical symbols are quoted as ratios on packets. Most fertilizers also contain trace elements like magnesium and iron which are needed in small amounts. Specific deficiencies

of other elements can occur, although these are usually required in minute quantities; find out from your garden center what the particular remedies are in each case. Synthetic fertilizers are very effective and they are easy to store in small spaces. They come in both dry and liquid form and should be applied in an ecologically sensitive way, which means not overloading the soil with chemicals and interrupting plant growth. Never exceed the manufacturer's recommended dose.

The choice of fertilizer can help to control or reinforce the pH of your soil. To increase acidity, add acidic organic matter like leafmold or use chemicals like sulfate of ammonia or sulfate of iron. There is a concentrated tonic known as sequestered iron, which is a pick-up for plants with yellowing leaves. If you need to reduce acidity, apply cautious amounts of lime in the form of carbonate of lime (ground chalk); wear gloves and scatter it thinly by hand. Check the soil's pH again after two to three years.

Most fertilizers are best applied in spring, before the growth spurt but after the last frost. Some, like proprietary liquid seaweed, can be watered in and will reach down to the roots easily. Plants such as clematis are greedy for water and food throughout the summer, so regular, bi-weekly liquid feeding is a good idea in a tiny clematis-filled garden. Put a length of tube alongside the climber at the time of planting to be sure that water and food will effectively reach the root system.

Fertilizers that enter the plant through its leaves are fast-acting. They can be sprayed on to foliage in emergencies, such as when builders working in your yard compact the soil and disturb the roots of established shrubs. Foliar feeding is best applied at dusk when the leaves are "breathing in." At the other extreme, slow-release pellets provide a steady, measured input of feed over time and are particularly valuable for busy people and ideal for containers such as pots, windows boxes, and hanging baskets.

Soil is not the only growing medium. There are soil-based composts and a number of lightly structured, soil-less composts for use in containers and for seed-growing, which contain sand, grit, and possibly a natural aggregate like perlite, which is a heat-expanded, volcanic glass that helps to retain moisture. Young plants establish easily in these light mixes. For roof gardens, where weight and water-retention are particularly important, vermiculite is used instead of perlite. This is a lightweight, flaked, mica-like material, also of volcanic origin. Even shrubs will thrive in this medium, provided it includes fertilizer.

garden hygiene

Gardens, like houses, need regular cleaning to prevent a build-up of problems, and one of the advantages of having a very small garden is that it is easy to keep under control. You simply need to remove all garden debris, like fallen leaves, accumulated piles of weeds, and clippings, on a regular basis. Sweep hard surfaces and resist the temptation to empty these sweepings behind shrubs, back onto the soil. Left to rot, these mounds become homes to colonies of insects and can harbor disease spores as well; even piles of dry leaves provide hiding places for slugs and snails. Instead, bag up all debris and remove it from the site. It will probably all have to be carried through the house, so use heavy-duty plastic bags rather than flimsy ones, as prunings can be sharp.

Dead-heading keeps tiny spaces looking neat; done by hand or with hand pruners, it takes only seconds each day in summer. It also prevents the plants from putting their energy into making seed and, in the case of many shrubs like roses, or small herbaceous perennials like *Anthemis punctata* subsp. *cupaniana*, will promote a second flowering later in summer. However, some plants, like honesty, poppies, achilleas, *Sedum spectabile*, and ornamental grasses, have seedheads that are too attractive to remove; if left on the plant, their skeletal forms will enhance the garden in winter.

control of insects

In very small spaces, where there are few natural predators and you have provided insects with a *cordon bleu* choice of plants, the problem of infestation is greater than in a larger space. On the premise that prevention is better than cure, it is worth knowing your enemy and its weak points to stay ahead of the game. So, where possible, choose cultivars with pest and disease resistance and establish good habits of hygiene, including regular watering and feeding. Tackle all invaders at the first sign of infestation. There are organic methods of control—which use non-chemical, as well as organic insecticides and biological controls—and a range of chemical-based pesticides.

Contact chemical insecticides are sprayed onto the plant's surface. The pest is either hit by the spray or picks it up from the treated surface. They work instantly, but do not necessarily reduce the population much because there are often larvae ready and waiting to take over. The other problem is that you can easily kill beneficial insects too. You may, therefore, choose systemic insecticides which are absorbed into the plant's sap through their root and leaf systems; they do not harm beneficial insects like bees, but will deal with sap-feeding insects. Chemical control works, provided you use the appropriate specific insecticide. Always

left Anthemis punctata subsp. cupaniana is invaluable for its soft gray, filigree foliage covered with masses of white daisies for weeks. In a hot summer, deadheading it by clipping will ensure that there is a repeat performance later on.

To discourage feasting by slugs and snails, grow hostas in raised containers, where the marauders are more easily seen and can be picked off by hand. This elegant, white-flowering Hosta *"Frances Wiliams" is valued for its huge, lime-edged, blue leaves.*

wear gloves and apply it strictly in accordance with the manufacturer's instructions. Spray in the evening, making sure that pets and children are not in the garden at the same time. Do not spray in windy, sunny, or hot conditions. Store pesticides in a locked cupboard in the original container.

Organic pest control involves some tried and tested approaches. Sometimes merely washing plant leaves with clean water can remove aphids, and in very small spaces it may be feasible to adopt this individual approach. Insecticidal soap deals with aphids, red spider mite, scale insects, and thrips. Larger pests like caterpillars and snails can be picked off by hand; some gardeners leave saucers of beer or upturned grapefruit skins to attract slugs and snails, which then wait passively for you to deal with them. Organic insecticides, such as pyrethrum and derris, can be used against most insects but their effectiveness is short-lived.

Biological control is what happens in the wild, where pests are eaten by their natural predators; ladybugs deal with aphids, while ground beetles feed on slugs, caterpillars, and cutworms. Now you can buy a range of predators and parasites which provide effective control against a number of specific pests. Only use biological control as an alternative to chemical control, as the parasites and predators are susceptible to most insecticides.

disease in small gardens

Good cultivation is the best line of defence when caring for plants because a strong plant may throw off disease, whereas a weak one will succumb. Always buy healthy plants and give them a good start by careful planting in clean soil. Some diseases are soil-borne and others are carried either by insects or in the air. In the enclosed small garden airborne disease is very easily passed from plant to plant; humidity in the air encourages fungal growth so some summers may be worse than others, depending on weather. Enclosed courtyards, undisturbed by wind, also foster fungi. Leaving a good space between plants will help to control fungal infection, such as mildew, to some extent, but for those wanting to fit in as many plants as they can, constant vigilance is the only answer. Bacteria, virus, and fungus are the three main sources of infection and you can find chemical remedies for most of them.

Once you have diagnosed the problem, chemical control—using the right contact fungicide or other remedy—should work, provided you follow through by repeated applications as described by the manufacturer. Systemic fungicides get into the plant, providing long-term resistance. The makers of

agrochemicals produce information booklets advising on the identification of diseases, together with clear instructions on how to use their products to treat them. Treat chemicals with respect, never transfer them to unlabeled bottles, and always follow the manufacturer's instructions.

dealing with weeds

One gardener's weed is another gardener's treasured flower; many plant species are seen as "weeds" in their place of origin. But once you are clear about what you regard as weeds, there are ecologically friendly methods of removal—apart from the time-honored practice of digging out—which work well. Mulching with bark, rotted manure, or a 2-inch (5cm) layer of gravel over weed-free soil discourages the initial growth of weeds and is not unsightly in a tiny garden.

The available herbicides include contact types, which act immediately, killing green leaves and stems above ground, or

translocated weedkillers, such as glyphosate, which get into the system of a plant, destroying it more slowly because, in effect, the plant moves the chemicals around. Avoid those weedkillers designed for use on paths, as they remain effective in the soil for some months.

Spraying herbicides in a small space is quite difficult because you may not be able to be sufficiently selective. A better solution is the use of systemic herbicides in the form of gels, which cause the plant to fail over a period of weeks. This "touch-weeding" involves painting the gel directly onto a leaf, leaving the soil unaffected. The most effective time to apply weedkiller is when the plant is in newly green growth; do this in dry weather when you do not expect rain, which could dilute the effect.

No matter what we do to prevent them, annual weeds are invariably present in fertile soil. These may include hairy bittercress, groundsel, and chickweed, all of which should be hoed out regularly or hand-weeded before they set seed and spread. This also applies to nettles, which should either be dug out or spot-treated with systemic products made from glyphosate.

Perennial weeds are more difficult to eradicate. In the small space they compete with treasured plants for nutrients and, if left will usually win. They include dandelion, which can have a root as long as 1 foot (30cm) deep, as well as bindweed, and ground elder, which regenerate from even tiny sections of creeping underground stem. Repeated digging out or drenching with glyphosate will eventually work. Docks spread by seed, so dig these out when you see them or use a systemic or contact herbicide. If using a watering can, keep it for weedkiller only: residues can be left in the can which you may subsequently water onto your favorite plants without realizing.

left *A very small courtyard overflowing with flowering plants like alstroemerias, roses, valerian, sisyrinchium, and lychnis is nevertheless orderly because immaculately clipped box hedges and topiary control and manage the space so effectively.*

plant care

The success of your small plot will depend upon your management of it. In particular, you must understand the needs of your chosen plants, being sure of what to do and when, and care for them as individuals. Bear in mind their spread and find out whether particular plants will need reducing or merely tidying. Consider their watering and drainage requirements and, knowing your local climate, decide whether they need any special care in winter. In a small site, none of this need be too onerous.

pruning and training

When plants in the wild do perfectly well without pruning, what is the gardener's reason for doing it? In fact, trees and shrubs in the wild do shed branches naturally because of age, damage, or their normal habit. But pruning in gardens also means removing all unwanted growth, which may be unhealthy or growing in the wrong direction. There is more than one reason for pruning. Firstly, cutting back improves

and prolongs the vitality of a plant, increasing its flowering and fruiting potential. Secondly, pruning keeps naturally unkempt plants under control, which is important to the owner of a very small space. A third reason for training plants is for their decorative effect (see below); many plants also keep in better shape if clipped over occasionally. Finally, some large plants can be kept smaller than is their wont in order to make them suitable candidates for diminutive gardens. Carry out most pruning in the dormant season, before the spring burst of growth, possibly pruning again lightly in summer. Use sharp, oiled hand pruners to cut cleanly, without ragged edges, at a point slightly above a bud, which is then encouraged to produce new growth.

Pruning stimulates growth, which is why many fruiting trees and shrubs produce an extra-heavy crop when treated severely. Mature flowering shrubs like the small lilac (*Syringa pubescens* subsp. *microphylla* "Superba") will bear more flowers if a third of the old flowering wood is removed. The small, gray satiny-leaved *Convolvulus cneorum*, ideal for tiny sunny yards, will produce better foliage and flowers if it is lightly trimmed back in early spring. And shrubby potentillas can often be persuaded to flower again if they are cut back hard. Removing dead or diseased wood should be done routinely, as this too encourages regeneration. Wounds heal quickly and healthy new growth soon replaces the old wood.

To maximize the flowering potential of ornamental shrubs you need to know whether your plant blooms on "new" wood, which grew in the same season, or on "old" wood, on the branches formed the previous year. Most spring-flowering shrubs flower on

below *Trained evergreen ivy, carefully pruned to hug diagonal trelliswork, forms decorative patterns throughout the year.*

old wood, so shrubs like brooms (*Cytisus scoparius* and cultivars) must be pruned immediately after flowering, giving them time to grow the wood which will support the next year's flowers. Buddlejas, in the second category, flower in summer on the current year's wood, so they can be cut back hard if necessary in early spring, which allows them time to grow new stems for summer blooming.

Clematis are a more complicated case, because some flower on old wood and others on the current year's wood. Cut all newly planted clematis down to the lowest pair of buds in late winter. The most important thing is to be sure you know the names of every clematis in the garden so you can make a record of when each one needs pruning. This is particularly important in small gardens because the tendency of some clematis, like *C. orientalis* and cultivars as well as the hybrids related to *C.* "Jackmanii," is to flower ever higher up the plant each year. You will want to prune back the new growths each spring to lower the flowering height to eye level. The small-flowered, lower-growing clematis such as *C. alpina* and *C. macropetala* are particularly relevant for compact spaces: if pruning is necessary for reasons of space, trim their laterals (branches off the main shoots) back to one or two buds from the main shoots after flowering. Clematis in the vigorous *C. montana*

group should be pruned hard in early summer, once they are growing well; if they are ancient and tangled, shearing will do no harm. With many of the large-flowered hybrids like "The President" you can get away with light pruning if they are entwined in other shrubs. But reducing their growth in early summer, after the first flush of flowers, will keep them under control if they are against a wall, and allow for more growth, as well as some flowers later on. Always follow the advice on pruning times for clematis given in gardening books or a clematis-grower's catalog.

Maintaining an orderly garden involves cutting back vigorous plants, like *Clematis montana* and honeysuckle, which otherwise become a tangle of dead-looking stems. Some plants grow quickly, but with an unbalanced form, which wastes space in confined areas. The attractive small shrub *Ceratostigma willmottianum* is a luscious blue in fall, but then degenerates into a brown, straggly mess; cutting it back hard to ground level in mid-spring will ensure a bushy, compact shrub by summer. Some plants tend to die back in a harsh winter and it is best to remove the straggly growth that remains. *Lotus hirsutus* is a small, gray-leaved leguminous plant from the Mediterranean which will do well in a sunny yard, yet it partly dies back in a temperate winter to become rather ragged in appearance, so you should tidy the old shoots in spring. Some plants become lopsided through reaching for the light in a shaded site, and others throw up random spurs which need trimming off to restore their form. The usually neat varieties of *Euonymus fortunei*

left ***Early-flowering* Clematis macropetala *"Markham's Pink," with its pretty, nodding, moth-like flowers, is a small-scale species plant ideal for growing in compact gardens.***

far left **The silken seedheads of Clematis *"Ernest Markham"* continue the aesthetic value of this climber long after its flowering has finished.**

sometimes do this but are not adversely affected by trimming. Lavender, santolinas, helichrysums, and brooms also need to be trimmed annually; they will not stand being reduced to the ground because they grow from a woody stem and will die if you cut into this. Keep them in shape by lightly clipping over the whole plant with shears to make a dome shape; do this after the last frost and again after flowering.

Detailed, decorative control can be a remarkably effective way of enhancing a small space. Pyracanthas cope with any amount of cutting and can be trimmed flat against your boundary wall or pruned as parallel horizontal lines. This pruning is best done in late winter to prevent fungal disease entering the plant. Escallonias can be controlled to behave as flattened wall shrubs, but they will not withstand really radical topiary-work as pyracanthas will. Small-leaved ivies, on the other hand, can be persuaded to follow the slimmest linear patterns and can even be grown on dark walls (see Practicalities, page 166.

training fruit trees

It may be possible to turn a fruit tree into a highly decorative feature of your little garden by growing it against the wall as an espalier, fan, or cordon (for these and other trained forms, see Practicalities, page 166). The espalier and the cordon are particularly suited to small spaces, provided you choose an apple or pear grown on a suitable dwarfing rootstock; pears grown on quince rootstocks will tolerate moister conditions than apples and are more responsive to manipulation by pruning. The Conference pear is self-pollinating and one of the easiest apples is "Discovery," which will cross-pollinate with other apple trees near you. Both apples and pears can be purchased ready-trained, and from then on their lateral growths should be pruned to encourage fruiting spurs. Training like this requires patience and it will take about three to four years for these trained plants to bear fruit.

If you wish to train fruit, stretch wires horizontally against the wall, spaced about 15–18 inches (38–45cm) apart

(see Practicalities, page 166). The aim of growing in espalier form is to create a central stem from which branches are trained horizontally on either side, growing along the wires and flat against the wall. Cordons, usually single-stemmed, are often trained diagonally and grown parallel to each other, although they can be trained vertically as well (see page 166). Fans require more space than the espaliers and cordons: their branches are trained to grow out radially from the base, in a fan shape. Whichever form you choose, training is not entirely ornamental: fruit trees grown against a warm wall benefit from its protection and reflected warmth, both of which are fostered by training.

The symmetry of a fan-trained cherry ornaments the wall in all seasons, seen here with its fringe of ferns and neatly edged with dwarf box.

If you feel inspired by such ornamental pruning, consider growing some trees or shrubs which are too large for your small space, but are adaptable enough to be cut back every year, making them manageable. Eucalyptus can be stooled— that is, cut down every year or biennially to ground level—to make a multistemmed shrub that is wider than it is tall and whose leaves are much larger than normal. In the case of the hardy *E. gunnii*, stooling encourages the production of the rounded, gunmetal-blue juvenile leaves, which are much prettier than the mature lanceolate adult foliage. Other trees which can be cut down include ornamental elders like *Sambucus nigra* "Guincho Purple;" reducing this plant to ground level before its growth starts each year has the effect of intensifying the color, as well as making it more manageable. The large-leaved, golden Indian bean tree (*Catalpa bignonioides* "Aurea") will survive down-sizing too, its already large leaves becoming even broader in the process. Catalpas can be trained as a fan on a warm wall which will protect them from wind and frost. The pineapple broom (*Cytisus battandieri*) does well against a warm wall if pruned early in its life, after flowering, cutting into only the young wood to improve the production of silvery, evergreen foliage and bright yellow, pineapple-scented flowers.

Freestanding, large shrubs, like the ornamental *Cornus alba* varieties, can also be hard-pruned to ground level every year to encourage them to produce the colored stems—from yellow to red—so characteristic of the dogwoods. *Salix alba* "Chermesina" is a willow that also responds to hard annual pruning to produce orange-red winter stems. Some naturally elegant plants, like *Chaenomeles*, need a restrained hand with pruning; it is important to prune them neatly, in accordance with their shape and natural growing habit. Other small shrubs, like daphnes, need very little pruning: remove only dead wood or, if they are getting crowded, thin out a few stems.

Tiered shelving makes a virtue of necessity in a small garden. It is used as a tidy way of storing functional watering cans in a decorative display with small pots of white impatiens, green helxine, trailing toadflax, and small saxifrages.

watering and irrigation

The soil at the foot of house walls and boundaries always tends to be dry and rooty. Where space is limited these planting areas are precious, so it is crucial to water them regularly. One solution is to install an irrigation system that operates on a timer. But automatic irrigation systems, both the steady drip type and the "pop-up" type, need tanks which take up precious space (a minimum of 2 feet 6 inches by 2 feet/75cm by 60cm), which is quite a sacrifice in your tiny haven. An alternative is to go for a slow drip-feed form of irrigation via a perforated, or soaker, hose which is laid on the garden and can also be put on a time-switch. The slow seepage is effective in penetrating the soil and the roots, but a snaking hose can be unsightly and the holes can eventually get blocked, which may leave areas dry.

Expensive irrigation may not be necessary unless you are often away. Hand watering is easy in compact areas and it makes you look closely at your garden on a regular basis, reminding you to resolve small problems before they become big ones. A garden hose attached to an outdoor tap is less heavy than a can, and nozzle attachments produce a fine spray that is preferable to the heavy pounding produced by the direct flow from a hose, which can damage petals and foliage as well as washing mulch away from the plants. Most hosepipes can be neatly coiled on a reel; the wall-mounted types are space-saving. Remember that an outdoor tap will need to be protected from frost in winter.

There are other effective methods of conserving moisture in planting beds. Mulching, which involves covering the soil surface with a thick layer of material to prevent evaporation, will prevent the growth of annual weeds. A dark layer of weathered chopped bark covering the ground to a depth of approximately 3 inches (8cm) provides an attractive mulch and gravel is appropriate in sunny areas: it may sweep continuously from a planted area to a path, where a ground-cover matting underlayer will prevent any weed growth.

For raised planters, troughs, and containers there are water-retaining polymers that absorb water, after which they can be added to the soil mix to help it retain moisture. They replace peat, which served a similar purpose in the past. A drip irrigation system can be used for containers; if liquid feed is added, it will encourage lush plant growth too. Hanging baskets, notorious for needing twice-daily watering in hot, dry spells, benefit greatly from these polymers. They may be fed and watered on a drip irrigation system of looped fine tubing which maintains moist compost. Pulley systems are neat and easy to operate: they lower the basket to an accessible level for hand watering. Soaked baskets are very heavy, so make sure wall supports are strong and sturdy.

winter care

Exotic and tender plants can be wrapped in horticultural fleece so they suffer no frost damage; these are lightweight and allow light, moisture, and air to reach the plant. But cold is not the only winter problem: winds dry out the soil as well as foliage. Wind is a particular hazard on roof gardens, but fine plastic mesh, secured on stakes, can be placed in front of vulnerable plants on the windward side to act as a temporary windbreak.

storage

Gardens create a build-up of equipment and if your living accommodation is also compact, you will have no room to keep it indoors. But even the tiniest site requires some tools

A narrow shed, glossily painted and with a stained glass window, is made a feature in this small garden. A line of clipped box spheres in white-painted pots partially separates off the shed, but without concealing it.

and they have to be stored. Try to reduce a list of what you might like to the essentials that you need: a hand fork and trowel, a small border fork and spade, a good pair of hand pruners, a fold-up pruning saw, and a watering can with a long spout. Buy the best you can afford: stainless steel will not rust and, if you are storing tools outside, this is an important consideration. You will also accumulate canes, garden string, and ties, but empty plastic containers should be thrown away rather than stored. You need a yard broom and a dustpan to clean paving, and a foldable, wide-necked plastic bag, which is thornproof, for outdoor refuse. It is useful to have a large plastic sheet for garden use so that when potting up plants or dividing perennials, for example, the mess is contained and the debris easily disposed of.

Good-quality hand pruners are probably your greatest asset. They are very versatile and will cut stems up to ½ inch (12mm) thick. The anvil type, which has one sharpened blade that cuts down on to a straight "anvil" edge. These are easiest to use but can produce ragged cuts. Curved hand pruners have two curved blades, so that the sharper blade cuts against the broad curved blade, making a clean, neat cut. People with arthritic or weak hands might consider lightweight ratchet hand pruners which are efficient and easier to use. Always keep them clean, sharp, and well-oiled.

garden furniture

If you have to leave furniture outdoors all year round, it must be weatherproof. Tables and chairs should be made from treated timber, plastic, or metal; timber will need no maintenance if made from renewable hardwood. Plastic is lightweight for roof gardens, but chairs can blow away unless they are anchored; plastic furniture is vulnerable to ultra-violet light and will deteriorate in time. Metal furniture varies in quality, but aluminum will not rust if left out in winter. There is no advantage to having collapsible furniture unless you have room to store it. If you are really strapped for space, a fold-down shelf would allow you to eat outdoors. And have you considered blow-up inflatable seats? The built-in style of garden design can be a great space-saver, with retaining walls of raised beds doubling as built-in bench seats, provided they are at the right height. The freestanding "Shaker bench" is movable and handsome enough for indoor use; the seat is hinged over a box, allowing it to double as storage.

above **Timber is one of the most practical and sympathetic materials for garden furniture. The brick retaining wall of a raised bed behind the blue-stained table doubles as extra seating.**

greenhouses and sheds

For plant enthusiasts, a tiny greenhouse or cold frame can be a great source of pleasure. A lean-to greenhouse against the house might be the least obtrusive, provided it would benefit from good light there. There are now some miniature glasshouses available that are big enough to allow you to grow cuttings or protect tender, favorite plants. Even smaller, a tiny cold frame can be made from recycled glass window

far left **Advantage is taken of a shady corner to display functional items with shade-tolerant plants, such as hostas and ivies, in pots.**

right *The boundary of a roof garden made from metal scaffolding provides an ideal support for a heavy climber such as the Chinese gooseberry (Actinidia chinensis).*

above *Wisteria, with its lavender-colored racemes and attractive foliage, climbs naturally in twists and turns around the uprights of this wooden pergola.*

panes, to be assembled outside as required. The same amount of space could perhaps be better used for a little garden shed. If you think you have room for this, be sure it will take garden furniture and a lawn mower, if necessary, as well as essential garden tools. If you do not have room for a freestanding shed, you could build a shallow "wardrobe" against a house or boundary wall, with racks for tools and a few shelves. Make it as waterproof as possible by using pressure-treated timber and cladding the coping with a sheet of copper or other metal to help with rain run-off; the door hinges should be brass.

plant supports and fixings

Many climbers need support, but in a small space this should be unobtrusive (see Practicalities, page170). Choose a means which is neat as well as effective; plastic-coated wire netting does the job, but it is far from elegant and old hose will always look like old hose. Consider fixing heavy-duty galvanized wire to the wall in neat parallel lines; stretch it tight because sagging wires are ugly. Use vine eyes to attach it as they hold the wire away from the wall or fence, enabling climbers to twine. Sturdy wooden trellis will support climbers and is a good way to mask an ugly wall. Buy trellis in ready-made panels or make your own using pressure treated softwood or renewable hardwood. Think about attaching it to fixed timber batons, hinged at the bottom so that both trellis and plants can be pulled away for repainting.

New plants like clematis and roses will need tying in as they grow. Use proprietary ties which will not cut into plant tissue and which will allow space for increasing girth as the plant grows. Green or natural twine or string is unobtrusive, but needs replacing every so often. Look at the care traditionally given to ties by Japanese gardeners to see the attention they pay to such detail; the result is stylish in its own right. Never forget that in small gardens absolutely everything is on show.

illusion

The mirrored window within a window brings a touch of wit to the garden scene; it is angled to reflect a stone head.

This larger-than-life bronze fish out of water gasps its last as water trickles back into the pool.

A vanishing country road painted on a boundary wall invites us to explore, as well as providing the necessary bicycle.

A verandah extends the house out into the garden and draws the outdoors inside. Climbers hang down from overhead beams.

Ever-extending distance defies the confines of an enclosed courtyard – and it is all done by mirrors.

Placed against a mirror, the central plinth mounted urn becomes silhouetted in front of a wall "pierced" by a window of light, flanked by matching urns and standard trees.

left *Two tiny yards share a "canal" of water, exploiting neighborly friendship so that each garden benefits from a greater space and is linked to the other by a strong unifying theme.*

concealing and exploiting

In the tiny garden absolutely everything is on show, the assets as well as the eyesores. Making the most of your space means coming to terms with the immutable features of your plot and either exploiting them or integrating them as discreetly as possible. With precision planning, even the eyesores need not remain so: a mask or a face lift can achieve wonders. While the least attractive features of the plot can be physically masked by hiding them behind something else, the overall look of your tiny estate can be greatly enhanced by treating it in a way that creates the appearance of space while bringing out its inherent qualities.

concealing

There are in all gardens some minor irritations, like trash cans, wood piles, and oil tanks, as well as power meters, that we would happily dispense with if we could. If you are

designing your space from scratch, the most effective way to deal with the functional components of a garden is to site them in one place, usually dictated by the location of major services, and box them in with timber. Conceal the structure with a climber, resisting the temptation to be seduced by the speedy growth of Russian vine or Japanese honeysuckle. Although they will cover very quickly, they do not stop, which makes them too big for your site; try instead the self-clinging vine, *Vitis vinifera* "Purpurea," and stop it every year at least 3 feet (1 meter) below the eaves of the house. Alternatively, conceal the structure with a wall of clipped box or *Lonicera nitida*, making a feature of your functional area; do not use the very dwarf *Buxus sempervirens* "Suffruticosa," as it takes too long to form an effective screen.

Walls accrue attachments to do with the workings of a house, like gas flues, air conditioners, and ventilators. Never

far right *Exploiting every square yard of space, these two roof gardens are superbly designed as individual green spaces. The bones of the upper garden are formal, the grid principle being evident in both the planting style and the overhead white pergola.*

below *This enclosed small plot uses sturdy trellis to separate the family garden from the quiet area. Although it partially conceals one from the other, a rectangular opening in the trellis allows sight of a mirrored wall-mounted clay mask.*

cover these with climbers as the consequences can be dire. Instead, if they are close to ground level, use small, neat wall shrubs, like cultivars of evergreen *Abelia* x *grandiflora*, for example the yellow-green "Francis Mason" or the more compact "Sherwood;" both are slightly tender. Drainpipes on walls could be quickly covered by climbing plants trained up wires or netting. The pretty perennial climber *Eccremocarpus scaber*, which flowers through summer, grows as fast as an annual in cooler climes; it is tender but will be protected in a small courtyard. Small-leaved ivies, like *Hedera helix* "Glacier," make ideal candidates, being self-clinging and evergreen as well as hardy. But they become heavy in their mature stage and could damage walls, so prune them back regularly. The large-leaved Dutchman's pipe (*Aristolochia macrophylla*), can be trained on wires and will trap flies in its rather odd tubular flowers, but it will need constant vigilance to check that it does not spread too far. Make sure the stems do not go behind drainpipes because, as they thicken, they would gradually force the pipe from the wall. Deciduous climbers can drop dead flowers and leaves in gutters, so cut them back before they reach such a height

Drains and inspection covers always seem to be in the wrong place, spoiling an otherwise perfect paving scheme or making it impossible to grow a special plant in a particular place. Since it is unlikely that the drain itself can be moved, you must either conceal it or ignore it. It may be possible to pave around a drain, but manhole covers are often set at an awkward angle which does not fit in with the geometry of your paving. If realignment is not possible, you can buy metal-framed, recessed covers which are made to fit over an inspection cover exactly. They have a shallow depression so that paving slabs can be cut to fit the top or a material such as gravel can fill in the space. The courtyard surface is then uninterrupted and all that shows is the thin outline of the metal cover, which can be lifted for access as necessary.

Other solutions include putting a large planter on top of the inspection cover. This will not work if the weight of the filled container makes it too heavy to move—although you could put the planter on non-rusting casters and roll it out of the way as needed. This type of cover-up often has the opposite effect from that intended, however. Since plants in containers are usually sited either in corners, for reasons of space, or

along design lines, such as flanking a path or at the edge of a terrace, they look awkward when isolated, with no reason for their placement except the one you wish to avoid, turning an inspection cover into a focus of attention. If you were to adjust your plan so that there is a soil bed next to it, the cover can be camouflaged by a spreading evergreen plant like *Juniperus sabina* "Tamariscifolia." This will conceal it all year round and its branches can be lifted to provide access to the drain when needed. Rocks or pebbles may be used just as effectively, and laying decking over the whole surface will neatly obscure any eyesores beneath it; design a hinged trapdoor into the decking to allow access to the cover.

boundaries

Boundaries are a shared experience but they need not limit either our space or our imagination. Tiny yards can be joined together in a celebration of neighborliness.

Poor boundaries can be an eyesore, being particularly prominent in small gardens where you are never far away from them. Fences in a poor state of repair can be replaced or mended, but a scruffy brick wall is more of a problem. Do not be tempted to paint it because bricks are porous and can never be satisfactorily restored to their original surface. No matter how well the paint is applied, it will peel at an irregular rate and become grubby along the mortared joints. Repointing will smarten up a badly pointed brick wall but, if the bricks are not to your liking, it is better to camouflage the wall with panels of ornamental trellis or with plants rather than paint over them. This can be the lightweight timber lattice-work known as *treillage*, which must be fixed to the wall with galvanized screws in wallplugs. If you intend to grow climbers up the trellis, put spacers between panel and wall to allow them to weave their way around the posts and laths. Wooden bobbins make good spacers.

If you inherit old walls that are already painted or if you decide to paint a dirty concrete wall, think twice before choosing white, even if you wish to lighten a dark area. White continually needs to be renewed, as the paint becomes stained with green algae and moss and streaked with dirt. Never use black paint either because it, too, demands perfection and, unless this is a specially designed, modernist garden, the black will be depressing and light-colored dust and dirt become strikingly obvious on a plain, dark surface. It is preferable to paint walls in a mid-tone, such as a neutral "mud" or "sand" color, which will recede discreetly behind plants or a trellis mask. The most effective camouflage is the color of its surroundings—which is why soldiers in the desert wear sandy-colored clothing and, in the jungle, mixes of green—and you should bear this in mind if you want to make something fade into the background. Sheds and oil tanks take some concealing, but an approach like this will serve its purpose, especially if you follow through with self-clinging climbers like *Parthenocissus tricuspidata* or ivies. You may prefer to take a bold approach and paint a wall or feature a bright color, deliberately focusing attention on it. Add spirited plants, large of leaf and brilliantly colored, like *Rheum*

*below **Adjacent houses and courtyards show two schemes which blend together extremely well, one painted pale terracotta and the other a mellow pink, both tones being ideal for a sunny climate.***

*far left **Behind the trellis the wall is painted a pale sandstone color. This shade is warmly flattering to the lilac-blue lacecap hydrangea (H. macrophylla "Blue Wave") planted against the wall in a container raised on a plinth.***

palmatum "Atrosanguineum" or smaller *Acanthus spinosus* and *Crocosmia* "Lucifer." A generously intrepid approach can be inviting as well as amusing in a tiny space.

improving the view

Some things are with us whether we like them or not. If you live in an urban environment, it is unlikely that the view from your garden will be an asset. Since visual pollution is not something you can tackle on the larger scale, devote your energies to improving your part of this unlovely view. If you have an eyesore, such as a ramshackle corrugated-plastic shed roof on your neighbor's side, screening is the only way to deal with it. But since you also need to keep good relations with the neighbor, use sturdy trellis that will not take away any light. The effect of covering the trellis with plants will be more gradual than planting a mature hedge or putting up solid fencing. As an impecunious student, I once shared a boundary with a nervous neighbor whose tiny yard was surrounded with chain-link fencing, topped with barbed wire. Any plant which attached itself was beheaded, so all I could do was create a freestanding system of parallel canes up which I trained a dense forest of hollyhocks for the summer. Neither of us was unhappy with the result.

On the larger scale of a truly industrial landscape or an overbearing tower block, both of which are dominating, a better ploy is to divert attention away from the surroundings by screening, both physically and psychologically, so that only your garden matters. Distract the eye by emphasizing a feature within your own space, planning your layout so that this becomes the garden's *raison d'être*. It could be a piece of sculpture, contemporary or traditional, a plant-covered arbor, or a small water feature. All else then becomes subservient to the chosen feature, the plants serving as a foil for it and all design lines, like paths or border edges, drawing the eye to this internal focal point.

On the other hand, even though your own space is minute, your neighbor's may not be and there could be a tree in an adjacent plot which so dominates your garden space that it is, in effect, on permanent loan. This will affect all your layout and planting decisions. If it cuts out a lot of light, you could ask for the tree to be thinned a little or for the crown to be lifted. To reassure the neighbors of your good intent you could even offer to pay—but do use a specialist tree surgeon, as this is a skilled and sensitive job.

exploiting

There are no absolutes when it comes to what is aesthetically pleasing: ugliness, like beauty, is in the eye of the beholder. The current craze for "distressed" furniture, where immaculate wood surfaces are deliberately destroyed to the point of beating them with chains, would have been nonsense a hundred years ago. For a long time we have seen immaculate perfection as being the ultimate in beauty and yet we look at "antique" wheelbarrows and watering cans, their edges rounded and scraped with age, and find them charming. This hit home for me when I was looking at a glossy magazine and saw a photograph of a weathered shack in the Australian bush. The paint had peeled, the door hung from one hinge, and the roof was of rusted corrugated iron—but against the raw red desert the image was beautiful. I am not suggesting that you destroy your surroundings or cultivate an abandoned look, only that you take a dispassionate look at what you have and assess to what extent it really needs "dressing up."

Even the smallest yard will already have some redeeming qualities, like mellow brick walls or ornate cast-iron railings, balcony, or fire escape. Treasure unique assets such as these and turn them into an important feature of your small space. To make the most of architectural detail, avoid any extra embellishments, which will only serve to distract from them. With other old features, the key is whether the function of

the object is what has aged it in the first place. So cast-iron coal-hole covers, air grilles, old galvanized buckets, and clay sinks may be regarded as potential assets and incorporated into even the most pristine little yard. Garden "antiques" are being re-evaluated and all manner of domestic items used for improvised containers. I found an original aluminum pressure cooker in my garden which, when brushed up, looked vaguely like a bomb-case but which is now upright and home to a magnificent miscanthus. The occasional discordant note has much appeal.

the inward-looking garden

When the surroundings lack interest or charm, the tiny garden should contain enough fascination and appeal to exclude the hinterland, all eyes being drawn to what the garden holds. Pieces of sculpture or *objets trouvés* will provide an attractive focus for all seasons. Sculpture has been a part of gardens in the western tradition since classical times, and today the potential of three-dimensional art has expanded to include abstract as well as figurative pieces. Found objects may take the form of naturally contorted wood, interesting stones, and shells, or could include parts of old machinery or manmade functional objects of intrinsic interest. Whatever your preference, the siting of a piece is crucial because attention is instantly directed toward it. You will judge whether it is important enough to be placed on a plinth or will be freestanding and touchable; you may decide partially to conceal it within the dark depths of foliage. Wherever you are in the small space, it will have a presence, distracting attention from anything beyond the boundaries.

far left Making the most of vertical hanging space, the owner has decorated a dark shed wall with a collection of personal, yet weatherproof, loved possessions.

One of the most compelling features a small garden can have is water, because it involves the senses of sound and touch as well as sight. A very versatile element, it may be moving, flowing, pouring, bubbling, or sliding over a surface. The effective "wall of water" at Paley Park in Manhattan is a

right *A tiny fountain for a restricted space is easily made of upturned ridge tiles from which water pours into a slate box on a black slate tray surrounded by immaculate coping stones.*

far right *This small inward-looking courtyard has a quality of stillness because it is focused upon a traditional central pool. The pool is surrounded by a grassy pebbled floor and the garden itself is bounded by warm-climate plants, such as fan palms and cordylines.*

to commission an artist to create an original wall-mounted feature. Otherwise, it is possible to buy a simple, enclosed wall unit made from terracotta or lead-filled resin and glass fiber, or a narrow pipe which drips into a stone trough or onto a mound of pebbles concealing the basin. You will also need a small pump, placed below ground, which will feed the pipe encased in the wall; a power supply connected to the house will allow you to switch on the water whenever you want it. If you have young children, the safest idea is a reservoir-based feature, as there is no accessible body of

classic illustration of the soothing powers of water which turn this tiny park, hemmed in by giant buildings on three sides and with roaring traffic on the fourth open side, into a haven of tranquillity. Within your own space, you could use the sound and flickering light of water to divert attention from external sights and noise. Either choose the stillness of reflective water, its surface broken only by very small water lilies, like the fragrant *Nymphaea* "Caroliniana Nivea," or a slide of falling water that glistens, perhaps in association with *Iris laevigata.* You may prefer to have a fountain rising from a shallow pool containing *Caltha palustris* var. *alba* and *Myosotis scorpioides*; try to avoid making too heavy a splash which will be more suggestive of an inefficient, constantly running toilet cistern.

If you have little more room than a passage, you can still make a focal point of water using a tub with a miniature water lily, such as *Nymphaea* "Pygmaea Helvola," and keeping the water fresh with oxygenating plants like *Lagarosiphon major.* Or try the simple idea of a water spout fixed to a wall, with a basin below to catch and recirculate the water. This need not be the conventional lion's mouth: some companies produce alternatives imitative of gargoyles, like a clown's head bursting from a hoop, or you may wish

water into which they could fall. There is a choice of low, bubbling features in which the water emerges from a millstone, a drilled boulder, or rocks; and then trickles down over cobblestones and a surrounding planting of small ferns, tiny *Astilbe simplicifolia* "Sprite" and the compact *Hosta lancifolia*, and then collects in the underground reservoir.

If you are contemplating making a pool or water feature of any kind, seek advice from a water garden specialist, who will recommend the balance of oxygenating plants to others, as well as discussing the size and type of submersible pump for your needs. You should employ a qualified electrician to make electrical connections. Subtle lighting, put in at the same time as the piping for the pool or feature, extends the effectiveness of water into the evening (see page 78).

changes of level

Not all gardens are flat. If naturally hilly terrain means that your tiny site rises steeply or drops sharply down, you will need to do some leveling of the area immediately beside the house, however you decide to tackle the rest. If you live in a basement apartment, your windows will possibly face a vertical wall topped with iron railings. If the brickwork of the walls is attractive, make the most of it or, if the wall is rendered and sunlight is a luxury, paint it a pale color to lighten the area and reflect what daylight there is. This is one occasion where white-painted trellis, hinged to fixed batons, would look effective against a warm terracotta wall. Seek out wall shrubs and climbers which grow in shade, like the 3-foot (90cm) evergreen X *Fatshedera lizei*, with its attractive, deeply lobed, glossy leaves, for ground level, and a fragrant rose,

like "Mme Alfred Carrière" to flower higher up. Swags of clematis will be appropriate if the trellis is ornate in character. The plants will all thrive if they are grown in large, well-managed containers. An alternative would be to train small-leaved ivies along canes, laths, or wires securely attached to the wall with vine eyes in a large diamond pattern (see Practicalities, page 174); this effect would be decorative all year round. Pots of shade-tolerant, white *Impatiens* and variegated, tiny-leaved ivy, such as *Hedera helix* "Adam," can be placed on every step. A long timber trough, big enough to support trailing plants, could be placed on top of the wall, at the foot of any iron railings, to add another dimension to the vertical surface. As there is more light at this level, you might fill it with small evergreens, such as periwinkle (*Vinca minor*) with trailing fuchsias, verbena, and lobelia for summer.

Perhaps the building cuts into a naturally steep bank, the only level being a path alongside the house. Terracing would open up opportunities which those gardening on flat ground

far left **Even in a very small space the water surface reflects the light of the sky. Flanked by Eucomis bicolor, the tiny bird bath has already attracted duckweed, but this is simple to remove by hand.**

below **Raising the level of this courtyard has provided a narrow planting bed, as well as an opportunity to site wall fountains which feed a slim water course. The steep steps arching over this resemble a flying buttress supporting the wall.**

right *Containers full of annual Swan River daisy (*Brachyscome iberidifolia*) line the steps down to the sunken, narrow passage of a basement flat, bringing color to a dark area. Evergreen pyracantha and ivies line the walls and climbers create greenery overhead.*

do not have: a chance to create your own hanging gardens. It is advisable to employ a landscape contractor to carry out the construction of terracing, as it is essential to have well-built retaining walls, of thick timbers or masonry, and good drainage to channel water into adequate drains. Once the terraces are made and planted with trailing and tumbling plants, you need never see the walls again unless you wish to.

If the steep bank is firmly made, you can plant it without the need for terracing, provided no landslips would slide against the house. There are many plants which revel in vertical or sloping sites: the contours of the ground might be followed by conifers like *Juniperus communis* "Green Carpet" or *Cotoneaster dammeri* and its smaller sibling, *C. astrophoros*, with red berries in fall. Add a few large rocks and some dwarf pines, plus alpines like saxifrages, campanulas, and the mountain avens (*Dryas octopetala*). In deeper shade, bugle *Ajuga reptans*), dead-nettles (*Lamium*), and ivies can be allowed to spread. Plants with an elegant, arching habit, like green- and red-leaved Japanese acers and pendulous fuchsias, will be shown to full effect from below.

raised beds

Sometimes you may choose to provide different levels for planting, both as a means of making a flat area more interesting and as a way of packing in a greater number of plants. Freestanding raised beds can be built from sturdy treated timbers, bricks, or stone walling. They must have "weepholes" incorporated into them to allow water to drain out, ideally into narrow, pebble-filled gullies running along the base of the retaining wall and leading off to planting beds or a drain. Raised beds about 1 foot 6 inches–2 feet (45–60cm) high can be built all around the boundaries of a small site, providing built-in seats and possibly a built-in barbecue area, with a storage cupboard beneath.

Raised beds have many virtues. They make gardening easier for elderly or disabled people, as there is no need to bend down, and they enable all gardeners to grow trailing plants, like annual verbena and lobelia, or the flowering prostrate shrubs, like *Ceanothus thyrsiflorus* var. *repens* or the more tender *Rosmarinus* Prostratus Group. Those plants which arch before they weep, like *Fuchsia* "Mrs Popple," *Acer*

the garden at night

As an extension of the house, the garden should be available after dark, even in winter, exploiting its special ambience and enhancing its atmosphere as evening turns into night. Lighting also has a safety role, illuminating steps and entrances, as well as providing security. A good outdoor lighting company will advise on all these aspects. Stone steps, for example, can be downlit on either side, beneath the lip of the tread, making them an attractive feature, as well as one that is safe to use. And light from wall-mounted downlighters or freestanding, hooded lights on poles, can bathe steps and paths in pools of light, providing an easy passage without blinding glare from above.

palmatum var. dissectum or the lovely wand-flower, otherwise known as angel's fishing rods (Dierama pulcherrimum), are shown at their best when elevated to a higher level.

The growing medium in a raised planting bed can be different from that of the local soil so that, in an alkaline area, you can fill a bed with ericaceous compost in order to grow rhododendrons. For alpine enthusiasts, a low raised bed filled with gritty soil and top-dressed with gravel is an ideal means of growing these dwarf treasures. Incorporate some large rocks and complete the mini-landscape with very small conifers like the silver fir (Abies balsamea f. hudsonia) or the flat-topped spruce Picea abies "Nidiformis," alpine geraniums, campanulas, and phlox, and the tiny bulbs of Iris reticulata and Narcissus cyclamineus growing from a sea of Raoulia australis or Thymus minima.

The best outdoor lighting is subtle, allowing some plants to be seen in silhouette and others to be spot-lit. The garden should never be illuminated like a football field, shadowless and flat; too much lighting reduces its depth and destroys any sense of mystery. In extremely small courtyards restrained lighting works best, choosing to focus on a particular feature, such as a piece of sculpture, an urn, or a plant. Side lighting emphasizes form most effectively, as well as revealing texture, whereas front lighting tends to flatten and smooth out surfaces. The light source itself can be hidden from view and the beam can be either wide or as narrow as a pinpoint, creating different intensities depending upon the object itself and the desired effect.

Again with the source hidden, lighting can "wash" across a wall from below, creating a theatrical effect against which plant shapes or other features, like a cast-iron staircase, are silhouetted in a decorative pattern. If you do this in a very

above **At night the intimate garden shown in detail on page 116 has a different emphasis. The focal sculpture is back-lit, making all other pieces subordinate.**

top left **Everything on this roof garden grows in raised planting troughs. Osteospermum cantescens produces daisy flowers all summer because it is open to the full brilliance of midday sun.**

far left **Alpine sink gardens are for naturally miniature plants; grown as a collection, they look well together, benefiting from sun and free-draining, gritty soil.**

small space, little else will need lighting. The garden is thus treated as a "set" in a purely theatrical manner with the stars of the show in dramatic silhouette and the supporting cast only hinted at. At the flick of a switch you can change the mood completely, replacing the low-level uplighter with lighting from above, putting the prima donna in the spotlight while the shadowy background plants of the chorus acquire limitless depths.

Another lighting technique involves uplighting from below, with the light source beneath glass bricks or purpose-made glass-covered lights set in the ground. Uplighting can be a revelation when winter trees are silhouetted against a velvet-black sky: the trunk and branches will show their solidity and rough texture, while some of the finer twigs appear as delicate as spiders' webs. In summer, with its leafy canopy, the tree will look quite changed, its growth habit revealed in a different light. Arbors, too, can be shown up well in summer, with light flickering through floating twists of

wisteria or tapering trails of vines overhead, making it a pleasure to sit in the darkened garden. If you have a water feature in the garden, lighting will enhance every tremor, ripple, and droplet. It should be subtle rather than startling, so uplighting from below the level of the water or along the water from beneath the edging stone is the best method, making the water surface wonderfully reflective in both senses of the word.

Low-voltage outdoor lighting is safe out of doors, it will not burn plants and it is energy-saving, yet the options are very varied. The fittings can also be small, which is invaluable in a tiny space. You may want to tuck them out of sight, but even if you will see the light source in daylight, there are many simply designed, compact fittings which are attractive in their own right. Paradoxically, it is the darkness which is so important when lighting a small space. Indistinct depths of shadow that hint—as opposed to light which reveals—are all part of the subtle qualities of lighting. This is why colored light is so rarely effective: it distracts from the purity of light and shadow, which is what nighttime is really about. If you are not sure what effects you can create or want in your small space, get a friend to help you by using powerful flashlights. These can be carried around the garden, trying up, down, and side lighting while you study the results from the house window.

The successful use of outdoor lighting can create a delightful feeling of intimacy while, at the same time, suggesting that the garden is part of something rather bigger. Lighting is just one aspect of designing a small plot so that you can exploit its assets to the maximum. Few garden sites are completely ideal and it is surprising how often, in resolving problems, we generate original and satisfying solutions which add completely unexpected charm and help to make the diminutive garden unique.

below **A narrow basement space is enhanced by subtle lighting, cleverly revealing an elegant modern staircase which, by being put in the spotlight, here acquires the status of sculpture.**

trickery

Small should not mean cute or precious because this defeats the object of enjoying and feeling at ease in your little garden. Similarly, prissiness and over-meticulousness have the effect of emphasizing smallness. But you can have fun playing with reflections and tricks of illusion which confuse the boundaries and widen the horizons of your space. The use of optical techniques, involving line, scale, and color, can be surprisingly effective in creating real deceptions.

using perspective

Perspective illusions have fascinated artists since Roman times. Wall paintings in Pompeii show complicated architectural background scenes which retreat in implied space. By the time of the High Renaissance in Italy, "rules" for drawing accurate solids and spaces had been devised and linear perspective became all the rage in European painting. What has this to do with your tiny plot? By using those same rules you can deceive the eye into believing that your garden is considerably larger than it is—but, like painting, this works from only a single viewpoint. Perspective illusions are based on the premise that objects appear to get smaller as we look

into the distance. Hold your hand in front of your face and look through your fingers at people across the room: you will see that they appear to be nearly as small as your hand. Of course, this is not reality but simply your perception of it.

Similarly, if you are standing on timber decking laid at right angles to the house wall, with the lines running away from you, the slats appear to get narrower the further away they are: if your view continued to a far horizon, they would eventually be seen to meet. In the same way, the boundary walls to either side of your garden also appear to diminish and get closer together the further away they are. From your viewpoint, the top and base lines of the wall appear as diagonals, tapering ever closer to each other. The eye accepts this, so we still "read" it correctly, knowing that the wall is actually a constant height. But what if you design this into your scheme physically? What if you foster the perspective illusion by planning a wall which really does get lower at the furthest end of your garden, or if you gradually reduce the height of a hedge by clipping the top so that it slopes down toward the far boundary? From the house, the garden will appear much deeper than it is. If you are building a pergola overhead, you can decrease the gaps between the upright posts and bring the sides closer together: gradually narrowing the width of the area beneath the pergola fosters the illusion of deeper space. Central vanishing-point perspectives like these reinforce the impression of depth most effectively if they are not obvious: it is the subtle reduction that completes the illusion.

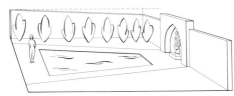

If your space is really too tiny for the above examples to be relevant, linear perspective can be made to work in a simpler way. Try a similar effect at ground level by deliberately tapering the width of a path from, say, 3 feet (90cm) to

left Looking surprisingly contemporary, this fresco painted on a wall in the garden of Loreius Tiburtinus in Pompeii shows a garden perspective of a small basin with fountain and accurate representations of birds.

garden with narrower slats. Similarly, large-leaved plants, like *Fatsia japonica,* could be placed beside the house with the smaller, but similar-leaved X *Fatshedera lizei* sited on the furthest garden boundary.

above left *Much is made of a triangular plot by siting narrow decking paths to follow a zigzag course to the raised sitting area at the far end. The effect is to lengthen the apparent distance.*

above right *The illusion of a doorway and distance beyond it is painted on the far wall of a garden, inside a raised "arbor." Despite its shallow depth, the suggestion is of a fantasy garden glimpsed through the open door.*

far right *In this same intimate, verdant garden, the addition of freestanding columns and mature leafy canopy make the dark, receding depths seem deeper than they really are.*

2 feet 6 inches (75cm). If you are paving the garden with rectangular paving stones, lay them running lengthwise from the house and use a jointing pattern to reinforce the lines, with the long sides mortared but the short cross-joints "butt jointed," that is, laid tightly together without any mortared seam. This will emphasize the long lines at the expense of the widthwise joints, increasing the garden's apparent length. Laying decking in parallel lines at right angles to the house is a simple way to achieve a similar lengthening effect.

the sense of scale

False perspectives make effective illusions when they refer to the human scale. Build features on the far wall slightly smaller than you would expect: for example, a "loggia," made to be looked at but not used, with three arches about 5 feet 6 inches (1.6 meters) high and a depth of only 3 feet (90cm), will look as if it were functional. Painting the interior dark will make it look deeper still. The inclusion of figurative statuary, approximately three-quarters life size, is another way of altering proportion to indicate distance because the eye will assume that the figure is life size. You could foster this illusion by siting a statue at the far end of a tapered pool, drawing the eye to a supposed distance.

Reinforce false perspectives by making elements of your garden larger in the foreground and smaller in the distance. Regular slatted fencing can be imitated at the rear of the

color perspective

All the suggestions above presuppose that the garden is viewed frontally, which is usually the case in tiny courtyards with one point of access. But other "laws" of perspective can be used where this is not the case. Color is surprisingly successful as a means of expanding or diminishing volume; bold reds seem larger in area and appear to advance, whereas cooler blue tones recede. Think of the "blue horizons" of islands in the sea which are, in reality, green— but distance adds a blue quality. If you wish to increase apparent depth in a small garden, plant the intense reds, like those of *Crocosmia* "Fireglow," or hot oranges and yellows found in annual *Cheiranthus* cultivars, at the front, and the cool blues, purple, and lilac, like those of campanulas and blue salvias, to the rear. Any red with bluish overtones, such as the coolly crimson monardas, will seem further away than their hot scarlet counterparts, the heleniums.

Color also has a dark and light value (see page 43) which is useful as a means of implying depth. Dark colors retire, while pale colors seem closer. So pastel flower colors, like that of cream *Eranthis hyemalis* "Ivorine," are eye-catching and project, while the contrasting deep blue *Aconitum* "Spark's Variety" retreats, fostering the illusion of a greater distance between them. In an enclosed small courtyard with rendered concrete-block walls, you could paint the far boundary wall a dark color as a means of creating implied depth, rather than a pale tone which would make it advance.

Use your plants to reinforce the illusion of depth, siting those with very fine leaf detail, such as *Lonicera nitida* or dark claret *Berberis thunbergii* "Dart's Red Lady," which give a uniform surface texture, to the back of the garden with large-, glossy-leaved subjects, like *Aucuba japonica,* or the large, shapely foliage of the oak-leaf hydrangea (*Hydrangea quercifolia*) near the house. All plants of character have a clear surface texture: there are those with fine foliage, like many artemisias; for shade, dicentras, thalictrums, or gypsophila make the same finely tuned, hazy effect. Take a leap forward by choosing plants with bold foliage and a clearly delineated profile for the front, like bergenias or hostas for shade, planting with them large, dominant, flowering perennials like brilliantly colored gillardias in sun or white foxgloves in shade.

reflections

Of all techniques the use of mirrors is the most effective for enlarging space. To understand the power of reflection for use in very small gardens, think of the mirrors not as mere decoration, but as a means of piercing through a solid

plants and perspective

Texture is an element that also comes into play as a means of suggesting greater depth, which is why landscape painters reduce detail in the far distance of their painted scenes. In the garden, you could use coarser gravels to the fore and finer gravels or even smoother paving at the far end, or you could pave your terrace with large flagstones near to the house, with smaller units of paving, such as granite setts, in a paved area that is further away.

boundary wall with a hole of light, extending into other gardens. Further the illusion by setting a large mirror inside a three-dimensional arch, making the arch appear double its depth and revealing a phantom courtyard beyond. A subtle extension is to make false lintels and frame the mirror "windows" with stone, brick, or timber, and complete the effect by concealing any give-away edges with an overlap of evergreen foliage like that of ivy or, at ground level, *Cotoneaster dammeri*. You could let plant foliage hide most

These two pictures (left) present an interesting contrast.
far left *This classically romantic courtyard contains trellis, topiary, and a wall painting whose image is entirely ornamental, describing another courtyard set in an idyllic Tuscan landscape of blue hills and narrow cypresses.*
left *In this garden, illusion is intended to fool the onlooker, convincingly revealing sunlit courtyards through the arches. In reality, the arches are backed with mirror and the other gardens merely phantoms.*

right and below *Arches again, but here the successful illusion is right, as a narrow strip of water flows through real space, then on into limitless "ghost" space.*

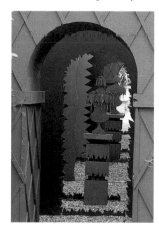

above *This garden also uses mirrored glass to provide brilliant light beyond what is clearly a theatrical, two-dimensional image made from flat-painted wood. The small stretch of water butting up against the mirror creates the illusion of a long rectangular pool.*

of the mirror, perhaps setting it among bamboos or lushly foliaged subjects, such as the larger astilbes, until the wind blows and flashes of reflection suggest places which do not exist. Kits are available with trellis fronting a mirror: these are effective for suggesting that a secret garden lies beyond.

The increased spaciousness suggested by a mirror is somehow credible, even when you are "in the know," provided you site

the mirrors where you do not face them when entering the garden. Seeing yourself initially would instantly destroy the effect. And never place a pot or statue in front of a mirror, as this, too, ruins the illusion. Make sure that the mirror is set directly on the wall and sits squarely onto the paving or path that leads right up to it. Then, standing slightly to the side, you will see what appears to be an entrance to another "ghost" courtyard.

For greater depth design the garden so that a long strip of water, such as a canal pool, runs up to a mirror on the far wall, so that no edge or coping is visible: this will become a convincingly continuous stretch of water, leading on into the fantasy world of the looking glass. Similarly, a rectangular stretch of water would appear as a larger, square pool. On the other hand, if the water stretches across the width of the yard and mirrors abut it on either side, the illusion goes on forever, like a veritable canal.

Mirrors will bring light into the gloomiest of dark recesses and double the verdant effect of shade-loving plants growing at their base. All you really need to see are flashes of a view,

so that they catch the eye and force you to look again. Even then, you will still find the illusion convincing. Add to the effect at night by using subtle lighting to foster elusive nightscapes, always ensuring the light source is hidden. Glass can be used to lighten effects in another way. Steps and walls made out of glass bricks and glass-topped outdoor tables are less heavy-looking than wooden ones and enable you to see the planting through them, increasing the garden's lush quality.

An attractive and economical solution can be achieved by combining linear perspective with mirror glass to create a *trompe l'oeil* effect. Trellis is normally used flat, but it can also suggest three dimensions if it is constructed along perspective lines. Covering a whole wall with a run of diamond or square trellis, pierced with implied round arches or "windows," is convincingly witty. Build the trellis by copying the rules of linear perspective to create an illusion of depth and fit a mirror within the central "window" to complete the effect. Although you can use ivy, provided it is kept under control, plants need not be part of the scheme. If you have a very dark wall, use trellis only and stain it a light color.

far left *The trellis perspective and painted door are intentionally and wittily obvious. But seen through the chink of the open door is a true reflection in a sliver of mirror. The implication of a real sunlit open space beyond the door is totally convincing.*

below *The floor level extends out from the house into the garden as a deck, linking the outdoor space with the interior. The lower garden is reached by steps from the terrace rather than the house.*

linking house and garden

Verandahs are a feature of houses in hot landscapes where the house reaches into the garden and the outdoors is drawn inside. In cooler areas, conservatories try to achieve the same effect, but the glazed walls remain a barrier. In a very small courtyard, a verandah could be built to stretch part-way into the garden, with only timber uprights as support: these can be made to vanish, becoming columns of green ivy. "Framing" a small garden in this way can appear to extend the outdoor space as the indoor room becomes an integral part of the garden. If the same paving—say, terracotta tiles—runs through the living room, verandah, and into the garden,

above **Verandahs are an excellent way of linking indoors and out. Here, overhead beams extend from the house walls into the garden space. They carry climbers which hang down and fill the outdoor space with greenery.**

the uninterrupted floor space will complete the unity. If the garden is little more than a passage, the verandah could extend across the whole space, a transparent glass or rigid, clear plastic sloping roof letting through sufficient light to support plants.

trompe l'oeil

Trompe l'oeil is an old French technique which grew out of the illusionist paintings of the Baroque period. It involved commissioning an artist to "paint away" the surface of a wall to create a fantasy perspective with a garden, fountains, cloudless blue skies, and whatever Fragonard fantasies appealed to the owner. In your own garden, painted trellis can relate to real trellis and painted plants to real ones, while fountains, arches, and bridges may lead the eye into distant landscapes far removed from the reality of your urban surroundings. If you want a more contemporary scene, you could commission an artist specializing in wall painting. Perhaps you could be inside a huge, tropical conservatory or you might like to see cows look back at you over a fence; maybe you always wanted a view of the Chrysler building and a New York skyline. All you need is imagination to make it yours. Remember that wit is an important ingredient for success. A smaller version would, of course, cost less, so if a real door or gate were to be attached to the wall and left open, it could reveal a glimpsed view. Fake windows or a metal grille could also be fixed to the wall above a small mural, or your shallow "loggia" (see page 81) could have views painted behind it.

If you are creating your own *trompe l'oeil*, make sure the wall surface is well prepared before you start painting. Old paint can peel and become powdery so it must be scraped and brushed off to remove any loose material. The surface on to which you will paint should also be stabilized with the right preparation which will soak into the surface and bind the paint to it. Provided you use exterior masonry paint, your horizons will last for years.

The Viennese artist Friedensreich Hundertswasser designed community apartments in which interiors and exteriors were merged together, with radiantly bold ceramic color, uneven terrain floors, and an overflow of plants. His roof gardens erupt with greenery, some of which trails down many floors, forming undulating walls below the roof. Can we take inspiration from this? Provided you have advice from an architect (nothing destroys a house faster than water and

above **Peacefully perusing the newspaper, a painted figure reminds us of the purpose for which an arbor is designed.**

left **A rural image is conjured artlessly on a wall in charming naive painting style. The real young girl with her cat turns to the camera with an unsure look, whereas the bicycle and chicken are assuredly solid.**

swelling roots), there is no reason why the greenness and brilliance that lights up the suburbs of Vienna could not be given a local interpretation elsewhere.

From the modest outdoor space defined by bricks and mortar with which you start, through the use of illusory tricks and the inspiration of fantasy, you can create an enlarged, other-worldly garden with an atmosphere all its own. If you carry through your ideas with confidence, it will become such a pleasure than even you will be content to suspend disbelief.

above and right **The Viennese artist Friedensreich Hundertswasser created a colored house for people to share. Architectural fantasy and trees are part of the rooftop skyline, while festooning climbers conversely trail down from high above and plants grown in architectural pockets in the building ornament the walls. Each person is entitled to a small open space, a tiny garden, each one different and entirely personal.**

atmosphere

What do we expect of our gardens? Are they just flower collections or are they a means of expressing ourselves? The way we decorate our exterior surroundings is, for many of us, our main creative output and whether your personal "paradise" is a place of extravagant fantasy or quiet reflection, it should not leave you unmoved. The best gardens set a scene and have a style of their own. Decide on the atmosphere you wish to conjure up and take inspiration from the gardens shown here.

There is just enough scope here to sit side by side among the scented lilies in an intimate, abundantly planted oasis.

Defying logic, granite setts are seen to be "floating" on the water which takes the place of cement jointing.

This contemplative, formal garden focuses upon a golden orb suspended on a slim wand over the shallow moon pool.

Fantasies are alluded to in this shady retreat, with a squat cherub half hidden by the foliage of ivy and a large vine.

Frothy green ferns surround orange drill-heads rising from the planting bed in this theatrical, totally original garden.

Beneath a canopy of huge, fanning palms, spiky yucca, and the sumach's pinnate fronds, the pool and colonial-style furniture create a sultry, inviting atmosphere at the end of a hot day.

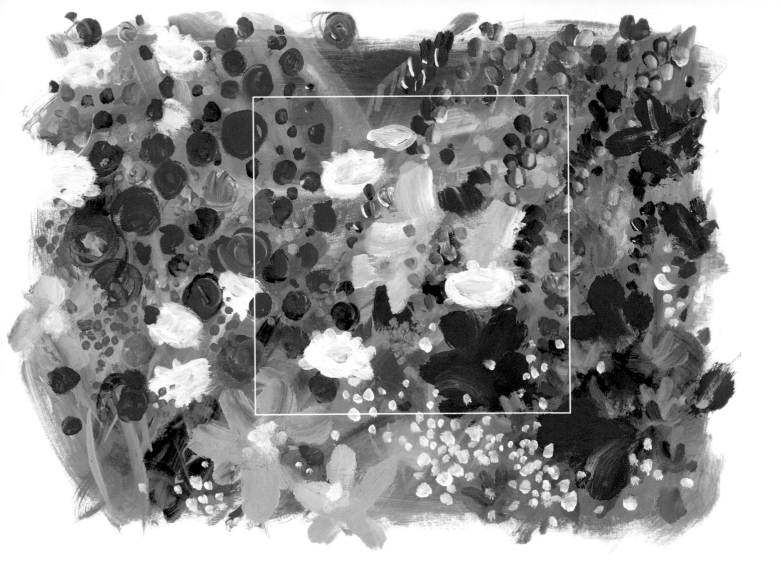

abundant gardens

Is a garden for people and for outdoor living, as described by the garden designer Thomas Church? Not always. For some, the whole reason for owning a garden, however small, is to grow as many and as wide a variety of plants as it is possible to cram in. The easiest way to do this is to festoon the boundaries with climbers, to amass containers over all the hard-surfaced areas, and to make the most of every piece of ground by working and enriching the soil. Supplement permanent planting with annuals and tender perennials. Although there will be little room to sit, this may be your choice.

1 *The bronze foliage of* Hebe ochracea *holds the attention among erect plants like* Verbascum chaixii, Verbena bonariensis, acanthus, *and the distant mass of salvias.*

2 *Yellows dominate in the flowers of Welsh poppies,* Alchemilla mollis, Phlomis fruticosa, *and the foliage of grassy carex, marjoram, and the golden hop.*

3 *There is barely room to sit in this small, scented garden crammed with clematis, hostas, phlox, lavenders, astilbes, lilies, and pelargoniums.*

4 *Blue, yellow, and pink irises, heucheras, columbines, and honesty rise through a hazy sea of pale blue forget-me-nots.*

Walls and fences are the first areas to use because the ratio of floor space to vertical growth is in their favor. Fences can drip with plants clambering over one another, while strong wall shrubs, like ceanothus and pyracantha, provide a frame for more slender climbers such as magenta *Rhodochiton atrosanguineus* or orange *Eccremocarpus scaber* (both grown as annuals in temperate climates) or the hardy passion flower. Securely fixed climbing roses can support the smaller species clematis as well as some of the hybrids, provided you avoid the top-heavy forms of *C. montana*. Vines, wisteria, and actinidia provide densely overlapping foliage patterns and some annuals, like black-eyed Susan (*Thunbergia alata*) and canary creeper (*Tropaeolum peregrinum*) can easily be accommodated too.

In very small spaces containers are the answer. Collections can be accumulated in pots of all sizes and at all heights, some raised on other, upturned pots, piled high, massed on tables, or standing on improvised plinths. You can buy octagonal shelf units, rather like a tiered wedding cake, which emulate the elaborate wrought-iron display tables made for showing pot plants in the nineteenth century. Similarly you could make rectangular tables from wooden slats to match trellis or use a pile of containers built on a foundation plinth of bricks; these will be simple to erect or dismantle as needs change. As long as the compost is suitable and the top layer is replenished every year, anything

left *Deep blue aconites and purple lavenders make a rich association with the yellow evening primroses (Oenothera tetragona) in this abundantly planted front garden. Clematis and the perennial pea (Lathyrus latifolius) cling to the railings.*

right *Among a mass of hosta foliage, white arum lilies (Zantedeschia aethiopica) stand erect behind the cream flower spikes of Sisyrinchium striatum. Pots of rich purple heliotrope provide contrast by the small pool covered in feathery milfoil.*

lobelias, petunias, nicotianas, and mallows for a copious display, assisted at the end of the season by alstroemerias, lilies, chrysanthemums, and penstemons.

In summer you can move rarities which do well inside the house outdoors to fill a sunny courtyard, still growing in their containers, to foster the exotic image; they will require the same care as they have indoors. With plants like monsteras, clivias, ficus, cannas, dracaenas, and cordylines, magnificent foliage is often the result. Handsome daturas, sought after by all who see them in hot climes, can be grown outdoors for summer in a generous container, where they will display their large, fragrant, tubular flowers. The dark-leaved false aralia (*Schefflera elegantissima*) can be grown in light shade as a 5-foot (1.5-meter) containerized specimen or the smaller, variegated *Dracaena marginata* "Colorama" in full sun.

As companions, some hardier plants may abundantly fill the scene. On the wall, X *Fatshedera lizei* with a clump of bamboo or *Miscanthus sacchariflorus* could back the large-leaved ornamental rhubarb (*Rheum palmatum*) in moisture-retaining soil, or the tough *Acanthus mollis* in freer-draining soil. These will help to create a jungle-like picture, into which pots containing the ginger lily (*Hedychium gardnerianum*), a

can be grown in a container; this even applies to trees, whether restricted in Japanese fashion or grown as young infants until they outgrow the root space and need replacing.

If you group together a plant collection in containers of various sizes, this could include a display of foliage subjects—sword-like, palmate, fluted, feathery, drooping, or mounded in towering heights. In sun, red-leaved heucheras, filigree artemisias, and spiky *Eryngium bourgatii* add texture as well as form, while, for shade, the rounded, variegated leaves of brunnera could be used with glossy bergenias and foaming astilbes. Some plants may trail at the foot of erect irises, verbascums, or phormiums, while others weave in and out of one another, competing for light and creating a glorious disarray that will need subtle management. Flowers will contribute a range of colors, as well as additional shapes and textures. Spring bulbs can be followed by summer-blooming

These rooftops overflow with plants to the extent that the tiny courtyards below are barely visible. Bamboos mix with ivies and vines, and pots house conifers as well as summery begonias, pelargoniums, and geraniums.

dark purple canna, a palmate-leaved castor oil plant (*Ricinus communis*), and powerfully scented datura could be inserted.

Passionate plantpeople cannot resist collecting, acquiring unusual plants, growing the "ungrowable," such as rare alpines or plants from foreign parts, with triumphant pleasure. Others concentrate upon particular groups of plants, such as ferns or alpines, or collect a genus which interests them, like *Fuchsia*. A fuchsia collection may be cerise, claret, violet, pink, white, or even orange, as in the tender "Thalia." Hardy forms, like carmine and purple "Tom Thumb," are subtle compared with the double largesse of the more tender "Dollar Princess." The fun lies in providing the conditions that each expects from nature.

A highly decorated glazed pot holds a standard wisteria, with a group of gracefully fading tulips filling in the center. This small garden is awash with plants: forget-me-nots, bellis, and geraniums at ground level, with taller foxgloves, dicentra, and rudbeckia rising above. There is even room for a two-dimensional sculpture.

Plants mass and mingle in beautiful disarray in nature, but in small spaces a "wilderness" of artless charm works best if some cultivars are substituted for species, because the flowers last longer. Many wild plants flower well, quickly reproduce themselves, then fade away. So mix in hybridized plants selected for the best characteristics that resemble the natural species: an example is the delicately structured *Hemerocallis* "Golden Chimes." Creating a wild scramble also means avoiding rigid plants, like hebes, which are unresponsive to wind, and missing out exotics like fatsia, with their heavy foliage.

The paving in an abundantly planted garden is a matter of choice or expediency. If all your money is to be spent on plants, then recycled paving slabs, engineering or reclaimed frost-proof bricks, railroad ties, or simply concrete, studded or not with chippings, would be fine, since the surface will mostly be obscured by foliage. Alternatively, you can throw down gravel where you need access, continuing its flow over the sunny plants as a cool encouragement to seed themselves shamelessly in every growable surface—irresistible for the plantaholic. There could then be a glorious disarray of Californian or Welsh poppies, pinky-white erigerons, foaming alchemillas, nodding aquilegias, sprays of forget-me-nots, and tiny violas, all of which will distribute themselves around freely. These can be selectively weeded out as necessary or allowed to increase every year with little assistance from the gardener. Nature is usually extremely abundant in the interests of survival.

*right **This tiny Californian garden is verdantly crammed with containers holding fragrant datura (Brugmansia), clematis, fan palms, heuchera, and tender abutilon.***

Two vertical shapes—a fine wire obelisk and a green cypress trained as a standard—catch the eye in a foliage mass, with alstroemerias, day lilies, and Rosa "Parkdirektor Riggers."

courtyard of abundance

It is clear from the layout of this small city garden that the priority is plants. Some space has been allowed for sitting out among the flowers and there is a cooling wall fountain which takes up little room. Axial paths cross the space, leading to the fountain and the sitting area. The high wall at the end is covered with trellis and the tiny garden feels enclosed and inward-looking, focused entirely on the green oasis within.

Wall shrubs and climbers mass around the perimeter of the site and the four beds are crammed with herbaceous plants, aided and abetted by those in containers. The foundation planting consists of wall shrubs, like blue-flowering ceanothus and the fragrant Japanese honeysuckle (*Lonicera japonica* "Halliana"), as well as many different ivies, including the vigorous *Hedera helix* "Oro di Bogliasco;" these cover the walls for most of the year. Other climbers on the wall trellis include *Vitis coignetiae*,

below **Cooling water is pumped through a lion's head to spout down into the tiny pool, from which it is eternally recycled.**

clematis, and roses. There are more evergreens in the form of a handsome *Fatsia japonica*, with its palmate glossy foliage, rounded mounds of clipped box, the yellow-spotted laurel (*Aucuba japonica* "Crotonifolia"), and the contrasting small-leaved *Pittosporum* "Garnettii," gray-green with white edges.

The designer-owner Patrick Rampton has extended the planting opportunities on the house side of the courtyard by building timber rafters out from the garden room; these carry overhead climbers, such as wisteria. But the centerpiece of the garden is the froth of summer color, supplied by flowering perennials like cerise-pink phlox, orange and white lilies, foaming creamy astilbes, daisy-flowered osteospermum, and the tall, purple-blue *Verbena bonariensis*. Small shrubs, like *Hypericum* "Hidcote" and low silver shrubs of lavender, and the satin-leaved *Convolvulus cneorum,* are assisted in high summer by tender plants, such as white marguerites, red and white variegated pelargoniums, deep blue lobelia, and masses of fragrant white tobacco plants (*Nicotiana alata*). No wonder the reclining chairs have a firmly reserved space: this is a plant world with accommodation for people, rather than the other way around.

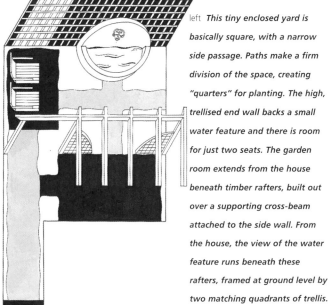

left **This tiny enclosed yard is basically square, with a narrow side passage. Paths make a firm division of the space, creating "quarters" for planting. The high, trellised end wall backs a small water feature and there is room for just two seats. The garden room extends from the house beneath timber rafters, built out over a supporting cross-beam attached to the side wall. From the house, the view of the water feature runs beneath these rafters, framed at ground level by two matching quadrants of trellis.**

above **In full summer, fragrant white nicotianas fill the space beneath the permanent hardy climbing roses and wisteria trained to clothe the overhead timber beams.**

right **Backed by evergreen ceanothus and ivy, and surrounded by climbing vines and evergreen shrubs, there is just room for a pair of reclining chairs among the glorious profusion of lilies, phlox, lavender, lavatera, and euphorbia.**

contemporary gardens

Changes in garden style generally take place over a period of time. Attitudes to design tend to alter gradually, as each generation absorbs the changes made by its peers and adapts these in different ways until a completely new identity has evolved. The blinding flash of "eureka" is given to very few and nearly all designers who have effected radical changes in different artistic spheres, like the English painter William Blake or the Spanish architect Antonio Gaudí, have had a unique and personal vision that was almost irrelevant to the time in which they lived.

1 Spare simplicity characterizes this cool garden. Meticulously laid pebbles create a textured grid at ground level, while a slim strand of water echoes the repeating linear pillars.

2 Mounted upon a copper monolith, three heavy gourd shapes carved from blackened timber are scooped out for plants and a fall of water.

3 Angles and uprights make the structure of this small city garden using modern materials. The silvery "fall" is made from cascading waves of steel.

4 Decking creates geometric ground patterns, with trellis behind and sentinels of matching bay and ferns on either side of this strictly green, contemporary environment.

In eighteenth-century England, "Capability" Brown made radical changes and swept away the superb, but no longer fashionable, formal garden style of the past, declaring that the way forward lay in creating new, "natural" landscapes with apparently random clumps of planting and no straight lines. The landscape style of garden design prevailed until the early twentieth century. Modern domestic gardens evolved on an "arts and crafts" scale, taking over from the large gardens of the nineteenth century, which had been maintained by ranks of gardeners. Once labor was no longer available, after World War I, designs were scaled down, although they continued to use the "new" plants that were being introduced to the West by intrepid plant hunters who brought them back from the East, Africa, and Australasia. With the social changes of the twentieth century, smaller gardens maintained by their owners necessitated a rethink. The phrase "low maintenance" crept into garden vocabulary and, with it, the notion that twice-yearly complete replanting of spring bulbs followed by summer bedding was over.

A further influence for change came with the development of architectural styles in buildings, which moved away from the conventions of classical order, the rhythms of symmetry, and a penchant for ornamentation. These building principles were replaced by a different set of ideals: the desire to simplify form, the strong link between design and function, and a tendency to reduce decoration to the minimum. This

way of thinking had an increasing influence on garden designers as the twentieth century developed.

Building materials have changed, too. Concrete is a fluid medium which can be given many faces—smooth, textured, stonily coarse, colored—or it can be made to simulate scarce resources, like sandstone paving or other quarried stone. The use of timber decking has become increasingly popular and the potential of manmade materials, like reinforced glass, synthetic plastics, rubber mixes, resin bonding mediums, and alloys of steel and aluminum, are all being explored for their use in the garden. Boundaries may be made from pierced concrete blocks, laminated toughened mirror glass, transparent rigid plastic, simulated timber made from recycled polystyrene, or short-lived materials like woven reeds. Pergolas need no longer be made from wood: stretched steel wire, slim aluminum rods, and even scaffolding are modern alternatives.

Many contemporary small gardens have taken a lead from the tiny, finely honed Buddhist courtyards of the classical Japanese era. Such gardens are for reflection, absorbing the mind without distraction. Everything has significance in the

Japanese garden and controlled, symbolic planting grows alongside carefully selected, sacred, natural materials, like stone, wood, and water. The Japanese appreciation of the essence of different elements is subtly reinterpreted in

contemporary Western gardens as understated, pared-down elegance, where each stone, slab, or plant merits attention, rather like theatrical one-man shows. In tiny contemporary gardens all materials, whether living or inorganic, have to earn their place in a space unadorned by fripperies.

Minimal, oriental-inspired styles of garden are especially appropriate alongside modern architecture. The planting should, above all, be simple and balanced, with one plant dominant and any others minor, however exquisite. A few rocks and one immaculate acer or the low-spreading *Pinus mugo* can provide the pared-down relationship which becomes the focal point of a courtyard. The ground is more likely to be graveled or laid with stone slabs than with lawn, and the boundaries evenly covered with an all-over pattern of self-clinging vines or ivy—or with nothing at all if the materials used are perfectly constructed, with meticulous attention to detail in the supports of a fence or the joints of a brick wall.

A growing ecological awareness of precious nature, so easily and irreversibly violated, has had its effect on garden design, too. It has made us appreciate the stability of plant communities and try to emulate them in our gardens by selecting only plants which thrive in the conditions on offer.

far left **A tiny enclosed Chinese courtyard garden in ancient Suzhou style is composed with the restraint of this classical period in southern China. The few symbolic landscape elements include rocks, gravel, and** *penjing,* **which is similar to Japanese bonsai.**

far left *Created with fastidious simplicity, the detail of this small garden shows Japanese influence. Green bamboo stems are underplanted with dwarf azaleas and ferns, beneath which spreading helxine, moss, and Thymus coccineus are green islands in a sea of gravel.*

left *In two green roof gardens atop modern buildings, one is carpeted with lavender and the other with ivy. The edging shrubs are yucca and bamboo.*

right *An extension of living space is seamlessly achieved here by a restrained geometric layout and cream paint. The discreet outside lighting continues the indoor/outdoor theme at night, top-lighting a wall feature and illuminating a group of plants from below.*

Plants like ornamental grasses and those grown for their serendipitous seed distribution affect the look of mixed planting and an effect of charming dishevelment is deliberately courted; this style is entirely in keeping with an approach which also values recycled materials.

If they are very small, contemporary gardens may be carefully planned as a celebration of foliage. Even deciduous leaves are likely to be seen in the garden for almost three-quarters of the year, compared with flowers which are usually on show for only a few weeks. Many foliage plants have strong architectural form and this is very much to the fore in terms of contemporary garden design. The small garden acquires much cachet with the inclusion of a dominant, over-scaled architectural plant, like melianthus or the exotic fan palm, *Trachycarpus fortunei*. Sculpture may be used instead of plants to draw the eye and this is more likely to take the form of abstract shapes or *objets trouvés* than a classical statue. Imagination has mixed form with function so that plant pots and water features are designed with a modern flourish, often unique to the small garden they dominate.

Water is highly valued in today's small spaces. It may take the form of "swallow holes" in the ground, bubbling up from pebbles, it may be contained in small bowls from which a tiny fountain fans outward, or it can spurt from small wall sculptures to be collected in a basin and then recycled. The sound of fountains or the faint splash of a tiny fall is especially pleasurable in enclosed urban yards. Some people like to see the movement of water, its ripples, splashes, and eddies controlled by unseen electric pumps, and others enjoy the tranquillity of totally still water, reflecting the light of the sky as it changes from cerulean blue to wispy clouds or even blackened by a threatening storm. Such sensory experiences are as important to contemporary gardens as they were to gardens of the past.

left above *Entrances must fit with the house style, and the linear geometry of this building sets the design for its Japanese-style courtyard. Flagstones of granite surround a rectangular pool and the rise of the steps is followed through across the space to create a weir of water. Feather palms, philodendron, and water hyacinths soften the angular effect and thrive in the warm climate.*

left below *Where a house is designed on bold contemporary principles, the garden must be part of the whole concept. Here, minimal planting makes an effective foil for the eye-catching sculpture, while the "mosaic" stone paving echoes surface detailing in the building.*

right *For a roof terrace with a view like this one in Paris, the design must be kept simple. A central block of built-in timber planters, placed to view the panorama, combines seating with a miniature landscape of rocks with clipped firs, pines, and box, alongside grassy mounds of green festuca.*

For some people, the absolutely new can be alarming and they prefer their garden to allude to a different culture; this has become another theme of contemporary gardens. Along with Japanese style, the Moorish theme, with its use of rills or narrow water courses, as well as monastic knot gardens with their geometric herb beds, have inspired modern designs. The past is often inaccurately recorded , leading to a pastiche of a time that never was. But it can be effective to use motifs of the past in a new way, avoiding the seduction of nostalgia, to create gardens with a contemporary integrity.

green peace

Many small gardens are narrow and rectangular and the usual solution is to edge a central open area with borders, but here bold, simple planning has created a garden which is undeniably modern yet inviting. Designer Cleve West has divided the space both horizontally and vertically into two areas. The "division" is made by a shed which extends via timber beams across the yard, bisecting the garden and providing a dominant, central gateway. The shed is roofed with meadow turf, the grassy mix containing daisies, clover, ragwort, dandelions, buttercups, and cranesbills. Beneath it is a layer of roofing felt covered by nondegrading plastic.

The two courtyards are distinct: in one a rectangular stretch of water flows across the garden from one side to the other, visually widening the area. The other, slightly sunken, provides a garden for sitting, in which a hammock gently swings in the distilled green calm.

Linking the two, the ground is paved with granite setts and recycled slabs; in the second

This narrow space has been made exciting by effective use of division. The garden is bisected by a shed, roofed in sod, which extends to become an arch, creating two separate spaces. One is dominated by a wide stretch of water and the other, virtually square, is used to sit in.

garden both materials have been used to make low retaining walls. At ground level, the setts have simply been bedded in; in place of mortar, water flows between them, making a watery maze for tadpoles. Where the setts are used for low walling, the absence of mortar allows plants to seed themselves in the walls, so construction materials and planting become interdependent. The rigid garden boundaries themselves have been dissolved into green velvety walls of shrubs and ivies.

Sensitivity to ecology is a major part of contemporary thinking and of this designer in particular. Noncombative toward nature, Cleve West allows many inhabitants to share his garden without recourse to chemical controls. The essence of this garden is the comfortable relationship between manmade and natural: while heavy setts appear to float in water, wildflowers grow on a roof.

The plants are a combination of bold forms, like the loquat (*Eriobotrya japonica*), *Yucca recurvifolia* and *Acanthus hungaricus*, interspersed by the large seedheads of *Allium cristophii*. They contrast with the delicacy of grasses such as *Eragrostis chloromelas* and *E. curvula* and the swaying grace of the tall feather-reed grass (*Calamagrostis* x *acutiflora* "Overdam"). Dwarf reedmace (*Typha minima*) edges the water and dwarf *Nymphaea* "Marliacea Chromatella" rests its leaves on the surface.

opposite *From the house, the garden invites exploration. Access via a large stepping stone leads across the water and beneath the sod canopy into the open space beyond. Two carved sculptural "pods" open to make solid seats with back support. Paving and granite setts link the two areas.*

below *Bold shapes are made by siting a yucca beside the gourd fountain. Water flows from the crocodile-like "snout" into the geometric pool below.*

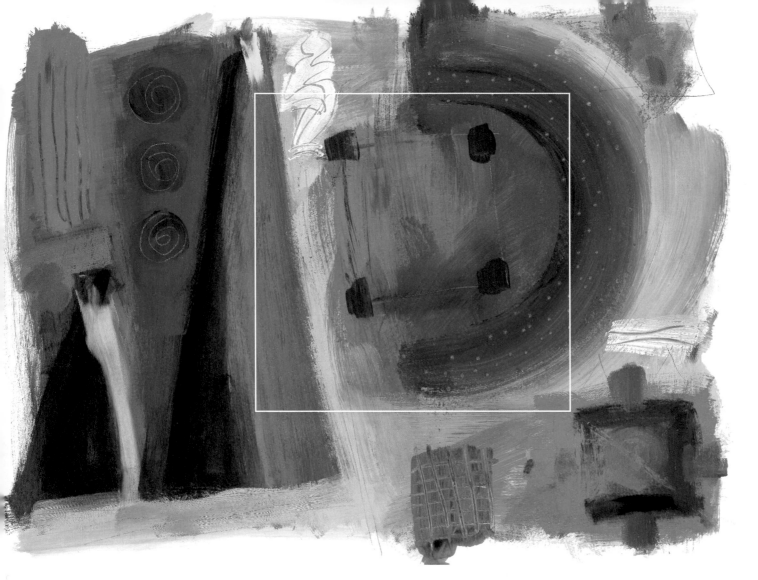

formal gardens

Designs based on symmetry are restful because, rather than exciting curiosity, they present a world of balanced order that is both peaceful and reassuring. Those of us who have busy and eventful days would be pleased to return to a simple outdoor space designed around parallels and right angles. You could reinforce the tranquil effect by keeping to a restrained palette of plants, using different tones of green to create contrasts of dark and light, or let planting beds echo the formality by pairing or making repeat patterns of plants like standard fuchsias or domed santolinas.

Throughout history and in all cultures, gardens have returned time and again to formal themes. Houses in ancient Greece were built around an inner courtyard, a tradition followed by the Romans, who used angular designs with straight paths around rectangular beds of formal clipped planting. In Pompeii the smallest garden found is only 7 feet 6 inches by 1 foot 6 inches (2.25 meters by 45cm), virtually a long window box. The wonderful hedges of the Villa Lante gardens in Italy, clipped with mathematical precision, take the visitor across contours in gently rising slopes.

From the Aztec gardens of Montezuma to the Mughal gardens of India, formality prevailed. In Montezuma's time, the Aztecs built small, highly formalized private courtyards; the Mughals in India made straight paths or water courses to divide their gardens into rectangular patterns. At the Alhambra in Spain symmetry also ruled, with narrow water channels leading the eye along straight lines. And in medieval Europe the enclosed monastery gardens were built on the same logical principles, with axial pathways and regimented beds trimmed with box and santolina. During the course of garden history, classical revivals sometimes held sway and now, with relevance to contemporary architecture, some designers have returned to pure geometry again. In our own personal and modest spaces we can learn from the best formal gardens: their spiritual presence is of great value in today's compact, but precious, outdoor rooms.

Straight lines can be just as effective in very small gardens as they are in large ones, leading us along a route and involving us with the plants or acting as dividers of the space. Repeated shapes, such as columnar conifers or small domes of clipped box, placed at regular intervals, can emphasize direction, while also making symmetrical patterns which frame or outline planted and paved areas. The effect of balanced order is pleasingly simple and, provided evergreens are used, maintains interest in the garden all through the year.

Formal designs are planned on paper using parallel or diagonal straight lines and all curves follow the form of radii, that is, parts of a circle. These lines enclose flat shapes like squares, rectangles, triangles, rhomboids, and circles. Linking the shapes together through the use of grids or as repeating patterns creates the two-dimensional layout plan of a garden. But as gardens are three-dimensional spaces, this is where the cube, the pyramid, and the sphere come into play.

Some people are averse to the idea of formality in a garden, thinking it to mean a hard-edged and unsympathetic style. In fact, more gardens are planned on formal principles than not, but the softness of planting complements such defined spaces and the garden's atmosphere may well be totally romantic. Traditional rose gardens, like those of Bagatelle in Paris, France, and Queen Mary's rose garden in Regent's Park in London, England, are both sensuous gardens full of color and scent in high season. Yet their underlying layout is symmetrical and

left **Absolute symmetry focused upon a geometric conifer "wall" is emphasized by a pair of standard** Cupressus arizonica **var.** arizonica **framing the view. They are grown in carefully placed matching containers, with carpeting junipers at their feet.**

Apart from the historical precedents, it is noticeable that all designs based on rhythmical repeated patterns, whether three-dimensional or flat, tend to sit well with buildings. Since all gardens are, to a greater or lesser extent, controlled and stylized versions of nature, those which are planned on a grid pattern, creating compartments and providing static areas, and those which depend on an axial focus are an acknowledgment that organizing nature in a formal manner can produce places which restore the spirit.

right *This elegant French roof terrace is simply laid out in parallel lines. Square sections are cut out of the decking so that seasonal containers, here filled with white chrysanthemums, can be slotted in. Gray-leaved mounding santolinas and erect clipped dark yews add to the formality*

right *Clipped dwarf box hedging and an arch covered with* Actinidia chinensis *emphasize the axial path which leads the eye to a white-painted arbor beyond the central circular pool.*

geometric. The same can be said of traditional herb gardens and potagers. These were historically planned with geometric precision, usually made more emphatic by outlining beds with clipped hedging of box, santolina, or lavender. Yet the atmosphere of these gardens is undeniably "such stuff as dreams are made on."

The idea of formalism is still valued in contemporary design, although stark minimalism has more often given way to a simple, refined elegance, sometimes with a touch of flamboyant self-expression. Even when using materials that are not traditionally used in the garden—glass, plastics, and metals—many designers still choose formality rather than a more random style. This is because the trend in contemporary architecture is toward geometric simplicity—to the point of severity with the use of concrete—which may or may not be adorned with surface decoration. The lines of the garden should always work with the building, so their design will inevitably have a formal bent. The roof garden designed by architect Rick Mather shown on page 122 is composed on geometric lines, yet his choice of lush, overflowing planting makes this contemporary garden green and romantic.

Many of the formal gardens shown on these pages could have been planned with a ruler to create their straight lines, measured distances, and symmetrical patterns. Each one has both style and charm and is the result of a bold decision to make the most of a defined and limited space by very simple, formal means. Peaceful and sophisticated rather than dramatic and flamboyant, they all employ restraint, often using the repeated shapes of clipped evergreens and perhaps adding just one color, usually white. Some show an entirely decorative treatment, with plants used to frame or to edge. Although they are all different in character, each garden creates a satisfying sense of order and sets a scene based on restfully patterned, small-scale spaces.

the sun and moon garden

Tightly designed for a very small space, this garden is a contemporary interpretation of seventeenth-century formal grandeur. Designer George Carter has translated it into the twentieth century as a moody, allegorical "vision of Versailles," with grottoes, *allées*, finialed stone pillars, and *treillage*, making the intimate space look far larger than it is. The courtyard is intended to be viewed centrally, and the scale is deliberately falsified to increase the apparent depth. The background is underscaled and the foreground overscaled by reducing the width between the trellis pillars, tapering the square pool very subtly, and altering the texture of the gravel, using a coarser grade to the fore and a finer grade further away.

The whole assemblage is more than just trickery, however. The overall color theme, based on reduced tones of gray, sets the

Clipped cones of box are a feature of formal gardens and are as static as the containers in which they may grow.

scene for contrasts of light and sparkling reflections to have maximum impact. Inside the dark trellis columns, deep green yews create dense living texture; seen beside them, the clipped pyramids of box become a more intense emerald green. A sheet of water skims the central "moon pool," reflecting light from the sky, and silvered glass spheres, or "suns," suspended on slim metal stalks, gleam in the mysterious depths of the garden.

Side *allées* cross the central square of the courtyard, leading on one side to an opaque glass panel backed with metal foil from which light is bounced theatrically from the wings of the "stage." The grotto is lit from above, while the circular moon-center of the shallow pool revolves gently, catching reflections of the sky above. The strong design concept gives the garden a stillness and calm.

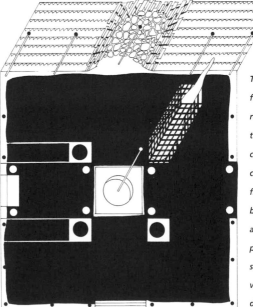

This symmetrical plan for a very small space revolves around a tiny, square, inner courtyard with a central shallow pool, flanked at each corner by small box pyramids and emphatic trellis pillars. These mark the side allées, each of which leads to a different focal point.

above **Directly opposite the glass wall is another small "apse," treated ornamentally by being lined at the end with gleaming metal sheets edged with a repeating jagged pattern. These mold into the curve, wrapping around a metallic orb which is poised in space and naturally lit from overhead.**

left **Formally restrained in an angular column of dark trellis, the even darker fastigiate yew aspires to greater heights.**

right *A view down the central axis of the garden shows the opaque glass wall with clipped silver santolina at its foot; the formality is intensified by finialed piers which flank it. The sense of depth is increased by the use of linear perspective.*

below *The grotto, seen along a side axis, is part of a small, semicircular space made from a receding curved wall textured with rough flints. It is framed on either side by rusticated masonry cornerstones, simulated in carved strips of wood and lit by the sky. The sparkling "sun" sphere seen in front appears to be suspended in the air, although it is supported from below by a slim metal wand.*

shady gardens

Are gardens at their loveliest in full sun? This is an idea that may need to be readdressed. The finest gardens are those with atmosphere, those which affect our mood, and fully involve our attention; whether they are in sun or shade is of no matter. It is, in fact, easier to create small gardens of mystery and character when working with shaded depths than in spaces that are fully exposed to the sun.

1. *Almost disappearing beneath a luxurious boundary of vine, this shaded garden is secretive and inward-looking. A paved central area reserved for seating is decorated with pots and statues.*

2. *An urn in shade harks back to traditional European garden styles. Here a low-growing fuchsia, with a hosta beneath, receives enough light to thrive.*

3. *The feathery pinnate leaves of Rhus typhina "Laciniata" create dappled shade in this tiny courtyard; fan palms behind the seats give further privacy.*

4. *Many of the foliage plants shown here thrive in shade, including the maidenhair and polypody ferns. Variegated small-leaved ivies trail from containers and, given more light, Acer palmatum var. dissectum completes the green grouping.*

Shade suggests green, large leaved lushness which people gardening in burning heat would envy. The richness of texture, with its overlapping patterns of foliage is usually associated with the misty dampness and low light of temperate climates, such as western Europe. So if you have a shady retreat, aim to work with the conditions of your site and, through the use of appropriate plants and materials, create an all-pervasive, verdant atmosphere.

Shade can present problems at ground level if the wrong hard surfaces are chosen because they take longer to dry out after rain. Smooth slate or glossy ceramic tiles become very slippery when skimmed with water and old bricks and clay paths attract moss in damp, dark places, although charming to look at, a mossy surface is dangerously unsafe to walk on. So for paving in damp, shady climates, choose coarsely textured flagstones of natural or imitation stone, or concrete slabs that are slightly ridged, for a secure footing. Bear in mind, too, that water features in dark shade become green and grotto-like almost overnight, producing an effect far removed from the one of sparkling freshness which you may have intended.

If the garden is enclosed by tall boundary walls to hide unpleasant views, this will further reduce the light. In such a case, view the walls themselves as a place to drape with flowering or evergreen twisters and twiners. Growing self-

clinging plants, like ivy, is the easiest solution in shade, but fine wires can act as supports for climbing plants, such as honeysuckle, which will do well once they reach toward the sun. Clematis, which take up little room and prefer to have their roots in shade, are ideal for small spaces as long as they are very well fed and watered regularly.

As far as the choice of shade-tolerant plants for ground level is concerned, there are plenty of woodland species to choose

In the heat of the sun, the shade offered by an arbor becomes the greatest attraction in the garden. Here, a trellis structure creates dappled light for eating comfortably al fresco.

from, even if the light levels in your garden are permanently low. Evergreens have an important structural role in small spaces and there are many that are reliably shade-tolerant: a green framework which never alters through the seasons will be particularly welcome in city plots where the immediate surroundings may be bleak. Some evergreens, such as mahonias, offer winter flowers with a strong fragrance and others, like aucubas, contribute leaves which are variegated

and polished; the bamboos are excellent in shade for their exotic, rush-like effects. If your soil is acidic, there is a range of smaller rhododendrons, like the yakushimanum hybrids, which carry large trusses of flowers as early summer approaches, in addition to camellias, flowering in spring, and the skimmias which produce their fragrant spring flowers, followed by bright red berries in the fall.

Beneath these shrubs many other plants will flourish, bringing textural effects as well as flower color to shady areas. Select ferns for their varied forms and fresh, textured green leaves unfurling in the spring, as well as hellebores, handsome of foliage, which may be tall, with green flowers, or shorter with flowers in plum-purple, soft pink, or creamy-white. Small spring bulbs, such as dwarf narcissi, will add cheerful color and, with them, the luminous hues of blue, pink, or white *Anemone blanda* can carpet dark, low levels; try, too, the tiny spring- and fall-flowering cyclamen or the taller *Lilium martagon*. The temporary inclusion of impatiens is always invaluable for brightening shaded areas in summer.

The soil in shade may be completely smothered by carpets as low-growing as moss, if you use plants like sweet woodruff (*Galium odoratum*) or the minute-leaved Corsican helxine (*Soleirolia soleirolii*). Purple-leaved bugles (forms of *Ajuga reptans*) or acid-loving *Pachysandra terminalis* make larger patterns at ground level. For the deepest shade there are ground ivies, like the large-leaved *Hedera hibernica*, as well as the wide-spreading evergreen *Lonicera pileata* whose tiny leaves will cover the surface of the soil. Brighten the darkness in spring with a spread of mid-height *Euphorbia amygdaloides* var. *robbiae*, their attractive lime-green flowers lasting for many months, or blue-flowering *Brunnera macrophylla*; in plain or variegated form, and for dry as well as damp shade choose the spreading, white-striped woodland grass, *Luzula sylvatica* "Marginata."

above **A green view from a balcony onto a small, shaded garden shows the contrasting foliage of fan palms, acacias and** Juniperus recurva var. coxii.

right **Even in deep shade, the variegated** Hosta undulata var. undulata **grows in overlapping lush layers in its container.**

far right **Foliage offers a wealth of textures and patterns which are very welcome in shade. Both** Choisya ternata **and the narrow-leaved fern,** Asplenium scolopendrium, **have glossy, light-reflecting leaves; the variegated** Euonymus fortunei **also brightens the depths.**

The damper the natural conditions, the wider the possibilities for lush foliage. A great advantage of being able to sustain a shaded and damp microclimate is that many plants which enjoy these conditions, like the magnificent rodgersias, offer large, interesting leaves that are very attractive in the small urban yard. Check first that these are in scale with your intentions: just one such plant could make a superb focal point in a tiny space. There is also a wide range of hostas that will thrive in damp, shady places, and whose foliage will provide form and greenery for half the year. Some of their leaves are symmetrically heart-shaped, like those of the compact, blue-leaved H. "Halcyon" (Tardiana Group), only 1 foot (30cm) wide and high, and others have rippling forms, like the variegated H. undulata var. undulata, while H. "Ginko Craig" is small with narrow, white-margined leaves. The tiny, plain green-leaved hosta, H. "Pastures New," grows to a mere 9 inches (25cm) high. Others can be huge.

If you wish to create a sculptural effect, include a tall, large-leaved rodgersia or ligularia to dominate the garden, or a white-flowering cimicifuga, whose spikes will tower up toward the end of summer. In damp conditions hydrangeas will add color at the end of the year. Some of the lacecaps, like H. macrophylla "Mariesii Perfecta" (syn. "Blue Wave") and the low mophead H. "Preziosa," are small and particularly fetching. In dappled light you can also include primulas if you are sure of constant dampness in the soil.

Paradoxically, one of the great assets of shade can be areas of light, particularly if plants with decorative profiles, like bamboos, foxgloves, or the tall, acid-loving ostrich fern (Matteuccia struthiopteris), are planted to be silhouetted against the sky. Sometimes the shady area is beside the house and one can look out onto a lighter space from beneath a dark canopy. If the area is densely shaded, use

Hosta foliage is often linked with the more ferny-textured leaves of astilbes, of which there are some excellent small forms, like the deep red A. x arendsii "Fanal" with dark foliage, the delicate A. simplicifolia "Sprite" and tiny A. x crispa "Gnome," only 6 inches (15cm) high. It is a good idea to leave the dead flower plumes on astilbes as their erect brown feathers will look beautiful in frost—a bonus for the small shady garden in winter.

brilliant or pastel color for the furniture and other detailing, or even for the surrounding walls. Reds and oranges are warmly welcoming, especially in the dark winter months. A great advantage of a dark background is that it makes a marvelous foil for color, intensifying strong hues and making pale colors luminous. And at night well-directed lighting can make it essential to leave the drapes drawn right back in celebration of the view outside.

a shady retreat

The design of this tiny, square space, only 16 feet by 22 feet (4.9 meters by 6.7 meters), is extremely simple, with a small raised dais at the end on which sculpture and pot plants are displayed. It was designed by the owner, John Sowerbutts, who planned it as an extension of his living space. It is entered from a conservatory densely covered by the vine that envelops the whole courtyard, merging the two areas into a private sunken living space. Paved with old natural stone slabs and old bricks, unity with the hundred-year-old house is maintained.

The planting scheme is planned to cope with deep shade. As can be seen, the courtyard is padded almost all around by a thick layer of *Vitis coignetiae*, which encompasses three of the boundary walls with layer upon layer of overlapping huge leaves, as well as partially covering the conservatory. This vine grows at least 10 feet (3 meters) in all directions every year. Beneath it are more large leaves, those of the evergreen *Hedera hibernica*, the green-leaved Irish ivy.

This shady garden is entered from a conservatory (at the bottom of the plan, although not shown). Several levels have been created, mostly in the form of raised beds, to extend the garden's scope. A rectangular pool at the far end is fed by water from a sculpted Neptune's head inside an arch. Its sound provides a soothing backdrop to this green retreat.

The design is effectively laid out to leave an open space in the middle, which catches all the light. Adding another dimension are the raised areas, some of which are planting beds and others to display sculpture on what is effectively a long plinth with steps to one side. This raised area also has a narrow, rectangular pool whose single fountain provides sound and movement. To the left of this, in an arch, is a carved Neptune's head from which water pours down into the rectangular pool, rippling its surface.

The one small tree-like shrub in the garden is a lovely white-flowered evergreen, *Eucryphia glutinosa*, a calcifuge which thrives on acid soil on the west coast. This shrub must have its roots in shade, in cool, moist soil, but its fragrantly flowering head in full sun, so it is well served here. The rest of the plants are shade-loving herbaceous perennials, with bergenias, hellebores, and some immaculate hostas growing in purpose-built beds. Every summer pot-grown groups of impatiens, which do so well in shade, make the courtyard vibrate with color. Additional color comes from petunias and pelargoniums, grown in containers so they can be sited where the light reaches in.

The garden also displays a personal collection of figurative sculpture on pedestals, including a heron. It is hoped that this figure may serve the purpose of keeping away real herons, as the pool contains nine Koi carp.

Over the years, statuary gets covered with ivy, giving a sense of time passing.

opposite *A dense canopy of* Vitis coignetiae *envelops this tiny square courtyard. Shade-loving hostas thrive and the invaluable impatiens add summer color.*

below *Against a backing of ivies, daphne, and camellias, Neptune's head and a Cupid are illuminated; a slim fountain catches the light.*

hot gardens

Open sunny courtyards may be enticing but, if they are not shaded by buildings or by the canopy of a tree, a practical approach is essential in the name of comfort. Provided you allocate a small area of the garden to shade, to protect people from the effects of over-exposure to strong sunlight, the rest of the garden can contain those plants which revel in dry soil conditions and bright sunshine.

1. **Cooling foliage, including asparagus fern in the window boxes, makes an attractive sun-filled courtyard from little more than a passage. Hibiscus and begonia suit the climate.**

2. **The Chinese gooseberry (Actinidia chinensis) grows in a ridged terracotta pot, protected and elegantly silhouetted in front of a translucent screen.**

3. **A layer of root-cooling gravel protects the roots of dwarf irises, Santolina virens, and a ribbed green hosta from burning in the sun.**

4. **The shady bower, covered with Parthenocissus tricuspidata, provides relief in a hot garden filled with sun-loving palms, a fig tree, and Centranthus ruber.**

Intense sunlight can be just as difficult for plants to live in as deep shade. And if your garden is deeply set among buildings, the heat from walls all around may rebound into the airless site, intensifying the heat and producing a microclimate that is hotter than the surroundings. However, nature has resolved the problem of hot, dry conditions by reducing the leaf size of some plants to cut down moisture loss, as is characteristic of many artemisias, eryngiums, lavender, and rosemary. Some plants are covered with mats of fine hairs which deflect the heat from the leaf surface, as well as preventing rapid evaporation; these include lamb's ears (*Stachys lanata*), the low shrub *Lotus hirsutus* (syn. *Dorycnium hirsutum*), and other species loosely described as "Mediterranean" which are often aromatic too. Some plants, such as the fleshy-leaved sedums, echeverias, and crassulas, carry their own reservoir of water. In the tiny open courtyard, where heat rebounds from paving and walls, these forms of protection can save lives.

Conserving water is crucial in hot or exposed situations and, because wind will also dry out soil as fast as the midday sun, some screening is essential. Lightweight, but firmly fixed, boundaries of close-meshed trellis or woven bamboo will filter the wind, reducing its power, and a small irrigation system and a gravel mulch will do the rest. Drought is the enemy of roof gardens, in particular, even though they are open to the sky and therefore receive rainfall. This is because

everything is likely to be grown in containers or in the shallow soil of raised beds and also because the rate of evaporation is very rapid in windy conditions, whether it is sunny or not. So choose plants that tolerate dry conditions, cover them with a mulch, and include water-retaining granules in the compost.

Because so many of the plants which thrive in hot, dry conditions are either silver-gray or strikingly formed, the hard materials associated with them can be bold. Rocks, pebbles, and gravel create a natural appearance against which exotics like agaves, cordylines, and cacti look good, if you have the climate for them. With the softer effect of perovskias, sages, and nepeta, decking may be a more appropriate surface.

In hot climates water is always a welcome ingredient. It cools and refreshes, whether it takes the form of a silently silver slit, as in Moorish-style gardens, or a fabulous playing fountain. Sometimes just the sound of moving water is soothing enough—it may be the restful patter of a tiny fountain or a small pool bubbling over pebbles. Moving water stirs and cools the air, as well as animating the garden with flickering reflections. Smooth marble and decking look appropriate in association with water and are cool to the

feet, while a layer of gravel cools plant roots. Terracotta or ceramic tiles make pleasing alternatives in frost-free climates.

Although we may revel in sunlight, there will be times of the day when shade is invaluable. If there is no tree canopy to give overhead cover, shade can be achieved by fashioning an arbor. You may stretch a canvas awning over a seating area, while timber trellis fixed overhead can carry a vine, a golden hop, or a wisteria, which will allow only dappled light through in summer. You could make a timber-framed arbor to enclose a shaded space in romantic rustic style, or design it instead with smoothly planed and stained wood to create a more sophisticated look. Whichever you choose, make sure it is sturdy enough to support those climbers which thrive in

far left *Timber trellis and wisteria-clad decking deflect the heat. On either side, sun-loving pelargoniums revel in it.*

left *Surrounding this balcony, the tall cordyline, a contained Japanese fern palm (Cycas revoluta), and, growing in the pool, the paper reed (Cyperus papyrus) all thrive in the heat of a Mediterranean environment.*

opposite *A cat cheerfully basks in the dappled light beneath a wirework arbor clothed by an equally contented climbing rose.*

heat. With a little care, summer jasmine, *Solanum jasminoides,* and a grapevine will cope in temperate climates. *Trachelospermum jasminoides,* although somewhat tender, is a superbly fragrant climber, and in totally frost-free areas you may be able to grow flame-colored bougainvillea or pretty blue *Plumbago capensis,* perhaps even an exotic passion flower.

At a lower level, gray is the natural foliage cover for dry heat and classic associations with it are white or pastel flower colors. If you find this rather stark for a sunny climate, warm things up a little with hot-color partnerships like *Helianthemum* "Ben Afflick" and *H.* "Ben Nevis," with their tawny orange- and rust-colored flowers. Add some of the smaller kniphofias, like *K. uvaria,* with spears of orange-yellow flowers or the lemon-yellow *K.* "Little Maid." Partner these with day lilies, like the little *Hemerocallis* "Stella de Oro," and try ornamental brown grasses such as the 1 foot (30cm) high bronze variant of *Carex comans.* For dramatic emphasis include clumps of the "black" grass (*Ophiopogon planiscapus* "Nigrescens") and associate with it *Heuchera hispida,* with its unusual bronze and orange flowers above evergreen leaf rosettes. Luscious dahlias, carnival alstroemerias, fiery crocosmias, and other plants with strong flower colors like these look their dramatic best under a bright sky and will make your small space sing out.

If an oasis outside your window is more to your taste, greens will make a hot garden feel fresh and cool. Try a foundation planting of *Euphorbia mellifera* with irises, day lilies, green fennel, and *Santolina virens.* Fragrant myrtle and blue-flowered ceanothus could provide the backdrop and the invaluable box will accommodate to any form or create the divisions needed in the garden space. And although pale, cool creams, mauves, and pinks seem to fade in strong sunlight, the range of blues, from deep agapanthus blue to the pure powder blue of scabious, are all effective.

above *Flowering aloes, crassula, phlomis, datura, erigeron, and an overseeing tamarisk are companionably suited to the dry conditions of a hot, sunny climate.*

exposed to the heat

The maker of this contemporary rooftop, architect Rick Mather, has designed his roof garden from the ground up. Everything evolves from the living spaces in the house below. From entering the house at ground level, the circulation spirals upward, through to the large room at the top of the house which gives entry to the double roof garden. The spiral flow is completed as you enter the lower garden from one side of the roof light, moving round it and up the steps to the summit. A sloping skylight is also a central light source from within the house, making the sky visible from the ground floor up.

When the original pitched roof, steep at the front and with a gentler gradient at the back, had to be replaced, a strong new roof was built, using joists able to support the weight of a garden. Drainage was dealt with at the same time so that water collects at one point. The area is 20 feet by 32 feet (6 meters by 9.75 meters) but, by making two levels, it looks much larger.

The garden boundaries are made of scaffolding which supports translucent rigid plastic panels, keyed

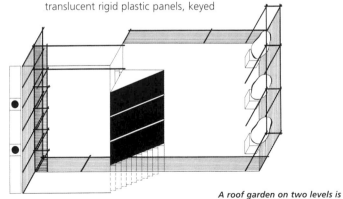

A roof garden on two levels is screened from the surrounding houses, yet light pours through the translucent panels. The entrance and steps are separated by a pitched skylight. The metal scaffolding framework around the boundaries provides screening.

together with a refined clamp system. This is easily adjustable so that the jointing can be altered as space is redefined. Once it became clear that winds from the north and east would damage plants, the chimney wall was raised and a second tier of boundary panels added, to provide better wind protection. They now reach to about 5 feet (1.5 meters) high.

At either end the scaffolding shelters a shallow arbor which runs the length of the wall. This draws climbers into the garden but leaves the central spaces open to the sun. Most of the plants are of Mediterranean or New Zealand origin and are suited to hot conditions. The Chinese gooseberry *Actinidia chinensis*, growing in a pot, runs along the boundary in both directions. Although wind and drought are the main enemies of plants on roof gardens, the protection wrapping around the site enables many tender plants, like the dark-leaved *Trochodendron aralioides* and *Brachyglottis repanda*, to be grown.

The overall impression of the garden is of lush foliage—it is easy to forget that everything grows in containers. But the owner is a plantsman who understands plant needs and provides conditions they love.

above **Looking over the skylight to the lower garden, the biggest plant on the roof is the evergreen strawberry tree (Arbutus unedo) in the corner. To its left is fragrant Trachelospermum jasminoides.**

opposite **White-flowering rain-daisies (Osteospermum) frame this group but one of the garden's prize plants is in the central pot: Trochodendron aralioides, an unusual and primitive evergreen tree with vivid green flowers.**

stage sets

The very small space lends itself to a theatrical approach because it is likely to be seen from only one viewpoint, front-on. You can frame the shallow, intimate stage of your small garden using evergreen shrubs as "wings" and timber beams to support a fringe of trailing greenery overhead, with a central backcloth of wall plants. The space becomes a stage in which striking plants or sculpture "perform."

The small outdoor building attached to the house has a pitched sod roof with carved timber edging resembling shark's teeth. Matching black twisted timbers frame the door.

2 *Primitive sculpture, adorned with bead necklace, suggests the South Seas. Its presence is strengthened by its placement beneath the canopy of a wide-spreading Japanese maple*

It is Halloween and bright orange pumpkins ornament the courtyard, bringing magic and mystery into it.

4 *A slim, elegant Corinthian pillar hints at the classicism of the old world; here it also serves the practical purpose of supporting the tree branch.*

The art of theater has long prevailed in gardens. In the eighteenth century, classical temples and statuary were glimpsed along *allées* or displayed in arborial splendor. Painters like Claude of Lorraine and, later, Fragonard depicted landscape and gardens as romantic unreality; this, in turn, influenced attitudes to garden design. Many such allusions are still used today: in some small gardens classical figures, half-concealed by ivy, peer out from the boundaries, while elsewhere Cupids become water sources at the center of circular pools. Grecian pillars and urns are placed simply to decorate rather than to support, their historical and symbolic use long forgotten.

Not all garden theater is classically inspired. With the "curtains" permanently apart, you might make a historical fantasy, transport yourself to another culture, or create a shangri-la of your own. Many of the world's famous gardens graft other cultures onto their own, like the Indian styling at Sezincote in Oxfordshire, England, the Moorish gardens in the Generalife in Spain, and the Palace of Queluz in Portugal. A tiny space can equally indulge such fantasies. You may decide to give your garden an oriental, Arabic, or some other exotic flavor by choosing types of trellis, certain plants, and appropriate paving and putting them together in a special way. Box can be clipped into almost any shape, like Moorish or Tudor arches, or even crenellations suggesting a Gothic fantasy. Real, but intimate, illusions of grandeur may

be achieved by reproducing the "grand manner" of formal French gardens in miniature geometric form, with clipped box defining small planting spaces and elaborate *treillage* camouflaging the boundaries. Wooden Versailles tubs could contain exotic summer plantings of dwarf citrus trees or figs, all of which can be brought indoors for the winter.

You can transform a small space into a cloister, creating an orderly monastic herb garden containing geometric beds edged by clipped santolina and lavender, with shallow, three-dimensional arches on the walls and a stone urn in the center. Fill the beds with hardy herbs, like thyme, sage, oregano, and rosemary, with summer additions of basil, parsley, coriander, and chervil. Add espaliered fruit trees and

clipped bay trees in terracotta pots (see Practicalities, pages 166 and 168). You could suggest an Arabic theme with a narrow rill of water leading to a circular pool with a slim, sparkling fountain. The whole garden might be paved with frost-hardy, colorful ceramic tiles, while freestanding Moorish arches made from trellis would provide shade, as well as concealing the boundaries. The courtyard thus becomes transformed into another place in another time.

Looking east, perhaps a Chinese style of garden might appeal to you. You could make a circular "moon gate" in a boundary wall from mirror glass and surround it by Chinese fretwork patterns; use white paving and intersperse it with blocks of naturally formed limestone standing erect among bamboos or peonies. Add a collection of bonsai landscapes mounted on plinths and some *chinoiserie* furniture to complete the scene. Traditional Japanese courtyards also lend themselves to imitation, often representing miniaturized landscapes. A graveled area, asymmetrically placed stone slabs and rocks, with bamboo fencing, carefully tied, are all appropriate ingredients, with acers, mountain pines, irises, and azaleas furnishing the restrained planting.

The ultimate theater is to create a garden in the sky, removed from the noise and bustle of the city, blessed with good light and fresher air, but where there is no natural earth and no surrounding trees. The special, unexpected environment of a roof garden is totally artificial and free from earthbound conventions, yet it can be transformed into a rural idyll or an elegant, modernist outdoor room, just as a theatrical play transports us to distant places.

Theater depends on a self-effacing background of lesser parts which do not upstage the star roles. In the garden context, plants may act as a background, behaving with the mass identity of a Greek chorus but demanding no attention for

far left **With a stylishly laid checkerboard floor and the pots of white and pink foxgloves placed as carefully as chess pieces, this small roof garden has an air of fantasy. The theatricality is fostered by the mosaic fruit on a mosaic table and by the tiny topiarized trees that hug the wall.**

themselves. The more exciting stars, like statuesque *Acanthus spinosus*, flaming red-hot pokers, pure white regal lilies, or sword-like phormiums, all benefit from a subdued backcloth. Provide for them a foil of greenery, the unlit background of your stage, with infallible evergreens like viburnums, prunus, and mahonias. *Viburnum tinus* "Eve Price" is a dense, dark green plant that can grow to 10 feet (3 meters), but it is amenable to pruning and regenerates quickly. The cherry laurel (*Prunus laurocerasus*) is tall, glossy bright green and spreading, but again its size can be controlled by pruning; select a smaller, narrow-leaved form like *P. l.* "Otto Luyken" for its vase-like shape which fans out to 5 feet (1.5 meters), with white candle flowers in mid-spring. The green assurance offered by such a background allows you to display other, more dramatic plants with confidence.

Plants alone can also be handled theatrically. The use of exotic plants in temperate areas immediately creates a sub-tropical scene. The look of the garden may be reminiscent of Mediterranean climates, with sharp forms like cordylines, the hardier fan palm (*Chamaerops humilis*), perhaps even agaves, like *A. filifera,* and some of the hardier opuntias. Soften these with the beautiful *Euphorbia mellifera* and *Pittosporum tobira*. In a protected microclimate, aloes, crassulas, and hedychiums add more drama, with gray-leaved santolinas and lavenders softening the whole effect.

Clipped box, used since Roman times, can frame spaces and direct the eye to a central focus or be trained into marvelous sculptural forms, such as twisted spirals, spheres, cubes, or "Popsicle" shapes on stems that will populate the stage all year. All gardens designed like a set become a permanent part of the interior too, when viewed from a window. Since imagination is the key, the inspiration may come from a familiar source, from an unknown world you have never experienced, or it may be a totally personal concept.

right above **The elegant geometry of this contemporary garden is enlivened by the diamond patterns of black and white tiles on the wall and the terracotta paving. Bright red pelargoniums around the boundaries introduce bold drama and the glass topped table gives an air of unreality.**

right below **A wicked-looking Pan plays his pipes in front of the golden setting sun. As daylight fades, artificial lighting takes over, intensifying the sense of theater.**

a sculptor's garden

This vision is not for the faint-hearted. The extraordinary tiny space behind his house is the garden of sculptor Johnny Woodford. Surrounded on all sides by tall walls, it should be dark, but the enclosed space is painted a fiery orange and glows throughout the year, rain or shine.

The tallest wall is almost 20 feet (6 meters) high. A wide raised bed has been constructed against it to fulfill the role of buttress, as well as being virtually the only place in which to grow any plants. It is faced with galvanized sheet metal and a heavy timber beam provides a solid coping on top. Ornamenting this retaining wall with suspended ball and chains creates a humorous allusion to medieval fantasy.

The chosen plants for the raised area are mostly the frondy fern, *Polystichum setiferum* Acutilobum Group, with spiky yuccas and *Phormium tenax*. All are "mulched" with chains to foil the local cats. In metal containers within coiled chains grows the black grass *Ophiopogon planiscapus* "Nigrescens." A tiny-leaved

Access to this tiny L-shaped yard is from French doors on the left; the small sod-covered outhouse is used for storage. A wide raised planting bed has been built against the tall wall opposite the French doors, with a bench seat below.

Muehlenbeckia complexa festoons the galvanized sheet, clinging to the ball and chain hangings or scrambling up on to the wall of the house. A permanent bench seat below the raised bed is shaped like a surfboard with the fins of a shark and painted to resemble rows of gnashing black teeth.

Sod covers the roof of the tiny outhouse, growing over a lightweight proprietary growing medium specially formulated for roof gardens. It is hand-trimmed, apart from the edge which is allowed to form a lush fringe concealing the galvanized gutter. The only other planting is a soft mound of helxine (*Soleirolia soleirolii*) growing among the paving setts, and some ivies which either climb or trail according to their situation.

Johnny Woodford spent some years working in forestry, where he acquired not only expertise in timber but also an affection for the equipment used by foresters—hence the heavy chains. Other baggage from his forestry years include the drill-heads, still coated in their original orange protective paint, which "grow" alongside the plants, as thrusting as the phormiums. Touches like this make the garden theatrically original as well as good-humored and inviting.

above **Looking toward the "small house" with its warped timber frame, you see the raised planting bed on the tallest wall, faced with galvanized steel and decorated with ball and chains.**

left **Small black grasses grow in copper containers, concentrically ringed with chains. Beside them, rising from the soil, is a spiral drill-head.**

right *The detail here shows the blackened timber door frame and lintel surrounding a door with an exaggerated keyhole; it is made from green English elm which is burned black and allowed to warp. Sod covers the roof of the outhouse. Allusions to medieval crenellations are interpreted as a line of carved teeth.*

below *Inverted narrow pyramids made from lacquered steel are wall-mounted and planted with small yuccas, described by the owner as "carrots."*

directory

The plants which make up this directory are mostly tried and tested subjects on which I have learned to depend for small spaces. A few are included to add piquancy, as no design should ever be too conservative, and the description makes clear which these are. Heights and spreads are based on my personal research, as well as my long experience of designing gardens and using many of these plants to furnish them.

The **mounding grass** *Stipa tenuissima* has fine foliage and tall, feathery plumes. It brings movement to small gardens, even in winter, if left in place.

Bergenia "Baby Doll" is the smallest bergenia hybrid. Invaluable in shade, it has glossy evergreen leaves and sugar-pink flower spikes in spring.

Tulipa kaufmanniana, the water-lily tulip, is one of the earliest tulips to flower. Short in stature, it is suitable for small gardens and easy to grow in sun.

Daphne tangutica is a very fragrant evergreen shrub which forms a compact shape. The purple buds open to white flower clusters in early summer.

The china-white fruits of *Sorbus cashmiriana* form in fall, when the gray-green leaves also turn yellow. This small hardy tree is ideal for small gardens.

Parrot's claw (*Clianthus puniceus*) is a semi-evergreen climber which will bring summer color to a warm wall. Wire support is needed and, being frost-tender, it may require winter protection.

ACER PALMATUM "SANGO-KAKU"

BUDDLEJA ALTERNIFOLIA

CRATAEGUS X *LAVALLEEI* "CARRIEREI"

ACER PALMATUM "SANGO-KAKU" (SYN. "SENKAKI")

The coralbark maple is one of the most elegant of Japanese maples. Sometimes described as a shrub, it grows initially from an upright single stem, eventually branching into fine twiggy growth. In winter the wood is brilliant coral red and the palmate leaves, which appear in spring, are pinkish-tinged light green, accompanied by tiny drops of red flowers. By fall the leaves are yellow and winged seedheads decorate the tree. Remove any leaves which revert to green and protect from frost damage and midday sun. Does best on neutral to acid soil which should not dry out. Height and spread 21 feet (6 meters) by 18 feet (5 meters).

BETULA PENDULA "LACINIATA"

This birch is fairly tall, but its habit is slender and graceful. The silvery bark and trailing branchlets are attractive in winter, when it makes a pleasing outline against the sky, and the delicate canopy allows light to filter through to a semi-shaded planting below. The fluttering, indented foliage turns from light green to yellow in fall. *B. pendula* "Tristis" is as tall, but narrower and more pendulous. Both eventually reach 52 feet (16 meters) by 24 feet (7 meters).

BUDDLEJA ALTERNIFOLIA

Sometimes treated as a bush, this plant is seen to greatest advantage when grown as a very small tree on a single stem, allowing it to form a cascading mophead. It is best purchased as a container-grown tree and staked in windy sites. *Buddleja* is commonly known as the butterfly bush and the graceful arching branches of this species are wreathed in fragrant, lilac flowers in summer, often made more colorful by butterflies. The pretty foliage is narrowly pointed and grayish, turning yellow in fall. Prefers rich, deep soil and a sunny situation. Remove old wood immediately after flowering. When controlled by pruning, it may be kept to 10 feet (3 meters) high and wide.

CARAGANA ARBORESCENS "WALKER"

This shrub can be grown as a very small, mopheaded weeping tree on a single, lightly spiny stem. It is suitable as a focus, especially if grown in a large container associated with rocks. Clusters of yellow "pea flowers" appear in late spring, among light green, feathery foliage. In fall it turns yellow and bears long brown seedpods. Likes any soil, even alkaline, and a sunny site, although it tolerates light shade. No

pruning needed, apart from removing dead wood. Usually grafted onto a stem 3–6 feet (1–2 meters) high.

COTONEASTER SALICIFOLIUS "PENDULUS"

Although grown as a very small evergreen tree, this shrub is really a hybrid of *C. frigidus* which, when grafted onto an erect stem, makes a stiffly weeping form. The branches trail down to the ground, but can be pruned clear of it. It will sculpturally dominate the garden or can be grown in association with rocks and Japanese maples. White flower clusters are followed by masses of brilliant red berries. Likes full sun and any soil, except extremely alkaline. It reaches just over 10 feet (3 meters) by 13 feet (4 meters) at maturity.

CRATAEGUS X *LAVALLEI* "CARRIEREI"

This hawthorn is densely foliaged and creates shade beneath, but it has two seasons of interest. It produces clusters of white flowers in late spring followed by rounded scarlet fruits that survive well into winter. Its glossy, oval green foliage is remarkably red in fall when the fruits and leaves together are a rich combination. It is wide-spreading, at 15 feet (5 meters), but ultimately in the open only 24 feet (7 meters) high.

MALUS X ZUMI "GOLDEN HORNET"

SORBUS CASHMIRIANA

MALUS CORONARIA "CHARLOTTAE"

This small ornamental tree has large, semi-double, fragrant shell-pink flowers in spring. Oval, coarsely toothed leaves color powerfully in fall. Reaches 36 feet (11 meters) with a spread of 18 feet (5 meters).

MALUS TURINGOIDES

This fruit tree has an elegant habit, with lobed, downy leaves which are highly colored in fall. Pinkish-white flowers are succeeded by small yellow fruits. It grows to about 24 feet (7 meters) tall and 18 feet (5 meters) wide. *Malus x zumi* "Golden Hornet" is taller and more upright, but the naked tree is covered in yellow fruit "baubles" for several months in winter.

PRUNUS "AMANOGAWA"

A narrow upright tree whose columnar form carries fragrant, semi-double pale pink flowers in late spring and whose foliage turns red in fall. Does well on most soils and in full sun. In heavy snow, tie in the branches with soft material to prevent them from breaking with the weight. Makes a fine vehicle for late-flowering clematis. At ten years the height is 20 feet (6 meters), but the width very narrow, about 7 feet (2 meters).

PRUNUS MAACKII

Known as the Manchurian cherry or the Amur cherry, this is a vigorous, but small, tree with a polished sheen of cinnamon-colored bark which encircles the trunk with peeling charm. Extremely hardy, it carries racemes of fragrant white flowers, followed by black fruits. The dark green leaves turn yellow in fall. There is a good form named "Amber Beauty." The ultimate height is 40 feet (12 meters) with a spread of 30 feet (9 meters).

PYRUS SALICIFOLIA "PENDULA"

The ornamental weeping pear has a wide spreading, rounded head, but it is not tall and its floating silvery, narrow leaves and weeping habit make it desirable for small gardens. The branches arch out widthways before drooping elegantly to touch the ground, but it can be carefully shaped to maintain a less dense habit by pruning out all the downward-growing branches to encourage the development of a wide canopy. This is likely to become the dominant specimen tree of your garden if you select it, and the light shade it casts will dictate what can be grown beneath. After about 20 years it can grow to as much as 26 feet (8 meters) high and 20 feet (6 meters) wide.

The mophead acacia is a very slow-growing, small tree for warm places. With protection from wind and well-drained soil, it produces a compact "Popsicle" shape, ideally suited to formal gardens. The foliage is a dense mass of characteristically twinned, mid-green, oval leaflets. It tolerates pollution, but rarely flowers. Grows to 20 feet (6 meters) in height and spread.

SORBUS CASHMIRIANA

A hardy small tree noted for its china white fruit clusters in fall. In late spring the flower clusters are pink in bud, opening to white among finely paired, gray-green foliage which allows dappled light through; the leaves later turn yellow. Copes with most soils; prefers sun. Height and spread 20 feet (6 meters).

SORBUS VILMORINII

This tree is even more gracefully structured. The delicate paired leaves, dove-gray with purple overtones, redden and deepen in fall; they catch the wind and filter the light. Its white flowers in spring are followed by clusters of small, rounded mauve flushed white berries. Height and spread about 20 feet (6 meters).

JUNIPERUS COMMUNIS "COMPRESSA" AND CHAMAECYPARIS OBUSTA "NANA GRACILIS"

PINUS MUGO "WINTER GOLD"

slow-growing and dwarf conifers

A very slow-growing plant which naturally forms a densely foliaged dome shape. The overall color is grayish-green with purple tips. It is not fussy about soil and quite hardy, given adequate moisture, good drainage and wind protection. Work with the proportions of 1 foot 6 inches (45cm) in height and 2 feet (60cm) in diameter.

CHAMAECYPARIS OBTUSA "NANA GRACILIS"

This is a genuinely dwarf plant with rich, velvety green foliage made of fanned branchlets growing in tiers. This habit creates a dense form, wider than it is high, and dwarf enough for rock gardens. With good drainage it will very slowly achieve an ultimate height and spread of 6 feet (2 meters).

JUNIPERUS COMMUNIS "COMPRESSA"

Diminutively erect and conical, this plant looks rather silly on its own, but is effective when grouped. The many small columns of naturally dwarf conifers can be attractive with tiny rhododendrons and spreading alpine plants among rocks and gravel in sun. The ultimate height in about 20 years is only 2 feet 6 inches (76cm).

JUNIPERUS HORIZONTALIS "BAR HARBOR"

Slow to grow, rather than dwarf, this plant covers the ground widthways, following its contours, making it suitable for terraces and banks. It is comprised of long, whipcord-like branches, the foliage a soft dove-gray with blue overtones. If not controlled by pruning, it is apt to become straggly. The carpet is only 8 inches (20cm) thick, but can spread to 6 feet (2 meters).

JUNIPERUS SABINA "TAMARISCIFOLIA"

This neat, wide spreader does not spread randomly, but grows in concentric layers so it can be useful in low-maintenance small gardens. This suggests use in more formal gardens, but it can also be attractive following a bank, where the layering becomes decorative. The Savin junipers are green with a gray overtone and they build up their height slowly to 2 feet (60cm) with a spread of 5–6 feet (1.5–2 meters).

PICEA PUNGENS "GLOBOSA"

A slow-growing, densely jade-blue bush which expands widthways faster than in height. Although it can be irregularly shaped, its overall habit is flattened and conical, created by congested branches with rigidly

prickly needles. The inert form is suited to gravel gardens in sun, where it will hold its fresh blueness through the summer. Prune out any awkward leading shoots which spoil the shape. Ultimately 4 feet (1.2 meters) high, it steadies at 3 feet (90cm).

PICEA PUNGENS "PROSTRATA"

This spreading spruce can be luminously blue and is unlike other spruces. It is grafted to retain a horizontal habit, but if a leader develops, it should be removed. Small, upright dusky-crimson cones are sometimes produced that look beautiful among the silver-blue needles. Resting on flagstones in good light, it associates well with low-growing cistus or rock roses. Height 6 feet (2 meters) and spread 10 feet (3 meters).

PINUS MUGO "WINTER GOLD"

The hardy mountain pines suit gardens with a Japanese air, looking fine with acers and gravel, or those which are minimalist with but a few simply formed evergreens requiring little interference. There are many lovely green varieties, but this one is noted for its yellow winter color, best developed in an open, sunny position. It makes a low dwarf 2 feet (60cm) by 3 feet (90cm).

Acer palmatum Dissectum Group

Carpenteria californica

shrubs

Abelia x grandiflora

This semi-evergreen shrub with a natural rounded habit is useful for smaller gardens because it can be fan-trained against a sunny, sheltered wall. Pink and white hanging bell-shaped flowers cover the shrub from midsummer to early fall, backed by glossy green, lightly coppered foliage. Prune out a third of the oldest stems in early spring to encourage new flowering shoots. Prefers soil which is not alkaline. The cultivar "Francis Mason" is a yellow-variegated form and "Prostrata" a low-growing one. Average height and spread 5 feet (1.5 meters) by 6 feet (2 meters), depending on variety.

Acer palmatum Dissectum Group

The slow-growing Japanese maples are treasures for small spaces. There are many different forms, some with more filigree foliage than others. The deep red forms are magnificent, as they flare in fall. but the green ones have great delicacy. Responsive to wind and with an elegant form, even in winter, they weep over raised beds in a pleasing manner. Remove any stems which die back. Japanese maples very slowly grow into small trees, but their average height and spread is 8 feet (2.7 meters) by 6 feet (2 meters).

Berberis calliantha

A small, slow-growing evergreen bushy shrub from Tibet whose prickly, holly-like leaves have glaucous undersides. The young growth is red and the pale yellow flowers hang beneath the branches in spring. In fall it has striking blue-black fruits. No pruning required. Hardy in sun or shade and tolerates all soils. Height and spread 3–5 feet (1–1.5 meters).

Berberis x stenophylla "Coralina Compacta"

This dwarf, evergreen shrub with mid-green, narrow oval leaves is extremely floriferous. The coral-colored buds open to dense, tiny orange-yellow flowers wreathing the spiny stems in late spring; small blue-black fruits appear later in very hot summers. Little pruning required, but will withstand cutting back hard. Hardy in sun or deep shade; avoid dry or chalky soils. Height and spread 1 foot–1 foot 4 inches (30-40cm).

Berberis thunbergii "Helmond Pillar"

A deciduous, narrowly upright berberis whose wine-red leaves hold their color from spring to summer, flaming scarlet in fall. White flowers are followed by red fruits. Best grown as a specimen. Occasionally remove old wood—that is, three- to four-year-old stems—to encourage new growth. Hardy in sun or light shade. A really dwarf red-leaved form, *B. thunbergii* "Bagatelle," is the size of an armadillo, making it appropriate for minute gardens. "Helmond Pillar" is ultimately 5 feet (1.5 meters) by 2 feet 6 inches (75cm).

Buddleja davidii "Nanho Blue"

This small, elegantly arching plant produces deep blue, scented flowers in short racemes. Hardy, it thrives in rich soil and sunlight. Every year, prune hard in early spring to cut back the previous year's wood to within 4 inches (10cm) for strong flowering. It is lower than the type, growing to about 6 feet (2 meters), with wider arched habit of over 6 feet 8 inches (2.2 meters).

Carpenteria californica

A tender evergreen suitable for a fan shape on a protected sunny wall. Bears large, white flowers with yellow anther, but is slow to flower when young. On established plants, prune out a third of the oldest wood after the last spring frost, to maintain shape and health. Prefers rich soil; protect with frost blanket in severe weather. Height and spread 8 feet (2.4 meters).

CERATOSTIGMA WILLMOTTIANUM

CISTUS X DANSEREAUI "DECUMBENS"

CERATOSTIGMA WILLMOTTIANUM

Deciduous low shrub with an open, rounded habit and intense blue flowers in summer to fall, when the green leaves turn wine red. Hardy, but protect the base with twigs in very cold areas. Rich soil, which may be dry or dampish, and full sun are essential. Cut back hard every spring. 3 feet (90cm) high and wide.

CHAENOMELES SPECIOSA "TEXAN SCARLET"

Ornamental quinces are outstanding shrubs, growing with an elegantly structured habit in sun or light shade. This is tomato red, but there are white, pink, and orange forms. Cut back all unwanted branches immediately after flowering, following the habit of the shrub. Prune out forward-growing branches to encourage a fan shape against a wall. Fruit forms at the end of the season. Any good soil, except very alkaline. Its average height and spread are 10 feet (3 meters).

CHOISYA TERNATA

A neat, glossy-leaved evergreen whose long narrow leaflets create a fine-textured effect. The highly fragrant white flower clusters appear in spring and in warm seasons may repeat. Hardy, although leaf damage may occur if exposed to severe wind or frost. Prune to within 1 foot 6 inches (45cm) of the ground every three to four years if it gets too large for the site. Does well in sun or shade and all soils except highly alkaline. Height and spread 6 feet (2 meters).

CISTUS X DANSEREAUI "DECUMBENS"

This evergreen rock rose spreads vigorously, but can be lightly trimmed for tidiness. It has narrow green leaves covered from early to midsummer in small white flowers with crimson blotches at their centers. Excellent trailing over raised planters. Frost-hardy and copes with all soils, including alkaline; plant in full sun. Height 2 feet (60cm) with a spread of 4 feet (1.2 meters).

CONVOLVULUS CNEORUM

Being low-growing and hardy, this rounded, bushy shrub is well suited to very small spaces, where it is grown as much for its evergreen foliage as for its flowers. The silken sheen of its narrow, gray leaves catches the light and it associates well with other gray-leaved plants, like lavenders and santolinas, all preferring sunshine and well-drained soils. White, typically bindweed flowers enhance the plant from late spring through to midsummer. Benefits from a light trim in early spring to promote flowers. 2 feet 6 inches (75cm) in height and spread.

COTONEASTER COCHLEATUS

Several cotoneasters make excellent ground covers: *C. congestus* is tiny and creates small mounds, whereas *C. salicifolius* "Repens" spreads widely and has narrowly pointed, evergreen leaves. The very hardy evergreen form is densely foliaged and ideal for small places, where it follows the ground or drapes over low retaining walls; it can expand up a wall. White flowers in spring are followed by large crimson fruits. No pruning required. Grows in sun or light shade in any soil. Hummocks reach 3 feet (90cm) eventually and it spreads to 5 feet (1.5 meters).

CUPHEA CYANAEA

This evergreen, rounded little shrub from South America is half-hardy to frost-tender, but if you have the right conditions and can protect it in winter, it will repay you with masses of brilliant orange, tubular flowers throughout the summer. Little pruning is

CUPHEA CYANAEA

X *FATSHEDERA LIZEI* "VARIEGATA"

required. It is ideal for very small, protected sunny sites, at 3 feet (90cm) high and wide, at most.

DAPHNE MEZEREUM

Deserving a place in most gardens, the mezereon is valued for its intensely fragrant, early flowers, which may be mauve-purple or white and grow in columnar form along the stiffly upright branches. They appear in late winter, before the leaves. The plant is hardy, preferring limy, well-drained soil and a cool situation, which may be lightly shaded. It needs no pruning. A pale pink form, "Autumnalis," can flower as early as Christmas. The height and spread are 3 feet (90cm) by 3 feet (90cm).

DAPHNE TANGUTICA

Like all the daphnes, this is highly fragrant and, being very low-growing, this species is ideal for small spaces. Purple buds carried in clusters at the end of the last season's growth open to white flowers among narrow, evergreen leaves with silvery undersides. Site in light shade and rich, well-worked soil which will not get waterlogged. It forms a compact sturdy shape which needs no pruning and has a diameter of 3 feet (90cm).

ESCALLONIA "RED ELF"

Restricted to west coast gardens, this diminutive, evergreen bush has small, glossy green leaves and is covered with crimson flowers from midsummer to fall. When established, remove one third of the woody stems after flowering. It grows to a height of 3 feet (90cm) by 4 feet (1.2 meters).

EUONYMUS ALATUS "COMPACTUS"

This dwarf form of the winged euonymus has the same intense fall color. For the rest of the year, when summer perennials take over anyway, this is a densely foliaged, undistinguished plant, but, by fall, the brilliant leaves provide a backing for its distinctive scarlet seeds amid purple casing. It needs no pruning. Hardy but best grown in sun and on rich soil, where it reaches approximately 10 feet (3 meters).

EUONYMUS FORTUNEI "EMERALD GAIETY"

An invaluable, low, evergreen, whose green leaves are margined in creamy-white and which will grow in shade. Similar cultivars include "Emerald 'n' Gold," with yellow variegation, and "Sunspot," which is greener than either, but slashed with yellow. All can be

clipped to shape and grown as dwarf shrubs or planted for ground cover. They are hardy, tolerate all soils and grow in any conditions, although the variegation will be slightly less in shade and the yellows are stronger in sunlight. If unpruned, they will grow to 3 feet (90cm) high by 12 feet (3.5 meters) wide.

X FATSHEDERA LIZEI

Thought to be a cross between ivy and fatsia, the tree-ivy is an adaptable evergreen for small, dark gardens as it is hardy and tolerates pollution. It spreads widely if fan-trained as a wall shrub, but accommodates well to pruning when the old shoots need cutting hard back. A useful plant for a difficult place, having glossy, light-reflecting, palmate leaves even in full shade. It copes on all soils, but grows fast in deep, rich soil. The inconspicuous green flower clusters are followed by clusters of black fruits. Look for the variegated form too. Average height and spread 6 feet (1.8 meters) by 10 feet (3 meters) if trained as a climber.

FUCHSIA "TOM THUMB"

Fuchsias are useful because they flower in late summer when many shrubs have finished. This dwarf form has

HELIANTHEMUN "FIRE DRAGON"

HEDERA HELIX "CONGESTA"

HYDRANGEA "PREZIOSA"

dark green foliage and pendulous crimson and violet flowers. The hardy fuchsias are usually cut to the ground in cold winters but they recover fast. They cope with most soils but revel in rainfall and will grow in sun or semi-shade. Other hardy cultivars include the red and white "Madame Cornélissen," "Mrs Popple," with larger red and purple flowers, and "Riccartonii," which has slim scarlet and purple flowers. "Tom Thumb" grows compactly to 2 feet (60cm) in both height and spread.

HEBE BUXIFOLIA

This dwarf shrub from New Zealand has small, glossy, evergreen leaves resembling box. The white flowers produced in early summer are lightly fragrant. Growing in most soils, unless drought-prone or waterlogged, it needs only an overall light spring trim to maintain a compact form and encourage new growth. There are other dwarf hebes which are gray-leaved, like *H. pinguifolia* "Pagei," which is the color of pewter, or the filigree *H. pimeleoides* "Quicksilver," which is more prostrate and has tiny silver-gray leaves. Approximate height and spread 2 feet (60cm) by 3 feet (90cm).

HEDERA HELIX "CONGESTA"

Not all ivies trail or cling to walls. There are erect forms known as "candelabra" ivies which, being stiffly and compactly upright as well as evergreen, can have a focal role in tiny spaces. The cultivar "Erecta" is bolder-leaved and taller, reaching 3 feet (90cm), while this one, although slightly less robust, is attractively slimmer with more pointed leaves and its height is about 1 foot 6 inches (45cm); although they may both spread wider than they are tall, remove any outward-spreading branches to retain their vertical habit.

HELIANTHEMUM CULTIVARS

Known as sun roses, helianthemums are suited to hot, more humid, and sunny small spaces, requiring sun and good drainage. These low-growing, hardy shrubs are covered in flowers all summer. Excellent with alpine plants among rocks and gravel, they also make good edges to paths. Trim sparingly with shears in early or mid-spring to encourage new flowering shoots. Look for the cool colors of "Wisley Primrose," "Wisley White," or "Rhodanthe Carneum," or the hotter colors, like "Fire Dragon" or "Henfield Brilliant." Height and spread 1 foot (30cm).

HELICHRYSUM ITALICUM SUBSP. SEROTINUM

Known as curry plants because of their aromatic foliage, these evergreen, low shrubs are grown for their fine, narrow, silver-gray foliage. This form (syn. *H. angustifolia*) is one of the hardiest; it is amenable to shearing to create dwarf hedging or round mounds. It needs full sun and well-drained soils, where it co-habits with lavenders, helianthemums, and artemisias. Height and spread 2 feet (60cm) by 2 feet 6 inches (80cm).

HYDRANGEA "PREZIOSA"

Among the many hydrangeas, this small hardy form stands out as ideal for small places, offering two periods of interest. The rounded heads of rose-pink florets appear in summer and as they age, become stained with a purple-claret hue at the season's end. This color is complemented by the foliage which gradually darkens to bottle-green with overtones of purple, making it distinctive among other fall color. It likes sun or light shade with deep, fertile, moist soil (the dryer the soil, the more shade needed). Flower color may turn blue or mauve on an acid soil. Remove old, weak, and dead stems every fall (or spring). Height and spread 4 feet (1.2 meters).

LAVANDULA ANGUSTIFOLIA "HIDCOTE"

OSMANTHUS DELAVAYI

LAVANDULA ANGUSTIFOLIA "HIDCOTE"

The compact lavenders are ideal in small spaces that are sunny and well-drained. The evergreen, silver-gray foliage is topped with upright spikes of dark purple flowers in summer. Lavenders suit the company of many flowering plants which enjoy the same conditions, like artemisias, helianthemums, and small "patio" roses. Highly scented, lavenders also come in other sizes and colors, so look for dwarf forms like "Nana Alba," which has white flowers, or French lavender (*L. stoechas*) with its distinctive purple bracts. Regular pruning is important: trim over the plant in spring to a dome shape and trim again after flowering. Remove dead wood at any time, but never cut into the main stem. May also be clipped as low hedging. Ultimate height and spread 4–5 feet (1.2–1.5 meters).

LOTUS HIRSUTUS

Small and silvery-leaved, this sub-shrub (syn. *Dorycnium hirsutus*) grows best in well-drained, acidic or alkaline soil in full sun. The stems carry terminal buds of pinky-white "clover" flowers on the current season's growth from midsummer. In fall these become dark reddish seedpods which are charming against the silvery, hairy leaves. Usually dying back to ground level every year, it rarely needs pruning except to remove dead material. It gradually expands over 20 years to 4 feet (1.2 meters) by 6 feet (1.8 meters).

NANDINA DOMESTICA "PYGMAEA"

Erroneously known as the heavenly bamboo, this plant is actually related to berberis. It is evergreen and delicately formed, with many slim, erect stems arising from a clump and attractively paired bronzed leaves. It is valued for its fall flare, like that of the smaller *N. domestica* "Firepower," sometimes with red fruits. This small plant has great character, particularly if associated with rocks, acers, and grasses, as well as with water. In cool climates it should be sheltered and it must have moist soil. No pruning needed, apart from the removal of old flowering spikes. Cut out one third of stems from time to time, to induce new growth. Grows to 3 feet (90cm) by about 3 feet (90cm).

OSMANTHUS DELAVAYI

Darkly gray-green, this Chinese evergreen shrub has sweetly scented white flowers in early spring. It is hardy and accommodates to all soils except very wet ones. Preferring a site with dappled light, it will grow in full sun. No pruning needed unless it becomes too big and you need to keep it within bounds. 12 feet (4 meters).

POTENTILLA FRUTICOSA

Potentillas are invaluable deciduous shrubs, small enough for most compact gardens and flowering for three months or more in full summer sun. There are silver leaved forms, like "Beesii" with yellow flowers and grayish foliage, "Manchu", white with gray-green leaves and a trailing mat habit, "Primrose Beauty," a reliable old favorite with creamy-yellow flowers, and "Tilford Cream," with larger flowers. Orange and pink forms do best in light shade. Any soil, but avoid extremes of drought, damp, and alkalinity. Prune every year by thinning out a third of old growth to ground level and shorten overgrown stems to neaten the plant. Average 4 feet (1.2 meters) height and spread.

PYRACANTHA COCCINEA "RUTGERS"

Known as the firethorns, these accommodating dark evergreens can be grown as freestanding hedges but are also valued as wall shrubs. They may be tightly clipped to any shape against a wall or fence; this

SALIX HELVETICA

SANTOLINA CHAMAECYPARISSUS

reduces both flowering and fruiting but makes flat, attractive patterns without intruding into valuable garden space. They are thorny plants, which may deter burglars, and have small, dense leaves. The white flower clusters in summer are followed by red, yellow, or orange fruits. *P. coccine* "Rutgers" has orange-red fruits and is resistant to fire blight. It will grow in any soil, except a very alkaline one, and in extremes of shade, exposure, and cold; the red-berried cultivar, *P.* "Mohave" is very winter hardy. Clip in late winter or early spring. Ultimate height and spread are 18 feet (5.5 meters) by 12 feet (4 meters).

RUSCUS ACULEATUS

This useful evergreen will grow in deep shade, even when the soil is dry. Known as butcher's broom or box holly, it is unusual in having no foliage, but flattened branches tipped with green spines. Very hardy, it needs no pruning except to remove damaged shoots. 3 feet (90cm) by 4 feet (1.2 meters).

SALIX HELVETICA

The very small Swiss willow is grown for its silver-furred yellow catkins, produced in spring, before the foliage

appears. Small, attractive branching habit with narrow silvery leaves. It can be bought trained as a very small standard tree or a slow-growing, small shrub which associates with water, rock, and acers, in full sun or light shade. No pruning required, except to neaten. Can grow to 3 feet (90cm) by 4 feet (1.2 meters).

SANTOLINA CHAMAECYPARISSUS

The santolinas are ideal small, twiggy shrubs for tiny spaces because they are evergreen, easy to grow, and can be clipped to fit any space. The silver foliage of cotton lavender is very finely divided and, in summer, covered with mustard-yellow flowers. The particularly small form, *S. chamaecyparissus* var. *nana*, has lemon-yellow flowers and there is also a charming bright green form, *S. rosmarinifolia* subsp. *rosmarinifolia* (syn. *S. virens*). All need well-drained soil and full sun. In spring clip over the plant to foster new growth and clip again after flowering to keep a compact shape of about 1 foot 9 inches by 3 feet (50cm by 90cm) if wanted.

SARCOCOCCA HOOKERIANA VAR. DIGYNA

Being low, evergreen and winter-flowering, this form of Christmas Box—also known as Sweet Box—suits small

city gardens well. The narrowly ovate, purplish leaves are borne on upright stems and the richly scented, white flowers appear in winter. Needs fertile, acidic or alkaline soil and grows in sun or medium shade to about 5 feet (1.5 meters) by 2 feet 6 inches (80cm).

SYRINGA PUBESCENS SUBSP. MICROPHYLLA

This hardy lilac is remarkable for its fragrant pink flowers in late spring. As a small, mopheaded "tree" it is effective in enclosed spaces. Remove one third of the old flowering wood in late summer every two to three years. Flowering later and adding claret-red foliage in fall, *S. pubescens* subsp. *patula* "Miss Kim" is rounded and densely foliaged. Also highly fragrant, the pink-budded flowers emerge ice blue. It is slightly taller than the other's 4 foot (1.2 meter) height/spread.

TEUCRIUM CHAMAEDRYS

Wall germander has dark green leaves with reddish-purple flowers in late summer; it associates well with fuchsias and "patio" roses. Frost-hardy, it benefits from a sunny, but sheltered, position in well-drained soil. Shorten last season's woody growth by two thirds in mid-spring. 1 foot 6 inches (45cm) high and wide.

ANTHEMIS PUNCTATA SUBSP. CUPANIANA

AQUILEGIA MCKANA HYBRIDS

perennials

ACANTHUS SPINOSUS

A statuesque habit and handsome basal leaves make this a bold architectural statement for small spaces. Tall, mauve, prickly flower spikes appear in late summer and will dry for winter use indoors. Preferring sun and well-drained soil, it can also grow in gravel gardens. Up to 5 feet (1.5 meters) high with a spread of 2 feet (60cm).

ACHILLEA X LEWISII "KING EDWARD"

Characteristically flat-headed, primrose-yellow flowers cover this alpine form of yarrow from late spring to midsummer; it creates a good contrast beneath spiky forms like *Sisyrinchium striatum,* which is also creamy flowered. With its feathery foliage it makes a compact, semi-evergreen rounded form. Prefers a sunny site, but tolerates any soil quality as long as it is well-drained. Plant in groups and replenish in two to three years. Grows to 4 inches (10cm) by 9 inches (23cm).

ANTHEMIS PUNCTATA SUBSP. *CUPANIANA*

Aromatic, finely cut, gray foliage provides a feathery background for masses of white daisy flowers in early summer. If trimmed off, the plant will flower again later. Must be grown in sun and well-drained soil,

where it looks attractive with lavenders and dwarf irises. It has a rounded, compact form, 10 inches (25cm) high and 2 feet 6 inches (75cm) wide.

AQUILEGIA MCKANA HYBRIDS

Invaluable early-summer spurred flowers among pretty, long-lasting foliage and requiring little planting space. There is a compact form, *A. flabellata* var. *pumila* f. *alba*, which is no more than 1 foot (30cm) tall and wide, but the hybrids provide much taller plants with flowers in mixed colors and extra-long spurs; there is also the old-fashioned columbine, *A. vulgaris,* which offers bluish-pink, crimson, purple, and white colors. In a sunny site aquilegias will seed everywhere but are easily removed if not wanted. They create transparent screening opportunities because they flower on tall, slim stems to a height of 3 feet (90cm) above foliage which forms a spread 1 foot 6 inches (45cm) wide.

ARMERIA MARITIMA

More or less evergreen, the grassy mounds of sea thrift provide rich green, dense tufts from which pink or white pincushion flowers are carried on wire-thin stalks in the first part of summer. There is a tightly compact

dwarf, *A. juniperifolia*, for really miniature-scale container gardens. Thrives in full sun and well-drained soil, including gravel, where *A. maritima* reaches only 6 inches (15cm) with a diameter of 1 foot (30cm).

ARTEMISIA SCHMIDTIANA "NANA"

Many of the silver-gray artemisias are suitable for small sunny gardens, but this dwarf alpine form is particularly lovely. Its fillygree-fine, silver foliage softly mounds in dry sunny sites, whether sprawling among flat gravel gardens or overhanging raised edges. The daisy-like flowers are insignificant. Height and spread 6 inches (15cm) by 1 foot (30cm).

ASTILBE "SPRITE"

This is a particularly dwarf and elegant form, ideal for small sites if planted in shade where the rich soil does not dry out. Mulching with leafmold will maintain these ideal conditions, encouraging the plants to be long-lived. Widely branching sprays of ballerina-pink flowers from mid- to late summer rise from dark green leaves. Like that of all *A. simplicifolia* hybrids, the textured foliage is attractive all season. Look also for *A.* "Bronce Elegans" with salmon-tinted flowers and

EUPHORBIA POLYCHROMA

HOSTA "GINKO CRAIG"

coppered leaves and *A. chinenis* var. *pumila*, a vigorous, ground-hugging form which is later flowering, with slightly mauve overtones. Both are smaller than "Sprite" which itself grows no higher or wider than 1 foot (30cm).

BERGENIA "MORGENROTE" ("MORNING RED")
A reliable and adaptable plant which is suitable for shaded gardens. Cherry pink flower spikes mass early in the year and again in early summer, finishing in mid-spring and leaving behind glossily rounded and evergreen leaves which may edge awkward corners and be a simple foil for ferny-leaved astilbes. Attains a height of 15 inches (38cm) by 2 feet (60cm) wide.

CAMPANULA PERSICIFOLIA
The peach-leaved bellflower has basal evergreen rosettes of dark green leaves which launch nodding bell-flowers on slim, wiry stems, forming a transparent "screen" through which other plants can be seen. White or blue varieties are available, flowering all through the summer and suitable for cutting. Easy to grow in fertile soil in sun or light shade. Usually 2 feet–2 feet 6 inches (60–75cm) by 1 foot (30cm).

COREOPSIS "GOLDFINK"
Large, deep yellow, daisy-like flowers in summer and very fine green mounds of foliage characterize this plant. It needs a sunny position and fertile, well-drained soil. Only 1 foot (30cm) in height and spread.

DICENTRA "LUXURIANT"
Many dicentras are suitable for small spaces, offering pink, crimson, and white hanging "locket" flowers for a long period, leading to their common name of bleeding hearts. All have delicate ferny foliage. This reliable hybrid has bluish-tinged, mid- to dark green leaves and "old rose" flower color, continuing from mid-spring to late summer. They need light soil and a cool, lightly shaded site where they will grow to 10 inches (25cm) in height by 8 inches (20cm) spread.

Epimediums are invaluable in lightly shaded places with moist soil; they will accommodate to sunshine and heat. Slow-growing, they gradually build up mounds of exquisitely formed leaves on thin, wiry stems. Flowering in spring, this one has deep pink flowers, others carry pale yellow flowers; some have red-edged foliage. The

slightly smaller, lovely *E.* x *youngianum* "Niveum" has white flowers. Height and spread are 1 foot (30cm).

EUPHORBIA POLYCHROMA
The early-season brassy yellow and green bracts, surrounding inconspicuous flowers, appear before the leaves. Reveling in sun and sharp drainage, euphorbias look good for the whole summer. Look for the purple form, "Candy," with bronzed early foliage. If seedheads are removed, the fresh growth is attractive. The plant forms a neat, round mound 1 foot 8 inches (50cm) in height and diameter.

GERANIUM
The vast number of available hardy species and hybrids of these plants makes selection for small spaces difficult. There are the low-growing, long-flowering "alpine" forms, like *G. cinereum*, often with pink flowers and attractive foliage, and there are weed-suppressing ground covers for difficult, dark areas, like the semi-evergreen *G. macrorrhizum*, with aromatic leaves and tiny white or pink flowers. *Geranium sanguineum* var. *striatum* "Splendens" bears pink flowers for two months in summer and is almost prostrate;

KNIPHOFIA "LITTLE MAID"

LIRIOPE MUSCARI

G. x *riversleaianum* "Russell Pritchard" has cerise-magenta flowers and sprawls in full sun, being only 9 inches (23cm) high by 1 foot 6 inches (45cm) across.

HELLEBORUS ORIENTALIS

Invaluable in winter and early spring, the evergreen Lenten rose will last for years, colonizing in a controllable manner. The open, nodding, and sometimes spotted flowers appear early in the year, offering a subtle range of pinks, white, primrose, and deep maroon shades, often with creamy stamens. New leaves follow quickly. They prefer shade and are particularly suited to a north-facing position; they will also grow under trees in most soils. Height and spread 2 feet (60cm).

HEMEROCALLIS "STELLA DE ORO"

The day lilies are reliable and attractive midsummer plants. Arching, rush-like, bright green leaves create a lush mass from which grow stems with gold lily flowers. This named cultivar is ideal for small gardens and easy-going as regards soil and aspect: only dense shade is to be avoided. As a slightly taller dwarf, it flowers repeatedly and grows to a height and spread of 1 foot 8 inches (50cm) by 1 foot 6 inches (45cm). Look for the, fragrant gold "Corky," which is one of the tiniest, being only 9 inches (23cm) high.

HEUCHERA "PEWTER MOON"

Most cultivars of these plants are small and ideal for limited space. Grown as much for their foliage as their flowers, they are good edgers because the evergreen leaves form neat rosettes at the base. "Pewter Moon" has bronze leaves overlaid with silver and sprays of tiny pale pink flowers which grow from slim stems in summer. They are suited to partly shaded or sunny areas and need well-drained, fertile soil. The foliage looks handsome from spring to late fall. Both height and spread are 1 foot 2 inches (35cm).

HOSTA "GINKO CRAIG"

Hostas are valued mostly for their superb ribbed leaves, which have great variety in size, color, and form. This dwarf form has narrowly pointed, white-edged leaves which quickly form an overlapping clump, from which small mauve flowers appear on long stems in summer. *Hosta lancifolia* is a slightly larger, but also a manageable form for small gardens, with brilliant glossy-green layers of pointed leaves and deep violet flowers in late summer. Both need moist soil and a shaded position. "Ginko Craig" is only 1 foot (30cm) tall and 1 foot 6 inches (45cm) wide, *H. lancifolia* is 2 feet (60 cm) by 2 feet 6 inches (75cm).

KNIPHOFIA "LITTLE MAID"

Flower spikes can enliven a plant mass and these are wreathed in brilliant, closely set, tiny, ivory-white flowers later in summer. The narrowly erect leaves are bluish-green. All forms make strongly architectural plants and appreciate full sun and sharp drainage. This one grows to 2 feet (60cm) by 1 foot 6 inches (45cm).

LIRIOPE MUSCARI

Lilyturf has low, evergreen grassy foliage, invaluable in small spaces where it can provide neat edging or clump among deciduous perennials. The plant spreads by rhizomes, but is easily controlled. It thrives in a sunny site and well-drained soil; it is frost-hardy, so reliable in enclosed small gardens. When least expected, in late summer, it produces mauve flower spikes to a height of 1 foot (30cm); the spread is 1 foot 6 inches (45cm), followed in the fall by black fruits.

OMPHALODES CAPPADOCICA

SISYRINCHIUM STRIATUM

OMPHALODES CAPPADOCICA

In spring and early summer the forget-me-not blue flowers are welcome in part or full shade. Good for ground cover, it is also easy to control. It does best in deep, moist but well-drained soil rich in organic matter. Leaves are broad and well-shaped; flower sprays reach 8 inches (20cm), the girth 9 inches (23cm).

PHLOX SUBULATA

Moss phlox is a small alpine which forms a ground-hugging, evergreen mat awash with small flowers of blue, pink, or white in spring. It grows best in light soil and full sun, and will trail over edges or grow in gravel. The mat is rarely higher than 9 inches (23cm) and spreads about 1 foot 6 inches (45cm).

SALVIA NEMOROSA "OSTFRIESLAND" ("EAST FRIESLAND")

Invaluably neat for small spaces, this compact, rounded plant has spikes of intensely deep blue flowers throughout the summer. Look also for *S. x sylvestris* "Blauhügel" ("Blue Hill") with light blue flower spikes. Both are easy to grow in any well-drained soil, being drought-tolerant in full sun or very light shade. Height and spread 2 feet by 1 foot 6 inches (60 by 45cm).

SCABIOSA "BUTTERFLY BLUE"

This is a dwarf blue-flowering plant with a compact habit. It is ideal for tiny gardens, earning its keep with a long flowering period of large, characteristic pincushion flowers lasting from late spring through to fall. It attracts butterflies and is generally trouble-free in light, well-drained soil and a sunny site. The height is only 1 foot (30cm) and it has a neat spread of 1 foot 2 inches (35cm).

SCHIZOSTYLIS COCCINEA

Late in the season, when most flowers are done, the kaffir lilies produce rich crimson, china pink, or pure white "lily" flower spikes which can last almost to Christmas in a benevolent season. Grassy foliage from a spreading underground root system is equally attractive. At the year's end they look wonderful, holding their color as the ornamental grasses fade to parchment coloring, and with infilling of now-bronzed *Sedum* "Herbstfreude" (syn. *S. spectabile* "Autumn Joy") They cope with sun and light shade but must have moist, rich soil. Cover in winter in extreme weather conditions. Growing 2 feet (60cm) tall, they take up only 9 inches (23cm) of ground space.

SEDUM TELEPHIUM SUBSP. *MAXIMUM* "ATROPURPUREUM"

For a small garden this form of sedum has much to offer, with thick, fleshy leaves of deep purple and flattened plum-pink flowerheads which by late summer have turned bronze and merged into chocolate-brown seedheads. The flowers branch above the leaves at a height of 2 feet (60cm); the spread is the same.

SISYRINCHIUM STRIATUM

Reedy, evergreen leaves make wide fan shapes from which spikes of cream flowers appear in summer. "Aunt May" is a smaller, cream-variegated form. Both grow in any soil in full sunlight. The height is 2 feet (60cm) and the width only 9 inches (23cm).

VERBENA BONARIENSIS

Thin, wiry, branching stems, growing tall over the main foliage base, are topped with tiny lavender-pink, fragrant flowers which grow as densely packed, tufted clusters from midsummer onward. It can be grown as a screen and planted to the fore of a bed. Although not long-lived, it redistributes itself by copious self-seeding, provided it has well-drained soil in full sun. Reaching 5 feet (1.5m) in height, it is just 2 feet (60cm) wide.

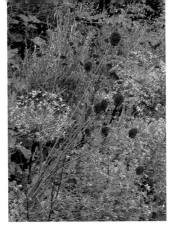

ALLIUM SPHAEROCEPHALON AND A. CRISTOPHII   ERANTHIS HYEMALIS

ERYTHRONIUM DENS-CANIS

bulbs, tubers, and corms

ALLIUM HOLLANDICUM "PURPLE SENSATION"

A highly ornamental bulb with large, purple, globular flowerheads, made from tiny star flowers in a dense spherical umbel, appearing in early summer on tall stems. The slender reedy foliage dies by the time the flowers appear. Plant bulbs in fall; given good drainage and a sunny site, they will increase over the years. Attractive as seedheads among late flowers and ornamental grasses. Can grow to 3 feet (90cm).

ALLIUM SPHAEROCEPHALON

The crimson-maroon "drumsticks" of the round-headed leek, produced on slender stems, mix in well with other perennial flowers in a sunny, well-drained site in summer; they are also effective in late summer as they fade. The flowerheads grow above semi-erect basal leaves to heights of 1 foot 8 inches–3 feet (50–90cm).

ANEMONE BLANDA

Small, easily grown bulbs which are best seen in quantity beneath trees, where they will naturalize. Attractive green foliage with cultivars of blue, pink, and white flowers, although they are possibly better seen as a single color mass than mixed colors. Shade-tolerant

and hardy, they flower in late winter, when snowdrops and aconites are still in bloom. Plant in fall and they will multiply over the years. Height 5 inches (12cm).

CROCUS SPECIOSUS

An excellent, fall-flowering species with slim, funnel-shaped, blue-lilac flowers appearing from late summer onward. They are hardy and need no winter protection as long as they are planted in well-drained soil where it is sunny. Plant corms the previous fall. About 4 inches (10cm) high.

CROCUS TOMMASINIANUS

The lilac and purple flowers are welcome in early spring and will naturalize successfully if grown in sunny or lightly shaded, well-drained sites. Plant the corms the previous fall in informal clusters. Height up to 4 inches (10cm).

CYCLAMEN COUM

Dark green, silver, or patterned green and silver, attractively heart-shaped leaves create the foil for pink, white, or violet flowers during winter. If planted in semi-shade and soil enriched with organic matter, they

spread rapidly. Protection beneath shrubs or trees suits them well and they can tolerate dryness. Always buy from reputable nurseries. They grow to 4 inches (10cm).

ERANTHIS HYEMALIS

The winter aconites are ideal for small shaded gardens, as well as sunny, open sites where their vivid yellow flowers are most welcome in midwinter to early spring. Plant the tubers in moist, but gritty, free draining soil and leave undisturbed to allow them to spread. They will naturalize beneath shrubs and need no further attention. They grow 3 inches (8cm) high.

ERYTHRONIUM DENS-CANIS

The dog's-tooth violet is a spring-flowering perennial which should be planted immediately after arrival because the bulbs begin to dry out. They prefer cool climates, must have soil rich in organic matter, and appreciate a top-dressing of leafmold. Two mottled leaves are at the base of a stem carrying white, pink, or purple pendent flowers with reflexed petals, which develop in late spring. Left undisturbed, they will thrive for many years. The height of the flowers is 6 inches (15cm).

Narcissus "Tête-à-Tête"

Tulipa aucheriana

Iris reticulata

The small, early-flowering irises are ideal for containers or graveled gardens where they can be sure of good drainage and receiving plenty of daylight. The species is scented and the flower color is purple with gold markings; there are pale and deep blue, yellow, and cream cultivars. Light, well-drained, alkaline soil suits best and they should be planted about 3 inches (8cm) deep in fall. They can grow up to 6 inches (15cm).

Lilium martagon

Turk's-cap lilies grow well in semi-shaded parts of the small garden, adding distinction with their deep purple or glowing white, nodding, summer flowers which are fragrant. Long anthers hang from the center of the reflexed petals. These are lime-tolerant lilies and will naturalize in well-drained, but fertile, soil. They grow to 2 feet 6 inches (75cm).

Muscari armeniacum

Small grape hyacinths are apt to spread easily, which is welcome in spring when their rich blue flowers seduce the eye, although they can be untidy in small gardens when the leaves die after flowering, so plant them among perennials which will take over rapidly and conceal their dying foliage. Randomly planted in fall amid shrubs and herbaceous plants in free-draining soil, in either sun or light shade, they will increase every year. They grow to 6–8 inches (15–20cm).

Narcissus "February Gold"

One of the earliest daffodils to flower, this delicately formed dwarf *N. cyclamineus* hybrid is ideal for the small garden. It is long-lasting and withstands wind. The trumpet is deeper yellow than the encircling petals, which are slightly reflexed and pointed. There is a white form too, "February Silver". Both will naturalize in sun or shade, growing to about 10 inches (25cm).

Narcissus jonquilla

There are many very pretty, small hybrids in this group, like the scented, multi-headed *N.* "Baby Moon." All are fragrant and will grow in containers or raised beds where they will best be seen. Flowering in late spring, they reach 9 inches (23cm) at most.

Narcissus "Tête-à-Tête"

This small hybrid is a favorite for all small gardens. It is reliable, grows in sun or light shade, will appear in early spring, and carries two or more flowers on each stem. The petals are lemon-colored and the flowers delicately formed, growing to 6 inches (15cm).

Tulipa aucheriana

Smaller-species tulips like this tiny, rose-colored plant add charm in early summer if planted where they can be seen along a path or among rocks in cool, but well-lit, sites. The flowers open out into stars before shedding their petals. These must be picked off the ground and not allowed to rot, to discourage the infection "tulip fire." All species should be purchased from reputable nurseries and never dug from the wild. Only 3 inches (8cm).

Tulipa kaufmanniana

The water-lily tulip is the earliest tulip to flower, usually as spring starts. There are many cultivars which are often brightly colored: *T.* "Concerto" is creamy-white but *T.* "Heart's Delight" has carmine flowers with pink edging and cream inner coloring. Striped foliage makes rich detail. In full sun and well-drained soil, these are easy to grow and will reach 8–9 inches (20–23cm).

ABUTILON MEGAPOTAMICUM

CLEMATIS "NIOBE"

climbers

ABUTILON MEGAPOTAMICUM

An evergreen, but tender, wall shrub which carries pendent, narrowly bell-shaped flowers. Slim branches can be trained in a fan shape against the wall, with butter-yellow and Indian red flowers hanging for weeks against dark green, unusual, heart-shaped and oval leaves. The height and spread are 10 feet (3 meters). In extremely cold weather, protect with a fleece or some other protective covering.

CLIANTHUS PUNICEUS

Parrot's bill or lobster claw describes the unusual, claw-like, red flowers which hang in groups from this semi-evergreen climber. Small twinned foliage with as many as 25 leaflets provides a textural effect but the stems are lax, so wire support is necessary. Frost-tender, this plant may need winter protection and should be grown on very warm walls in free-draining soil, where it will scramble to a height of 13 feet (4 meters).

CLEMATIS

Ideal climbing plants for intimate gardens because many can easily be fitted into a tiny space and will ramble over fences, walls, trees, and shrubs or weave in with herbaceous perennials. Highly floriferous and in some cases with wispily whorled seedheads, they climb by twining and can be evergreen or deciduous. They will thrive in sun as long as they have a cool, deep, moist root run, and need regular feeding and watering throughout the summer. There is a clematis to flower in every season, from spring to late fall, and even some for winter, so these plants will be an asset nearly all year. All clematis can, in fact, be pruned or left unpruned. But to achieve the best a plant can deliver, especially in the context of small spaces, you should prune each according to the group into which it falls.

Group 1: Early-flowering species, like *C. alpina*, *C. macropetala*, and the very vigorous *C. montana* cultivars prefer warm walls, but tolerate more exposed positions. Flowers are borne on the previous season's ripened shoots in late winter or spring. *C. montana* may become very tangled and will need a fairly tough approach; otherwise, prune lightly after flowering to allow new growth to ripen for the following season.
Group 2: These include the early to mid-season, large-flowered cultivars which bloom on the previous season's ripened shoots, as well as on new shoots.

Prune to where the new leaf-axil buds are visible, before new growth starts in early spring.
Group 3: In these late-blooming cultivars, the large flowers are borne on new summer and fall growth. This groups also includes the late-flowering species and small-flowered cultivars which flower on the current season's wood. Prune early down to a pair of new leaf-axil buds, removing the previous season's stems.

C. ALPINA "FRANCES RIVIS"
Group 1. Small, nodding, lantern-shaped blue flowers in late spring. Up to 8 feet (2.5 meters).
C. CIRRHOSA VAR. *BALEARICA*
Group 1. Evergreen, ferny leaves with creamy-white, bell-shaped flowers in winter. Silky seedheads in early spring after flowering. Up to 30 feet (10 meters).
C. "GÉNÉRAL SIKORSKI"
Group 2. Early-summer flowers are large, with overlapping, mid-blue petals and creamy-yellow anthers. Grows up to 10 feet (3 meters).
C. MACROPETALA "LAGOON"
Group 1. Masses of small, semi-double, nodding, blue flowers, late spring to summer. Grows to 12 feet (3.6 meters).

Parthencissus henryana

Rosa "Guinée"

C. "Niobe"

Group 2. Early, large-flowered type which flowers through summer. Velvety, red flowers with greenish-yellow anthers. Grows up to 10 feet (3 meters).

Group 3. Vigorous cultivar from the late-flowering viticella group, it has deep purple-blue flowers with cream anthers. Reaches to 15 feet (4.5 meters).

C. "Royal Velours"

Group 3. Vigorous viticella type with late-flowering, small purple flowers. Grows to 20 feet (6 meters).

Eccremocarpus scaber

The Chilean glory flower is a tender, fast-growing evergreen which climbs via tendrils that attach to wires. Grow in any soil, as an annual, or in a protected site all year. Rich, orange-red, narrowly tubular flowers are followed by seedpods. Will grow to 10 feet (3 meters).

Hedera helix "Oro di Bogliasco" (syn. "Goldheart")

This is one of the most useful evergreen climbers as it will grow in full shade, its creamy yellow leaf centers providing a cheerful sight in a dark area. Remove any branches which revert to plain green.

Hedera helix "Sagittifolia"

This ivy is popular for the narrowly fingered leaves which make patterns on walls; alternatively, it may be used as ground cover or to trail over retaining walls. It is hardy, densely foliaged, and fast-growing.

Parthenocissus henryana

This invaluable, smallish-leaved vine has deep green, velvety foliage, marked with silver-white veining, which becomes gloriously scarlet in fall. It is better in shade, since these characteristics are less well developed if it is on a sunny wall. Self-supported by tendrils with tiny sucking pads, it will grow 33 feet (10 meters) high.

Passiflora caerulea

The blue passion flower has arresting blooms: the central corona of purple filaments is surrounded by a ring of blue-white, flattened petals; in warm seasons large, orange, egg-shaped fruit are produced. This climber creates quick effects in new gardens because it is fast-growing and semi-evergreen, but it should be given protection as it is tender. Climbs by tendrils which grip onto wires, trellis, or other plants. Needs full sun and a fertile soil. Reaches 33 feet (10 meters).

Climbing roses

There is a rose for almost every site, even a cold one. For really small spaces, choose the stately, restrained climbers, whose large, single flowers occur in flushes, with recurrent repeats through the summer to fall. Look at the foliage because all detail is valuable; some also carry hips, adding to fall brillance. Most climbers have large flowers which grow on the current year's wood; these need pruning in early spring. They are ideal for trellis, pillars, and pergolas; clematis will fill in the quieter periods.

"Aimée Vibert"

This noisette flowers early, with clusters of pure white flowers. Vigorous, it reaches 12 feet (3.6 meters) by 10 feet (3 meters).

"Guinée"

Dark, velvety red, this adaptable fragrant climber even flowers on a cool wall. Allow 15 feet (4.5 meters) by 8 feet (2.4 meters).

"Madame Alfred Carrière"

This pretty noisette will grow on a cool wall, its creamy flower clusters tinged with pink. It is vigorous, growing to 12 feet (3.6 meters) by 10 feet (3 meters).

ferns

ADIANTUM PEDATUM

This maidenhair fern is semi-evergreen and the new growth appears in spring, lasting through winter. Black-stemmed, it has delicately lobed, mid-green fronds. It needs moist soil rich in organic matter and some shade to thrive; 1 foot 6 inches (45cm) by 1 foot (30cm).

ASPLENIUM SCOLOPENDRIUM

Known as the hart's tongue fern, this is ideally suited to small, enclosed gardens where wind is not a problem. In a shaded area the glossy, leathery leaves benefit from well-drained, alkaline soil. Look for the frilled-edge form, "Undulatum." It can reach 2 feet (60cm) by 1 foot (30cm).

ASPLENIUM TRICHOMANES

The maidenhair spleenwort is a small, pretty, evergreen fern. Bright green, it grows tucked into rocks, paving, or crevices in shady walls, where it will cope with poor, dry soil and grows from 2–6 inches (5–15cm).

ATHYRIUM NIPONICUM VAR. PICTUM

The Japanese painted fern is well worth hunting for. The graceful foliage provides lovely detail for small sites; its wine-red stems support green fronds, touched with silver. When first unfurling in spring it is particularly beautiful. Easily grown in dampish soil and protected in light shade, it grows 2 feet (60cm) high and wide.

CYRTOMIUM FALCATUM "ROCHFORDIANUM"

This cultivar of the Japanese holly fern, or fishtail fern, is a half-hardy evergreen, whose dark, glossy, pinnate fronds make wonderful ground cover in shade. In warm climates its depth of color and striking spikiness make a good contrast among more flamboyantly hued flowering plants. It is not particular about soil and varies in height from 2–3 feet (60cm–1 meter) and in width from 1 foot–1 foot 6 inches (30–45cm).

DRYOPTERIS ERYTHROSA

The buckler ferns are long-lived and hardy. They come in many different sizes and textures, offering choices for small sites. The fall fern comes from the Far East, so-called because of its color at the year end. Unfurling green tinged with pinky-bronze in spring, it matures to rich green by midsummer. The plant is adaptable, doing well in deep shade or very lightly shaded areas. It forms attractive clumps in acid or alkaline soil which does not dry out, growing up to 2 feet (60cm) by 1 foot (30cm).

ONOCLEA SENSIBILIS

Known as the sensitive fern, this has two frond types: light green, triangular, sterile ones which turn brown in fall and narrow, persistent, fertile ones with bead-like frondlets attached. Ideal for a wild-looking, woodland area, in semi-shade and moist soil it will spread vigorously, making it necessary to weed out the young ones in small spaces. Apply a protective mulch in colder areas. Grows to 2 feet (60cm) by 3 feet (90cm).

POLYSTICHUM SETIFERUM ACUTILOBUM GROUP

The decorative soft shield ferns are evergreen and easy to grow. There are many permutations of fronds with intricate differences, so look at the cultivars available. This group is taller than some and elegantly structured, ideal in shade where the fresh green fronds unfurl in spring. Remove old foliage as necessary. They will adapt to dry and alkaline conditions, but do best in free-draining soil, rich in organic matter, beneath trees, where they will reach 2 feet (60cm).

CAREX ELATA "AUREA"

PENNISETUM ORIENTALE

grasses

CAREX ELATA "AUREA"

Also known as Bowles' golden sedge, this plant is grown for its bright, elegantly arching leaves, which for most of the year are bright yellow with green margins, gradually becoming greener as summer progresses. Fluffy brownish flower spikes appear in summer. The plant needs a fairly moist soil and a sunny position; it is slow to increase. Grows to an ultimate height of 1 foot 8 inches (50cm) by 1 foot 6 inches (45cm).

CAREX HACHIJOENSIS "EVERGOLD"

A useful evergreen grass which stays bright in the dark days of winter. Grows best in rich soils which do not dry out. Because it will grow in semi-shade, it is indispensable for tiny gardens with low light. Grows to a height and spread of 10 inches (25cm).

DESCHAMPSIA FLEXUOSA "TATRA GOLD"

Fine, acid-yellow greening foliage carries flowers on reddish stems which shimmer in the sunlight of early summer. It grows well in either full sun or light shade and in moist, rich soil which is slightly acidic. Can be cut for use in flower arranging. Height and spread are 2 feet (60cm).

FESTUCA ESKIA

This small, tufted grass is brilliant emerald green and can be used for ground cover or grown as porcupine-like mounds grouped among other plants. *F. gautieri* is very similar but has a really dwarf form, "Pic Carlit," which is a tiny, mossy green 4 inch (10cm) miniature. Both will grow in sun or dappled light and soil which drains well, but which never completely dries out. The height and spread are 8 inches (20cm).

HORDEUM JUBATUM

Known as foxtail barley or squirreltail grass, this short-lived, sun-loving perennial carries softly fanning, silken flowerheads, catching the light throughout the summer. Preferring well-drained soil, it can be grown as an annual, but is seen at its best when massed. Each plants grows 1–2 feet (30–60cm) tall and has a spread of 1 foot (30cm).

MILIUM EFFUSUM "AUREUM"

In light shade this butter-yellow, fluttering grass, known as Bowles' golden grass or golden wood millet, brightens early borders where ferns and pulmonarias are on show. Although short-lived, the seeds succeed easily and stay true, so the grass appears in many unexpected places where you may easily weed it out or leave it in its chosen niche. In flower it grows to 1 foot 6 inches (45cm) and is 1 foot (30cm) across.

PENNISETUM ORIENTALE

Clumps of slender, bluish foliage carry iridescent, fluffy, pink flowers from mid- to late summer. Aptly described as oriental fountain grass, it may be grown as a specimen in full sun to light shade, in moist, yet freely draining, soil. Makes a distinctive association in fall with bronzing *Sedum* "Herbstfreude". Suits small spaces with its height of 2 feet (60cm) and with a spread of 1 foot 6 inches (45cm).

STIPA TENUISSIMA

Mounding, soft clumps of bright green, hair-fine leaves carry narrow, creamy-feathered plumes which respond to the slightest breeze. Can be cut down in winter or left as parchment-colored, fine-leaved mounds and cut before spring. Will thrive in sunshine and well-drained soils or among gravel-garden plants where it grows over 2 feet (60cm) tall; allow a spread of approximately 1 foot 8 inches (50cm).

ARCTOTIS VENUSTA

ESCHSCHOLZIA CALIFORNICA

HELIOTROPIUM "DWARF MARINE"

annuals and tender perennials

ARCTOTIS VENUSTA

Summer planting of the blue-eyed African daisy, a
South African native, is a means of creating rich color
association. Rust, bright orange, coppered red, old gold
yellow, milky cream, and mulled wine pink are the
flower colors. Bluish centers and gray-green, finely cut
foliage make these daisy flowers more interesting, to
my mind, than the startling gazanias. This tender
perennial is usually cultivated as an annual. Sow the
seed indoors for transplanting outdoors later or sow
directly where they are to grow. Better still, buy grown
specimens from a garden center to be sure what colors
you are getting. They require fertile, well-drained soil
and sunshine and are excellent in containers, where
they reach 1 foot 8 inches (50cm) high by 1 foot
4 inches (40cm) spread.

BEGONIA SEMPERFLORENS COCKTAIL HYBRIDS

The waxy, tender perennial begonias grown as annuals
prefer lightly moist soils, but will cope with some
neglect and full hot sunshine. These compact hybrids
are useful summer fillers, expanding gradually through
the season. Flowers may be pink, red, white, and
permutations of these with brilliant green, rounded,

succulent leaves, which are sometimes red-edged or
bronzed. The flower color seems always to be offset by
the natural leaf color. Sow seeds indoors and transplant
only when any danger of frost is over—or buy ready-
grown plantlets. Good in containers or as quick-effect
mass bedding. Height and spread no more than
6 inches (15cm).

ESCHSCHOLZIA CALIFORNICA

Californian poppies are easy to grow, making few
demands on the soil and self-seeding in later years.
They need full sun and will thrive if sown directly into
gravel gardens, subsequently spreading themselves
among gaps in paving. Cup-shaped, single flowers,
formed by four satiny petals of yellow, orange, scarlet,
or white, gleam on slim stems above fine, bluish
foliage. Massing the colors together works superbly
and continual deadheading maintains the effect
through summer. They are 1 foot (30cm) tall and
6 inches (15cm) wide.

HELIOTROPIUM "DWARF MARINE"

For some time rather out of fashion, the heliotropes
are worth considering for the sheer intensity of their

purple coloring and their evening fragrance. Ruched,
dark green foliage sets off massed heads of tiny,
densely packed flowers. New small forms have been
bred for use in containers as "patio" plants, against
the former practice of using them only for bedding.
Any well-drained soil will do but they must be in full
sun. They grow to a height of 1 foot 2 inches (35cm).

IMPATIENS HYBRIDS

When grown as annuals, these are the best value
among tender perennials. Continuously blooming
through the summer, they have particular relevance to
small gardens because they thrive. The familiar pinks
and reds add color, but the white ones are luminous in
dark corners, once the hellebores and pulmonarias are
over, provided the soil is moist, but well-drained. Their
bushy habit makes them ideal for containers and
hanging baskets, too. The "Duet Series" have a height
and spread of 1 foot (30cm).

LATHYRUS ODORATUS

Fragrance is of such value in small gardens and the
annual climbing sweet pea is noted for this
characteristic, as well as offering many color choices,

PETUNIA "PURPLE PIROUETTE"

VERBENA X *HYBRIDA*

like the old-fashioned "Painted Lady" which will grow up to 10 feet (3 meters) high, climbing by tendrils up wire, trellis, or canes. The flowers can be cut for the house. They demand little of the soil so long as it has been well prepared for sowing on site, is well-drained, and in full sun. They are not suited to southern areas. For very small spaces dwarf cultivars, like Bijou Group, which may be pink, blue, or red, are 1 foot 6 inches (45cm) high and need no support.

NICOTIANA

Whereas most half-hardy annuals are grown for container planting, the tobacco plants consort very well with permanent plants. The soft flower colors of *N. alata* are dusky pink, reddish-purple, lime, and creamy greens, all of which blend in easily if put in as small plantlets in early summer. Grown as scented annuals, these are a tallish 2 feet (60cm). Some distinguished relatives, like the very tall, 5-foot (1.5-meter), elegant, white perennial, *N. sylvestris,* can be grown outside in containers for fragrant sophistication. But the smaller, more bushy annuals called *N. x sanderae* Domino Series may better fit your space, at a height and spread of 1 foot (30cm).

PELARGONIUMS

So many forms, with different habits, foliage, and flowers, make this genus of tender perennials one of the most justifiably popular of temporary summer plants. Distinct types include the more common round-leaved zonals, such as pink- and white-flowered *P.* "Maverick Star." Many of these become top-heavy, with huge, round flower balls. The shrubby regals, like *P.* "Purple Emperor" with pink and purple markings, have fussier foliage and these are more vulnerable to inclement weather. Delicate, ivy-leaved forms are prettiest in both foliage and flower, like *P. peltatum* "Summer Showers," which trails and shows well in hanging baskets. The scented-leaved and species types tend to be less showy, having tiny flowers, but attractive, fragrant foliage; if planted in containers, they can be moved outside for summer. All pelargoniums can be raised from seed, but for the small garden it is easier to buy established plants, where you can be sure of the color and leaf. They are better used in window boxes and containers than planted in the ground with other plants, where they look unnatural. Frequent deadheading, regular feeding, and not over-watering are the keys to success.

PETUNIA

Soft, trumpet-shaped flowers in a range of crimsons, purples, pinks, and whites can be expected from these half-hardy perennials which are usually grown as summer-flowering annuals. There are single forms, doubles, some with a central dark blotch, and other white-striped forms. Perfect as container plants, all they require is regular feeding, deadheading, and some cover in really wet weather (unless you have chosen the Celebrity Series), in addition to the use of an anti-slug program. If these needs are met, petunias will reward you with flowers all summer. Most grow to 6–12 inches (15–30cm).

VERBENA X HYBRIDA

Traditionally used as bedding plants, many of the widely branched, spreading forms are ideal for trailing in window boxes and hanging baskets. They grow in any soil, as long as it is not damp, and they need a sunny site. The clustered flowerheads can be carmine, lilac, white, or deep purple. *V.* "Sissinghurst" is a very low-spreading, pink-flowered cultivar and *V.* "Showtime" is crimson and widely branching, being 8 inches (20cm) high with a 1 foot (30cm) spread.

practicalities

The art of successful garden design depends upon using the space fully, and the best way to achieve this is to plan the layout on paper first. This chapter shows twelve different designs for small plots, all of which resolve the constraints of the space and the conditions of the site in individual ways. The craft of gardening relies on both a respect for nature and an understanding of good husbandry. In small spaces we should value each plant's natural habit and we can use this both to shape a plant to suit our needs and to create good planting compositions.

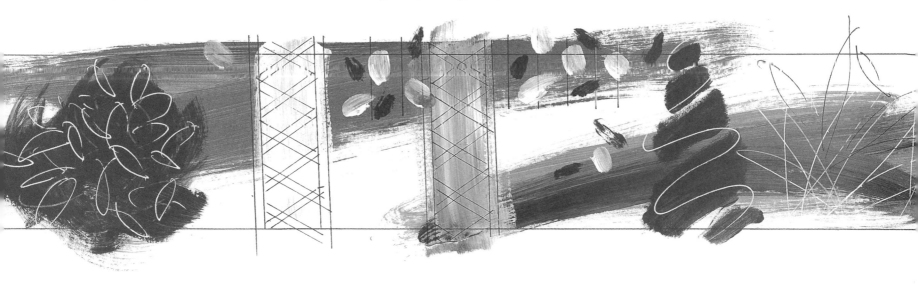

garden plans

All garden designers know how invaluable it is to plan a garden on paper. No special drawing skill is required, but an accurate scale is needed to show what is possible in terms of paving, seats, paths, and plants. These plans are all drawn to a scale of 1:50.

Square gardens

Square gardens present a challenge because the square is a more difficult shape to design with than a rectangle. One solution is to divide the space to create sympathetic rectangular spaces, dividing it with the geometry of pure symmetry, another is to fully utilize the square by adopting a circular theme, ignoring mathematical precision completely. One approach may appeal to you more than another as a starting point for your own space.

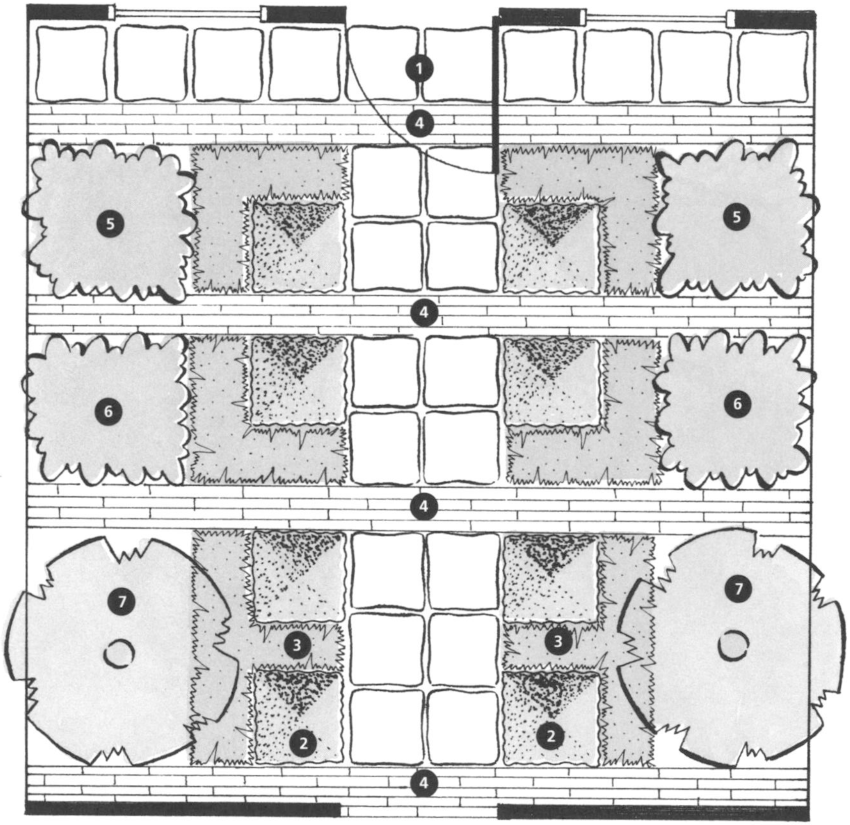

a formal front garden

While the design of the formal front garden shown above emphasizes the geometry of the square plot, its layout is less predictable. Areas of uneven depth are divided off by four lines of tile-on-edge running across the site. The dominant planting is of clipped evergreen forms; these are placed to either side of the central axis comprising eight sentinels of clipped box pyramids, fringed by low lavender hedging, which make the approach dramatic. Unity is maintained by the rhythm of repeated shapes and textures. Planting to the far side is less formal: two *Cistus corbariensis* make low flowering mounds, *Prunus laurocerasus* "Dart's Low Green" provides a shiny evergreen foil, and two standard roses (*Rosa* "Sander's White") are the most relaxed element of the planting.

1. *The design acknowledges the symmetry of the double-fronted house; the central-axis path leading to the front door is about 3 feet (1 meter) wide.*

2. *Formal plants of box (Buxus sempervirens), clipped as four-sided pyramids, flank the path.*

3. *Clipped lavender (Lavandula "Hidcote") hedging wraps partly around the pyramids, "widening" the access area.*

4. *Four lines, comprising a triple row of slim tiles-on-edge, run across the site, dividing it unequally.*

5. *Informal shrubs like matching Cistus corbariensis are planted on the far boundaries, separated from the main axial path.*

6. *Paired evergreen shrubs, Prunus laurocerasus "Dart's Low Green."*

7. *Standard roses (Rosa "Sander's White"), underplanted with white-flowering Narcissus "February Silver" and Viola cornuta "Alba" for seasonal color.*

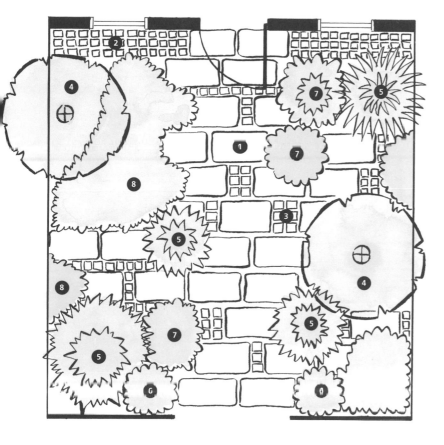

an informal front garden

The design of the open space is invitingly casual and irregular. The surface of concrete flagstones and smaller granite setts is laid informally, with spaces left for planting. A direct route from the gate gives variable access width, ideal for families, and allows clear access as no plants interrupt this line. Elsewhere the planting is informal and not all of it is evergreen. Two small acers, set diagonally across from each other, dominate the space; as they slowly grow taller, they will reach the height of small, stylish trees which are elegant even when leafless in winter. Although their canopy will eventually reach above head height, it will not make deep shade. Other plants include evergreen shrubs, mountain pines, carpeting thymes, and cheerful flowering perennials.

1 *The front door is easily reached, although access varies in width.*

2 *The house is defined and fronted by a triple layer of granite setts.*

3 *Granite setts are randomly interspersed among bands of informally laid concrete slabs. The setts vary from a single to a triple row, but are always parallel with the slabs.*

4 *Planting pockets, which must be planned from the start, allow for two acers:* Acer palmatum *and A. palmatum "Osakazuki."*

5 *Conifers include* Pinus mugo *"Pumilio,"* Juniperus *"Pfitzeriana," and J. sabina "Tamariscifolia."*

6 *Two small hebes (Hebe "Margaret") flank the entrance to the front garden.*

7 *Flowering plants include small shrubs like lavenders, helianthemums, and* x Halimiocistus sahucii.

8 *Herbaceous plants include alpine geraniums,* Phlox subulata, *and* Liriope muscari, *with the addition of small spring bulbs like* Chionodoxa luciliae, Anemone blanda, *and dwarf narcissi.*

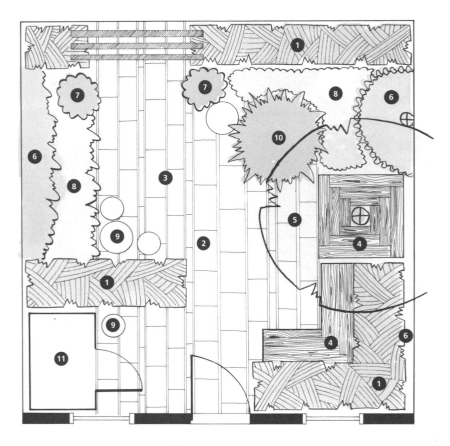

a formal back garden

The square space of this back garden has been divided by means of clipped evergreen box hedging used as walling to create a series of rectangles. At the far end it is approximately 5 feet (1.5 meters) high and elsewhere it is clipped to 3 feet (1 meter), so the garden is visible from the house. The greenness stretches along the back wall with a seat beneath a timber arbor placed to catch the morning sun, while the central area of the garden is left empty enough for furniture to be put out in summer. Another seat, lightly shaded by a small tree, faces the evening sun; this fixed timber corner seat is designed for people to converse easily. In the north-facing corner of the site is a functional shed, unnoticed from the garden because of the hedge and not visible from the house window either. Lengths of green slate paving in different widths run at right angles to the house.

1. Clipped box hedging divides the space in such a way that access involves turning right into the main part of the courtyard.

2. The paving is made from long rectangles of roughened green slate in varying widths, including some very slim ones.

3. Butt-jointing the paving across its width but mortaring it lengthwise appears to lengthen the square courtyard.

4. A built-in treated timber seat and table are permanent fixtures.

5. A small tree (Betula pendula "Tristis") grows through the central space in the table, providing shade.

6. Wall shrubs on the boundaries increase privacy; behind the bench seat and hedge are five cordon-trained ivies (Hedera helix "Sagittifolia").

7. Two matching clipped domes of box flank the timber pergola, below which a seat faces the morning sun.

8. Planting in front of the wall shrubs is mainly herbaceous, with some carpeting alpines.

9. Extra plants for summer color are grown in containers.

10. A low-growing Acer palmatum is sited beside the wooden table. A shed is screened by hedging.

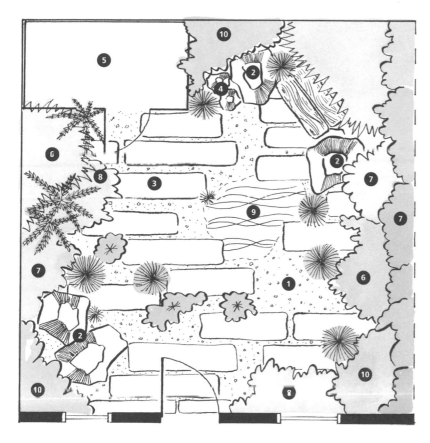

an informal back garden

This plan is loosely devised to create a casual, relaxed feel, with rural associations. There are no hard edges anywhere in the garden and no soil is visible, although it would have been well prepared initially to ensure free drainage. The open space is laid with gravel, in which railroad ties act as stepping stones. In the middle a shallow depression has been dug, lined with sand and heavy-duty plastic sheeting to create a small pond 1 foot 6 inches (45cm) deep; gravel, rocks, and timbers conceal its edges. Large rocks double as seats beside a permanent seat made from blocks of railroad-tie timbers. An attractively built shed, visible at the end of the garden, provides storage. Plants are chosen to echo the informality of the design: there is a large stand of the ornamental grass (*Miscanthus sacchariflorus*) with ferns and hellebores in shade. Species roses grown as wall shrubs provide flower, foliage, and fruit.

1. Gravel provides flooring and top-dresses the plants. Rocks, pebbles, and gravel are from similar rock types and are the same color.

2. The few large rocks have been carefully chosen to provide extra seats; they make more impact than many smaller ones.

3. Railroad ties make large, solid paving units and, laid in parallel, create a "stepping stone" path.

4. Large pebbles edge some of the rock groups.

5. There is just room for a dark-stained, sawn timber shed.

6. Informal planting includes all-green, tall ornamental grasses.

7. Rosa primula, R. moyesii, and other species roses are trained against the wall, with Viburnum tinus *opposite.*

8. A collection of ferns, Helleborus orientalis, foxgloves, and easy alpine plants grow elsewhere.

9. Gravel masks the edge of the randomly shaped, shallow pool. The few marginal water plants include Caltha palustris, Butomus umbellatus, *and* Typha minima.

10. Evergreen shrubs, including hollies, cotoneaster, and Nandina domestica, *associate with climbers like honeysuckle and clematis.*

the effects of orientation

The direction of the sun influences the layout plan of all gardens. On this and the following pages the designs for four identical L-shaped gardens show how orientation affects major decisions. The sun dictates where we sit, how we plan the views, and which plants will grow around the site. Shade is a consideration, too, because we do not wish to sit in full midday sun for reasons of comfort or, indeed, safety. Evening sun is important to those who arrive home from a working day to spend precious time in their gardens. Access to the garden is from the house doors at the base of the plan.

north-facing garden

This design is planned to make the most of the heat and light received only at the far end of the courtyard; the house end of the garden receives no sun. The courtyard is divided into two by rectangular trellis which runs across the garden, silhouetting it. Beyond this is an open space containing a timber pergola for shade. The flooring is built of timber decking, taking the opportunity to alter levels slightly. From the house the decking steps down and from the end of the passage it then steps up, and at the "entrance" to the second area is another slight change of level. All the steps are 4 inches (10cm) high, making the main courtyard 8 inches (20cm) above the passage. Variations in levels and changing the direction of the decking add interest to the design. A pergola is built over a permanent seat around which fragrant, sun-loving plants and climbers grow. The climber-covered trellis has an opening about 4 feet (1.2 meters) wide cut into it, partially to reveal the further garden.

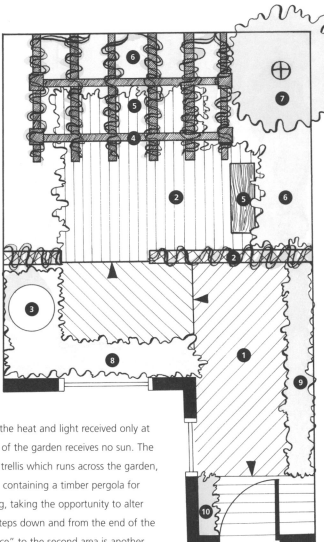

1. Decking, built over a concrete or graveled base, is laid in different patterns, but using timber all the same width (4 inches/10cm).

2. Seen from the house the garden is half-hidden behind trellis and invites further exploration.

3. On turning left from the passage, the view is of a large ceramic urn that needs no plant.

4. The timber pergola is a solidly constructed frame made on site that can support a heavy climber.

5. There are two sitting areas, one in the shade of the pergola, the other open, to be used in the evening with the benefit of the setting sun.

6. Around the seats are fragrant and aromatic plants. A myrtle planted against the wall grows with pinks, lavenders, oregano, thyme, and scented nicotiana and lilies.

7. The very small tree in one corner could be the fastigiate Prunus "Amanogowa" or a tree with a canopy, like Sorbus hupehensis.

8. Around the north-facing window grows Parthenocissus tricuspidata, its trails framing the view.

9. Ferns grow alongside the passage boundary, planted with spring bulbs like Anemone blanda.

10. A small-leaved ivy grows up the house wall in the shade.

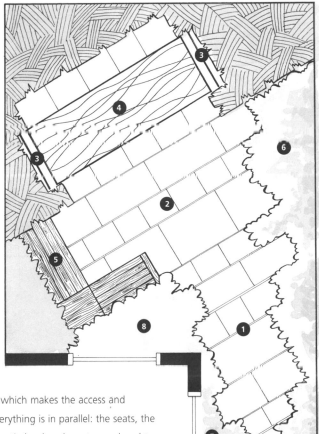

east-facing garden

This site has been planned on the diagonal, which makes the access and apparent width of the space seem larger. Everything is in parallel: the seats, the water, the paving, and the planting beds. The timber bench seats are placed to make the most of the sun and there is enough room for temporary seating as well. The most dramatic feature of the garden is that the planting bed surrounding the water is filled with a solid mass of evergreen box (*Buxus sempervirens*). This will need clipping twice a year to a height of approximately 5 feet (1.5 meters); a paved strip at the far side of the pool facilitates clipping. The rectangular stretch of water has mirrors set into the box at either end, so that the narrow tank becomes a virtual canal; this is visible from the house as well as the sitting area.

1. Planning the garden on the diagonal, at 30° to the house, increases the apparent space.
2. Cream limestone paving slabs are used in three widths of 1 foot (30cm), 1 foot 6 inches (45cm), and 2 feet (60cm). The light color increases the sense of spaciousness. They are mortared along the diagonal and otherwise butt jointed.
3. Two mirrors are set into the box at either end of the water. They are sealed around the back and edges with plastic, and backed with pressure-treated wood.
4. The water is clear, but dwarf water lilies or irises, which would reflect well, could be added.
5. Timber or metal bench seats are built-in to fit the space.
6. The plants opposite the bench seat, in the north-facing border, include tall, eye-catching subjects, such as a variegated yucca, as well as herbaceous perennials.
7. The "passage" from the house is planted on the south-facing side with sun-loving climbers, such as *Clematis viticella* and *C. cirrhosa* var. *balearica*. Carpet plants include herbs and creeping thymes.
8. Low plants grow below a window. Behind the bench seat *Sorbus vilmorinii* gives dappled light.

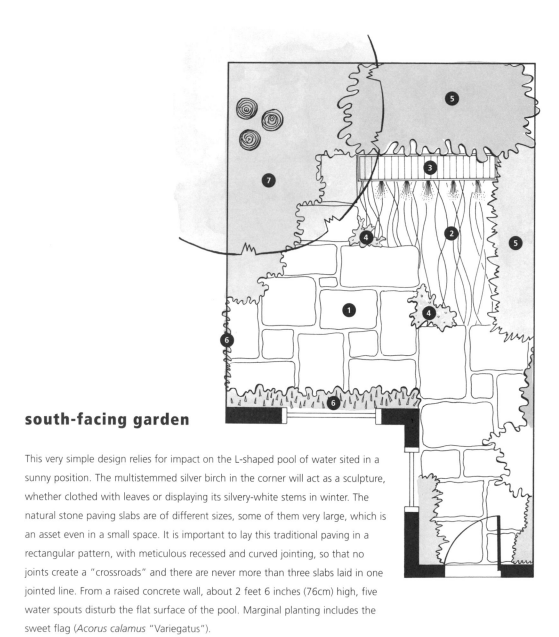

south-facing garden

This very simple design relies for impact on the L-shaped pool of water sited in a sunny position. The multistemmed silver birch in the corner will act as a sculpture, whether clothed with leaves or displaying its silvery-white stems in winter. The natural stone paving slabs are of different sizes, some of them very large, which is an asset even in a small space. It is important to lay this traditional paving in a rectangular pattern, with meticulous recessed and curved jointing, so that no joints create a "crossroads" and there are never more than three slabs laid in one jointed line. From a raised concrete wall, about 2 feet 6 inches (76cm) high, five water spouts disturb the flat surface of the pool. Marginal planting includes the sweet flag (*Acorus calamus* "Variegatus").

1 *Sandstone paving slabs pave a surface that complements the pool; they overhang it by 2 inches (5cm). An area large enough for seats has been left open.*

2 *The pool is about 2 feet (60cm) deep, sufficient to contain some fish. There will be enough sunlight to establish an ecological balance.*

3 *The 2 foot 6 inch (76cm) concrete wall behind the pool is faced with tiles; it conceals the pipes and pump. Water arches from the small pipes which pierce the wall.*

4 *Aquatic plants like* Myosotis scorpioides *will grow in 3 inches (7cm) of water on marginal shelves, deep enough for planting baskets. The pretty* Hottonia palustris *helps keep water clear. Variegated pygmy bamboo grows along the water's edge.*

5 *The mostly evergreen planting at the back includes* Aucuba japonica *"Rozannie" and a variegated fatsia in the corner, with small hostas and* Astilbe simplicifolia *"Sprite."*

6 *The window is fringed with lavender; a jasmine planted in the bed climbs the boundary wall.*

7 *Beneath the specimen multi-stemmed silver birch in the far corner grow epimediums, schizostylis, and omphalodes.*

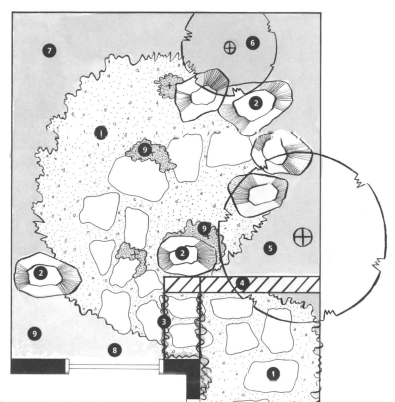

west-facing garden

This sunny garden has been designed on informal principles based on a circular theme, with an arched, climber-covered entrance leading from the passage to the house. The main sun-filled area, with its grouping of informal, flat-topped rocks, is visible through a vertically louvered wooden screen from the French doors of the house. The hard materials are gravel, randomly shaped flat paving slabs, stones, and a few large rocks. The main planting consists of two small trees, one an acer and the other with a wider canopy to shade the stone seats from midday sun. The other major plants around the perimeter include sun-loving species of bamboo, cotton lavender, *Euphorbia characias,* and *Cistus* "Silver Pink." With these are herbaceous plants like *Sisyrinchium idahoense* var. *bellum, Alchemilla mollis,* feverfew, foxgloves, violas, the smaller ornamental grasses, and annuals such as *Eschscholzia californica.*

1 The main circular area is surfaced with gravel; flat, rough-surfaced sandstone paving slabs create an informal path.

2 A group of large, flattened sandstone rocks provides seating; while two other "seats" are sited elsewhere.

3 A double timber arch carries a climbing rose (Rosa "New Dawn") overhead; it will be seen from the window, but not take the light.

4 A vertically louvered timber screen, covered by the early-flowering Clematis macropetala, provides a fragmented view from the door.

5 A standard Pyrus salicifolia planted behind the screen is visible from the house and provides shade over the "seats."

6 A low weeping Acer palmatum var. dissectum is planted behind the rock group.

7 The far corner is filled with a group of evergreen bamboos. Below the window is Chaenomeles x superba "Pink Lady," while Parthenocissus henryana is planted in the corner to cover the house wall and garden boundary.

8 Carpeting plants include green-leaved cultivars of Thymus serpyllum and gray-leaved T. pseudolanuginosus.

long narrow gardens

Many gardens are long and narrow, almost a passage, creating a strip of land whose dimensions can be discouraging at first. But if you have a clear idea of how you wish to use the garden, there is a choice of interesting approaches. The designs shown here are people-oriented, with plants secondary although still important for endowing the space with beauty.

three gardens in one

This scheme uses all the garden's length to create small "rooms." The division of space is made by two trellis screens which run across the garden, making three areas, each with a different character. The first rectangular space has a small, still pool. The paving is a simple geometric grid made up of units in two sizes to "break up" the floor pattern. Passing through an arch, the visitor enters the second garden, a sitting area, secluded by being intimately enclosed by trellis. Almost all the plants are climbers and the paving is made from the small floor tiles of the first garden. Two built-in seats face one another and a collapsible table folds down against the side wall for occasional use. The third room has a very informal atmosphere, its floor being covered with chopped bark and self-seeding plants. A mass of containers allows plant lovers to grow what they will.

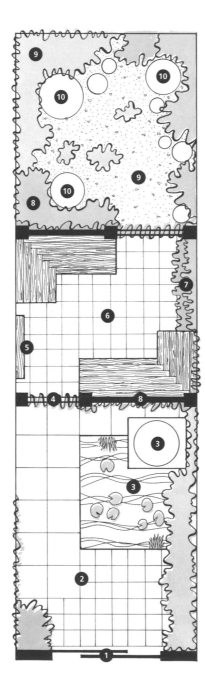

1 From the sliding doors the view is of a still, reflective pool in a tranquil, rectangular space.

2 Concrete aggregate square slabs and smaller units made by tiles pave the ground. The slabs slightly overhang the water's edge.

3 Dwarf water lilies float on the water's surface. In one corner a wide concrete bowl mounted on an 8-inch (20cm) plinth has a small evergreen shrub growing in it.

4 An arch gives access to the second garden room.

5 The fold-up table is positioned between the timber corner seats facing each other; it is used for occasional entertaining.

6 The small-unit paving is intimate in scale and appropriate for the sitting area.

7 A narrow planting bed allows for a run of Hemerocallis "Corky."

8 Climbers, including Clematis montana, grow on the trellis and over the arches; they are planted in beds in the outer gardens.

9 In the informal garden, bark chips allow plants to grow through. Good, free-draining soil conditions are important.

10 Containers may be used to grow collector's plants, or simply bulbs, or bedding.

borrowing scenery

There are two examples here of "borrowing" scenery: one is a distant church spire in view from the end of the garden and the other is the two neighboring trees next door. This garden uses both, with the idea of making the plot appear much larger than it is. From the house, the church steeple is "framed" by two box cubes about 2 feet (60cm) high and, along the bottom of the "picture," by a run of box which is 1 foot 6 inches (45cm) high. For this reason the steps are turned through 90° to step down onto the grass. To the east of the site, the two birches in the neighboring plot have been matched by planting a third well-grown specimen in this garden. The boundary between the gardens is obscured by ivy, strengthening the link. The paved terrace outside the house is enclosed by trellis on the boundary walls. The rest of the garden is informally grassed and planted with bulbs and summer-flowering "wild" plants.

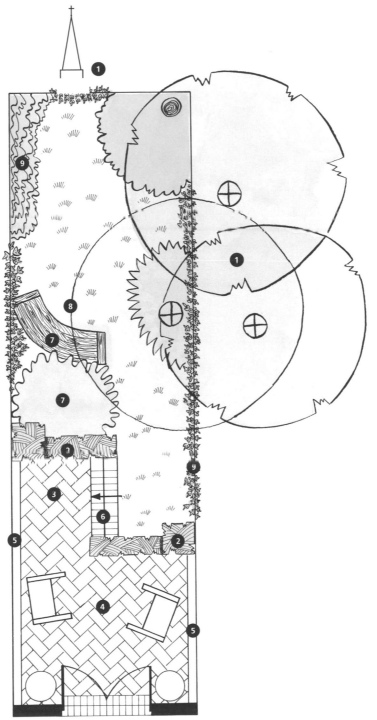

1. The two views are incorporated within the garden.

2. Formal clipped box marks the perimeter of the upper terrace, separating the paved sitting area from the "wild" garden, as well as framing the view from the house.

3. The terrace has space for sitting and containers, but access to the rest of the garden is made more interesting by progressing down into it from the side.

4. The upper garden is paved with brick-on-edge laid in a decorative herringbone pattern.

5. Unadorned trellis encloses the upper garden but wall plants cover the walls of the informal garden.

6. The lower garden is reached down two brick steps, 4 inches (10cm) deep.

7. A purpose-built, curved, double bench seat is backed by a low evergreen shrub.

8. The views from the seat look outward, as there is much to see and use beyond the boundaries.

9. Controlled pyracantha, dogwood, and guelder rose, with small- and large-leaved ivies, evergreen honeysuckles, and clematis conceal the lower boundaries.

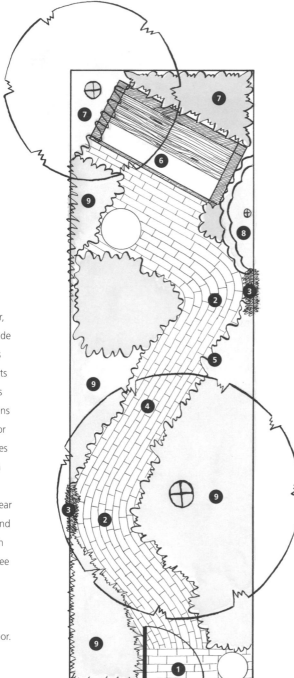

an illusion of width

The basis of this design is a wide path which curves from one side to the other, making maximum use of the space. Made from coursed brick-on-edge, the path is 3 feet (1 meter) wide, allowing for plants to spill and spread over its edges. This is the most plantable of the narrow gardens because there is only one small space for sitting in. At two points the path touches the boundaries without the benefit of a planting border, but a climbing ivy will cover this part of the wall or fence all year so that it "vanishes" among greenery and the garden's limits are masked. The path curves around a small, light-canopied tree and finally around a substantial low evergeen shrub before reaching the far end, where there is a paved area, large enough for one seat, and a covered arbor.

1 A paved stepping area runs across the site, with a large container to one side.

2 The path swings in generous curves around a tree (Robinia pseudoacacia "Frisia"), then Viburnum davidii, *leading eventually to a small paved area in front of the arbor.*

3 Ivies like Hedera colchica *"Dentata Variegata"* and H. canariensis *conceal the boundaries all year.*

4 *Lines of brick-on-edge create the sinuous curves of the path.*

5 *Plants flop over the edges of the path along its length, softening the whole effect.*

6 *The metal-framed arbor has a double seat inside.*

7 *Planting behind the arbor is a mass of evergreen* Garrya elliptica *"James Roof;" to the left is the fastigiate* Malus *"Brandywine."*

8 *To the right of the arbor a clipped pyracantha conceals the wall and links in with the ivy.*

9 *The width of the borders here provides planting opportunities for climbers and flat-trained wall shrubs, such as pyracantha and escallonia. It allows room for herbaceous plants like geraniums,* Phlox subulata, *and* Anthemis punctata *subsp.* cupaniana.

a bold rural strip

This is a bold garden which aims to create a particular style, ignoring the urban surroundings. The ground is coarsely graveled and the stepping paving slabs and flat railroad ties are randomly placed among raised seats. All the features are large, from the timber to loose cobbles and big rocks. The plants to go with them must be bold too, which means using bamboos, tall grasses and ferns, bold ground covers, and large-leaved wall climbers. The color is emphatically green; no variegated plants are chosen. Plants seed themselves among the gravel, being selectively weeded out as control becomes necessary.

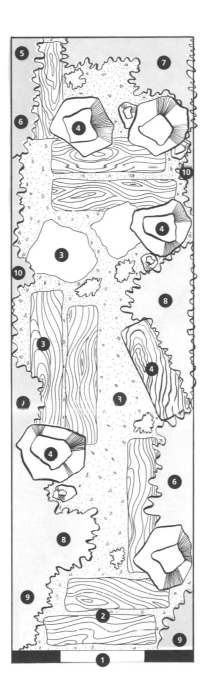

1. *The entire length of the garden is visible from the house.*

2. *The scale of the features make this an unusual outdoor space for a city garden.*

3. *The gravel floor covering is interspersed with timber and random stone slabs.*

4. *Large rocks are placed for sitting on, together with a raised block of recycled railroad ties used for the same purpose.*

5. *If a tree is required for screening,* Sorbus aucuparia *or* S. cashmiriana *would fill the bill.*

6. *Shrubs include cultivars of* Rosa rugosa *and a purple-leaved elder.*

7. *Stands of bamboo are contained below ground:* Arundo, Fargesia, *and* Sasa veitchii *fit in superbly.*

8. *Grassy-leaved plants like the large* miscanthus *and other ornamental grasses are planted with flag irises, lilyturf, sisyrinchiums, kniphofias, and schizostylis, all of which suit the rural style.*

9. *Shade planting includes many types of fern, the larger hellebores, and brunnera.*

10. *Along the sides the huge-leaved climbers,* Vitis coignetiae *and* Actinidia deliciosa, *are compatible with the other plants.*

shaping

Most shrubs and climbers benefit from some pruning, but in small gardens this becomes an essential form of control, both to restrain their growth or keep them flat against a wall, and to make their use more versatile.

trained 2-dimensional shapes

Fruits, figs, and vines were cultivated on the walls of the earliest known gardens, but it was the Romans who recognized that, by cutting fruit trees back severely, they could increase the crop. Initially, therefore, climbers and wall shrubs were pruned to improve yield, but ornamental designs soon developed which, in monastic gardens for example, were taken to

sophisticated levels. It was found that the natural growth habit of certain shrubs created different shapes, and various patterns evolved for growing these shrubs flat against a wall. Today, this ornamental manipulation of plants can serve as a focus in a restricted site. The patterns illustrated on these pages are especially suitable for small courtyards where, trained almost flat against the boundaries, the plants take up little depth in the garden space.

The principle behind fan training **(1)** is to tie in branches so they radiate from the base of a central trunk to form a more or less symmetrical pattern. Branches can be trained onto canes, timber slats, or stretched wires (for tying in, see page 170). Fan training is ideal for fruit trees, such as figs, peaches, apricots, cherries, plums, apples, and pears, all of which produce better fruit when trained against a warm wall. Ornamental shrubs suited to being restrained in this way are those whose natural habit is not to protrude forward too much. They include: *Chaenomeles japonica*, *Abeliophyllum distichum*, *Bupleurum fruticosum*, *Euonymus fortunei*, and the maidenhair tree (*Ginkgo biloba*). Some shrub and species roses also look magnificent as flattened fans.

1 *A fan-trained peach is created by shortening the main stem to 1 foot 4 inches (40cm) and training two main laterals to produce the "ribs." A new branch is pulled toward the center each year.*

2 *Espaliers are created by continually shortening the leader to encourage lateral growth. Each year the top lateral is trained horizontally, then pruned.*

3 *Dwarf espalier apples on dwarfing rootstock can be grown freestanding, trained on a sturdy low fence. They may be single or double tier.*

Creating espaliers **(2)** involves training shrubs and trees in horizontal parallel lines to create tiered patterns. This aids the fruiting of trees grafted on dwarf rootstock. Ideally suited to walls where they are trained against wires and posts, or trellis, if they are grown on a freestanding frame, they can also be useful as slim screens to divide up space. Pears and apples are the traditional fruiting trees grown in this way, as well as grapevines (*Vitis* species) and Chinese gooseberry (*Actinidia deliciosa*). Ornamental shrubs suited to this form of management include pyracantha, camellia, escallonia, chaenomeles, winter jasmine, and, in warmer areas, poinsettia and lantana. Climbers like honeysuckles and the warm-climate bougainvillea, and *Campsis* x *tagliabuana* also respond well to such training.

Dwarf espaliers **(3)** are grown on a strong, freestanding frame and may be useful in confined spaces to provide a low edging to paths. This is most useful for apples and pears grown on a dwarfing rootstock. Only 1 foot 6 inches (45cm) tall, they are known as "stepovers" when they are grown in this way.

Many fruit trees are trained on a single shoot or cordon **(4)**, with all side-shoots greatly reduced to encourage flowering and fruiting. Cordons are grown as uprights or at an oblique angle (usually 35–45 degrees); in either case they are trained on taut wires, sturdily supported canes, or slats of wood against a wall. Pears and apples are often grown as cordons; gooseberries and currants will do well, too. For purely decorative purposes, ivy

can also be trained in this way, clipped tightly to the supports; if plants are trained in opposite directions, an open diamond lattice pattern is created.

A once-popular but now less often practiced style of training is known as candelabrum **(5)**. The laterals are encouraged to grow sideways and the branched growth trained upward. Very stylish, it can be used for pears, apples, chaenomeles, pyracantha, evergreen ceanothus, *Cotoneaster dammeri*, and *Magnolia grandiflora*. Another rarely seen but very decorative means of training is called l'arcure **(6)**. Originating in France and Belgium, this method is based on creating arcs. Apples and pears were traditionally used, but pyracantha and ivy could be treated the same way.

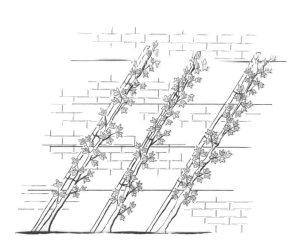

4 *The main stem of a cordon carries fruiting spurs which are cut back in summer. Cut a too-tall leader in late spring to keep 1 inch (2.5cm) of current year's growth.*

5 *A candelabrum is like vertical cordons all grown from a single stem. Train to wires and summer-prune to encourage flower buds and check growth.*

6 *L'arcure is trained obliquely from the start. Each year a branch is tied down to form an arc. A shoot growing from the top of the curve forms an opposing new arc.*

trained 3-dimensional shapes

The art of topiary, a word of Latin origin, involves pruning evergreen shrubs tightly to create a dense, solid shape. This horticultural art form has been practiced for over two thousand years, yet is still very much in fashion today. Symmetrically placed abstract forms often furnish formal gardens, contributing to their geometry, while animals, familiar or fabulous, fulfill a fantasy role in singular gardens of imaginative design. Topiary will ornament the small garden all year round, being enjoyed from the windows of the house even in the coldest months. From geometric crenellations to serpentine hedges, snapping dragons, and dancing demons, the scope for creating green, living sculpture is unlimited.

Solid geometric shapes like cones, three- and four-sided pyramids **(2)**, spheres and cubes **(3)**, as well as tapering spirals **(4)** can all readily be created in topiary. Working more sympathetically with the habit of the plant can produce simple effects, like cylindrical "cake stand" tiers **(1)**. The plants that best lend themselves to really tight shaping are traditional dark evergreens, including yew, box, and many hollies, all of which are foliaged to ground level and regenerate easily along the trunk.

Other shrubs are equally suitable for some kind of shaping. Common privet (*Ligustrum ovalifolium*) is adaptable to most fantasy shapes, and the denser-leaved Japanese privet (*L. japonicum*) can be clipped to a very sharp profile. The boxleaf honeysuckle (*Lonicera nitida*) and small-leaved evergreen azaleas also respond to being pruned into geometric shapes. However, these shrubs have a tendency to become lopsided or otherwise less than perfect over a period of years if they are subject to heavy snowfall or exposure to strong winds. The naturally erect bay tree (*Laurus nobilis*) lends itself to the creation of large topiary shapes or mophead standards on its central stem. And you can use the flowing lines of spreading savin junipers (*Juniperus sabina*) or Japanese white pine (*Pinus parviflora*) to make "cloud" topiary, in which cumulus formations sweep spectacularly downward from bare woody stems.

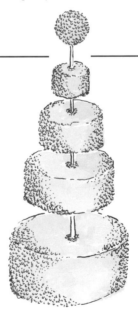

1   *Remove all unnecessary branches to create the densely tiered form of a wedding cake, and trim each year.*

2   *Squat pyramids work well with dwarf hedges, while tall narrow ones are eye-catching.*

3   *The combination of cube and sphere suggests a plant grown in a container. Two different-colored yews could be used.*

4   *Spirals add a French feel to a garden. Use a plumb line to keep them vertical.*

Many topiary shapes can be bought ready-trained and you can then continue the training yourself. Depending on the plant's rate of growth (dwarf box grows at half the rate of yew, for example), topiary will need clipping one to three times a year, using sharp hedge shears. Make sure a geometric shape stays symmetrical; if you do not trust yourself to do this by eye, hang a plumb line a little distance away to check the verticality.

In a small space, dividing the space or isolating a bed is neatly achieved by planting low hedging; Dwarf box (*Buxus sempervirens* "Suffruticosa") and little-leaf box (*B. microphylla*) are both ideal. Plant 6 inches (15cm) apart, clip in spring and in late summer. A single row makes a neat outline, a double row has greater effect.

False topiary

An artificial form of topiary can be preformed on a specially shaped wire frame over which tightly clipped small-leaved ivies (*Hedera helix* cultivars such as *H. helix* "Sagittifolia" or the variegated *H. helix* "Glacier") are trained. Commercially available frames are made out of galvanized or enameled wire, but it is possible to fashion your own shape out of chicken wire over a simple framework of galvanized wire. You could ask a blacksmith to make one for you. There are small topiary frames too, which sit on a container.

Ivies have flexible stems which can be twined and twisted around the frame. They will need encouraging to attach themselves to the frame initially: use small wire circlets to train them accurately along the wires until the shape is fully formed, after which they require trimming only once or twice a year. Pinching back the bare stems encourages the plant to respond by forming dense growth. Because these "topiary" sculptures are hollow, slim elements—like the tail of a bird—can be stretched elegantly out into space, which would not be possible with the more densely foliaged box or yew. But solid effects like chessmen **(7)** and peacocks are also convincing; you need several plants to fill a large frame.

5 *A globe suggests worldly matters, adding weight to a small garden. Use wire rings to secure the ivy strands to all parts of the circular frame.*

6 *Obelisks suit the seriously formal garden as they are static and have great presence. Plant an ivy at the base of each vertical on the frame.*

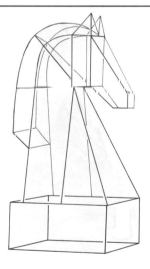

7 *Chess pieces may be simple or elaborate. Is this a knight from a game of chess or could it be Pegasus? Either way it brings a touch of wit to the garden.*

supports and fixings

Plants may be grown against walls and fences to create a two-dimensional cover or they may be encouraged to grow into a freestanding feature of the small garden. In either case, they will need to be given support and securely fixed to it; the materials generally used for this purpose are timber, bamboo canes, metal, or taut wire.

upright supports

Traditional obelisks and square-sided columns are ideal for small spaces because they allow plants to grow upward and not occupy too much floor space. Most freestanding types are made from metal or timber and many can be simply pushed into the soil **(1b)**, needing no other support provided the chosen plants are neither too tall nor top-heavy. They come in a range of heights to suit different plants. Some wooden obelisks are made to sit on top of a square-sided container, such as a Versailles tub **(1a)**. Wire-framed obelisks **(2)** are generally slimmer and more delicate in appearance and make ideal supports for climbers such as clematis.

Hollow columns built from timber or plywood **(3)** can be used as freestanding features in the garden or they may become the upright piers for an arch. If they have open diamond-trellis sides, this allows a rose or clematis to be planted inside.

The traditional "wigwam" support for string beans may take the form of a tripod or be a more continuous line **(4)**; these supports can be cheaply made at home from stripped branches or bamboo canes, lashed together with twine or raffia. They look effective for a season supporting lightweight annual or tender climbers, such as sweet peas, asarina, or *Cobaea scandens*. A line of simple upright supports, such as these twisted metal rods **(5)**, can act as a freestanding space divider when clad with plants.

Traditional trellis can also stand alone or be fixed to a wall. Purpose-made panels come in different patterns **(6b–e)**, like diamond, square, or rectangular. Always choose sturdy trellis, rather than cheap, panels.

Elaborate tops and finials are optional, but bear in mind that these will become a major

a   b

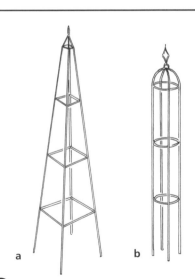

a   b

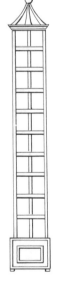

1 Freestanding timber obelisks add height and carry a climber. Frames may be built to fit a planter, the shrub inside trained to shape.

2 Metal obelisks are light and easily moved around the garden. They can support delicate perennial or annual climbers.

3 A hollow pillar built in square section makes a good upright for an arch.

4 Bamboo canes lashed together with a bracing crosspiece will support twining annual climbers.

decorative feature of the garden and may dominate the plants. A particular combination of trellis panels can be used against a wall to create a perspective illusion **(6a)**. If you want plants to be the main attraction, keep to a simple, flat-topped design of trellis and stain it a dark or neutral color. Trellis panels also make slim space dividers for the small garden

fixings

The fitting and fixings of garden features are especially important in very small spaces where any untidy details will be immediately visible. The effects of weather eventually corrode or rot fixings, so choose only the best quality: nonrusting screws, twine made for outdoor use, and plastic-coated wire.

If attaching trellis to a wall, make sure it is not tight against the wall's surface because all climbers need air circulation, and twiners, as well as those climbers which adhere by means of tendrils, need space between the timber slats and the wall. Provided there is a gap, plants like clematis, which thicken to make woody stems, can be threaded in and out of the battens while still soft and green. To maintain this separation, use either small pieces of timber of equal thickness as fixed wedges or insert cotton bobbins between wall and trellis **(7c)**.

Vine eyes **(7a, 7b)** are made specifically for the purpose of holding wires firmly about 4 inches (10cm) from the wall surface; masonry nails will last no longer than for one or two seasons. Drill and plug holes in the mortar

before screwing in the vine eyes. The parallel wires stretched between them are usually fixed about 1 foot 6 inches (45cm) apart. They must be very taut: there is no worse sight than a heavy climber on sagging wires. Plastic-coated netting can be attached in the same way and is suitable for climbers, like evergreen *Clematis cirrhosa* var. *balearica*, which will completely cover it. Supporting wires which run vertically up the piers of an arch are attached inside the arch **(7e)**; wire rings allow climbers leeway to follow their natural habit of growth.

There are some meticulous ways of tying the canes of a bamboo fence which will contribute to the beauty of a small space **(7d)**. If you wish to try these traditional Japanese methods, look at alternatives in a specialist book.

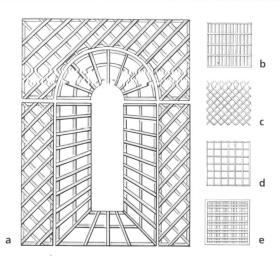

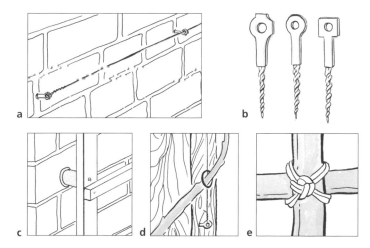

5 *Decorative, lightweight metal spirals are easily inserted into the soil.*

6 *Laid flat against a wall, these perspective trellis panels give a surprisingly effective illusion of depth. Many different patterns can be deployed for other trellis.*

7 *Fixing plants to their supports can take several forms: vine eyes and taut wires or trellis panels hold plants clear of a wall, wire clips and stretched wire up a post. Investigate Japanese knots to tie bamboo canes together.*

arbors, arches, and canopies

Any overhead cover, however light, makes a small space feel secure and protected, and provides an excellent opportunity to grow plants vertically.

arbors

The inclusion of a covered seat, known as an arbor, is particularly appealing in hot, exposed gardens or rooftop courtyards where shade is always welcome. It is possible to buy a small, ready-made wooden arbor as a complete unit **(1)**, attractive in its own right. Or you could make an enclosed sitting space on site, constructing it against the backing of a wall **(2)** using timber for the upright posts and overhead rafters.

arches

There is a role in every garden, even in tiny spaces, for an arch, with its suggestion that you are entering a new and special space. The slimmest, ready-made arches are fashioned from rods of solid steel or steel tubing and they are strong enough to carry climbers, yet easy to put into the soil. The style of the top may be simply rounded or pointed, or may take the form of a Tudor or Gothic arch **(3)**.

Heavier alternatives, like timber-framed arches **(4)**, must have more secure foundations. The upright posts need to be set firmly in concrete or held in special metal fittings whose long pointed ends are knocked into the ground to a good depth. The arch itself may be rustic

in appearance if made from rounded larch poles, or may be simply constructed from straight, rough-cut overhead rafters supported on 4 x 4 inch (10 x 10cm) solid timber uprights **(4a)**. The rafter endings may vary in detail **(4b–e)**, being shaped to suit your preference.

The timber posts supporting the arch must be at least 4 inches (10cm) in square section. A weak-looking support makes an arch appear very flimsy. For the same reason, the cross beams, which run the length of the arch, should be 6–8 inches (15–20cm) deep. The rafters, which run across it, may be only 1½–2inches (3–5cm) wide, but they can be up to 8 inches (20cm) deep. Once they are covered with plants, they will look strong rather than overbearing. The timber uprights could be

a   b

1   *This covered seat is a traditional design which can be bought as a ready-made unit or constructed from timber at home.*

2   *This "pergola arbor" is built using solid timber posts and overhead beams. Although open to the sky, if carrying heavy climbers like wisteria, it will give shade.*

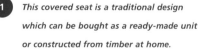

3   *Timber posts may be sawn with a rough surface or planed and grooved to give a more elegant finish.*

smoothly planed and grooved **(3)** if you want to create an elegant, less solid-looking feature. They may incorporate more or less elaborate finials if desired. If trellis is used on the top or the sides of the arch, this will produce an even more delicate-looking structure which casts attractive shadows on the floor. If you are constructing your own arch, always choose pressure-treated softwood or hardwood from a renewable source and, for preference, use brass screws which are countersunk.

canopies

In many gardens people need to be protected from strong sunlight, especially at midday. The overhead screening of small spaces is most simply achieved by an open, large-scale, timber trellis, built using pressure-treated timbers. Alternatively, tightly stretched yachting wire, which is nonrusting and very strong, can be fixed in parallel lines overhead, perhaps running between the house wall and a trellis panel to give shade over an eating area. Both the wires and the timber rafters of a canopy should be sturdy enough to carry large-leaved climbers, such as *Actinidia chinensis*, a fruiting grapevine, or even the huge-leaved *Vitis coignetiae*.

Another shade-giving option is to attach a length of strong, unbleached canvas securely between four upright posts **(6)**. The effect of such stretched canvas sheeting is to create parabolic curves against the sky, while its neutral cream color provides cool, but light, shade. The posts need to be lower at one side than the other, to allow rain to run off easily, preferably into a planting bed of some kind. Since the canvas itself is heavy, the support posts must be rigidly vertical. Stretch the canvas very tightly between them, avoiding a droop in the middle at all costs, as this would collect water and greatly increase the weight overhead.

Wide parasols of unbleached cotton on timber frames can also be left outdoors for the summer season; they may be secured on a heavy, freestanding base or held within the center of a table.

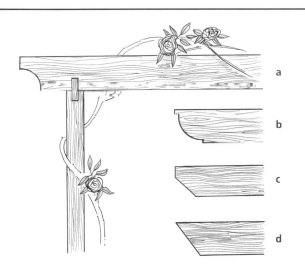

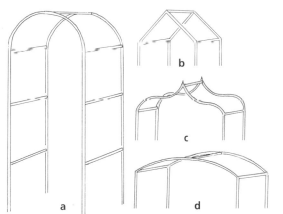

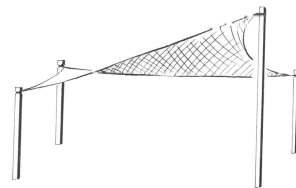

4 *Creamy limestone suits this elegant sunny courtyard where warm sunlight is reflected from the walls.*

5 *Purpose-made metal arches can be bought in different forms., their width influencing the arch's style. Place the "legs" of an arch in a bed where climbers grow.*

6 *A canvas awning is tied at its four corners to sturdy timber or steel posts and stretched tightly between them. Ensure that it does not sag in the middle.*

planting effects

Plants are the materials used by the designer/gardener who will exploit their magnificent variety of form, habit, and texture to create effects. A plant's distinctive habit of growth can be harnessed to bring style to the small garden.

1 Hedera hibernica *"Deltoidea" with Liriope muscari.*

2 Chaenomeles *x* superba *"Nicoline" beside* Ceanothus *"Burkwoodii" and* Clematis *"Ernest Markham," with* Sedum *"Herbstfreude" at its foot.*

3 Myrtus communis *subsp.* tarentina *and* Pittosporum tenuifolium *"Irene Paterson" with* Clematis alpina *"White Moth" and* Santolina rosmarinifolia *"Primrose Gem."*

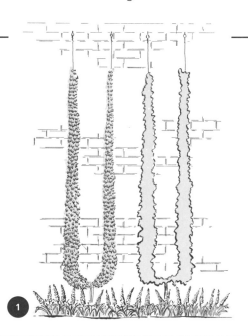

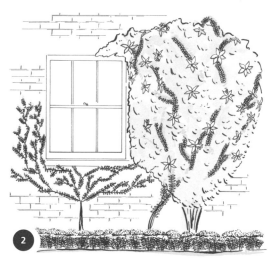

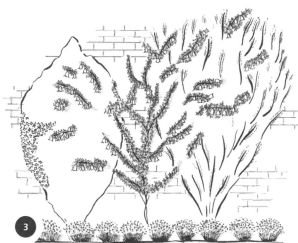

up

Those plants which reach upward to become controllable climbers and those which are naturally erect are both invaluable in small gardens, where horizontal space is at a premium. The associations suggested in the planting groups on these pages are based on choosing wall shrubs, which provide a climbing frame for more delicate climbers, or on combining upright-growing plants which flower at different times of year. I make no apology for

including many clematis which are ideal plants for small spaces and it is nearly always possible to fit in another one. As long as they are well fed and watered throughout the summer, they will reward you with plenty of colorful blooms. Their flowers may be huge plates, as large as the striped "Nelly Moser" whose flowers are over 7 inches (18cm) diameter, very small like those of *C. viticella* "Etoile Rose," nodding and bell-shaped as in the delicate *C. texensis* cultivars, or cluster-flowered like the lovely white species, *C. flammula*.

a formal group (1)

This small-leaved ivy can be trained on wires to grow in formal verticals, creating a year-round pattern on a wall. It should be clipped tightly to ensure that it retains its geometric form. Below it, in a narrow bed, a mass of the grassy evergreen lilyturf (*Liriope muscari*) will provide a duplication of the verticals with purple-blue flowers in late summer. As these plants are drought-resistant, they will do well at the foot of a brick wall.

a seasonal group (2)

This group will provide color from early in the year until the fall. The framework of the deciduous ornamental quince is valued for its elegantly branching structurer. Large red flowers appear in early spring, and the shrub can be trained flat against the wall by removing all forward-growing branches. Its height and spread are about 7 feet (2 meters). The ceanothus is a rich blue, hardy form which flowers in

fragrant white flowers appear through the summer. It is wider than its height of about 8 feet (2. 4 meters). Beside it the cultivar of pittosporum is evergreen but marbled with jade-green coloring; it will reach about 5 feet (1.5 meters).

roses and clematis (4)

This hybrid musk rose is a vigorous plant reaching 5 feet (1.5 meters); its semi-double fragrant flowers are

4   Rosa *"Buff Beauty" and* Clematis *x* durandii *with* Heuchera micrantha *var.* diversifolia *"Palace Purple."*

5   Ficus carica *"Brown Turkey" and* Clematis *"Abundance."*

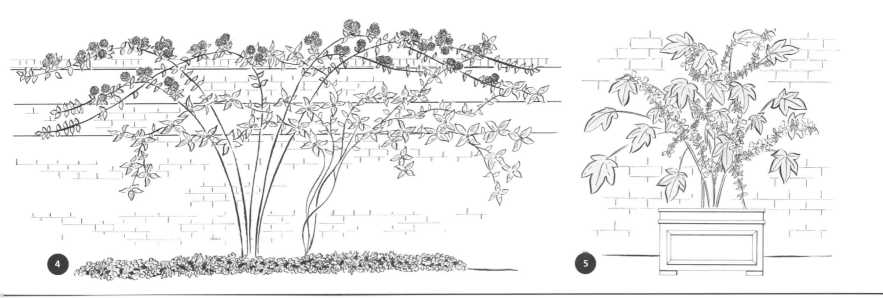

summer and on into fall; prune after flowering. The clematis flowers all summer, its blooms a rich pink which does not fade; cut back all last season's growth in early spring. This easy-to-grow group thrives in fertile soil which does not dry out, with some shade for the roots of the clematis, provided here by the sedum, whose flowers last until fall.

a fragrant white and green group (3)

The myrtle (*Myrtus communis*), an evergreen shrub from the Mediterranean, needs a warm, sheltered site where its

carried in trusses all summer. They are apricot-yellow fading to buff, so the association with the deep violet-blue sepals of the chosen clematis is pleasing through until fall. The clematis blooms are more sparsely formed, with four to six oval sepals, so each flower flatters the other. The clematis should be cut back to the ground in early spring. Both climbers do well in full sun to light shade, but they need rich soil which does not dry out. The clematis roots are kept cool behind the bronze-leaved heuchera.

container planting (5)

Restraining the roots of the fig in a large pot contains its vigor and helps with fruiting. Encouraged to grow in a fanned shape, it will make an eye-catching wall shrub in a protected sunny courtyard. Its large palmate leaves turn butter-yellow in fall. The late-season viticella clematis has small wine-red flowers in late summer; it does not have to be pruned unless it becomes too tangled, in which case it can be tidied in spring. Cover the container with a layer of gravel to cool the roots.

1 Wisteria floribunda *"Alba" with* Rosa
"Climbing Lady Hillingdon."

2 Buddleja alternifolia *with* Acer palmatum *var.*
dissectum *and* Hemerocallis *"Golden Chimes."*

down

Plants which flow downward have quite a different effect from dynamic, upward-growing shapes. They soften the look of a garden, sometimes conveniently clothing walls as they trail down, sometimes following contours as they hang down over raised planting troughs. Most attractive of all are the weeping forms which float downward, creating arcs which touch the ground far from their foundation. Responsive to wind,

they animate the garden with changing patterns of light. There is an important role for small trailing species in containers and hanging baskets, too.

suspended climbers (1)

The white-flowered wisteria ornaments an arch with its pendent racemes of flowers. Attached to a wall, it is trained over the cross beam, where its trailing flowers can be fully enjoyed from below. A strongly scented, apricot-yellow rose is planted on the other side of the

arch and trained to climb up the post and over the beam, where its famous recurrent nodding flowers can be viewed properly from beneath. Both do best in a warm, sunny situation.

weeping and arching plants (2)

Grown as a very small tree on a single stem, the cascading branches of this buddleja are wreathed with fragrant lilac flowers in summer; finely lanceolate, grayish leaves flutter from the branches. It stands behind a small formal pool with an accompanying mound-forming acer; if the leading shoot is trained upward, this maple will weep effectively, its leaves constantly swaying on all but the stillest days. A mass of the small day lily (*Hemerocallis*) merges with both plants. Such a planting group would do well in either sun or light shade.

hardy evergreen juniper and the spreading persicaria, with its pink candle flowers. This is a pleasing association for a sunny or lightly shaded position.

trailing plants for containers (4)

Fuchsias are ideal summer plants for containers. A standard would weep downward from the single stem

3 Cistus x dansereaui *"Decumbens"* with Juniperus horizontalis *"Prince of Wales"* and Persicaria affinis *"Donald Lowndes."*

4 *Trailing fuchsia and* Verbena *"Sissinghurst" with* Helichrysum petiolare, *trailing lobelia, and ivy.*

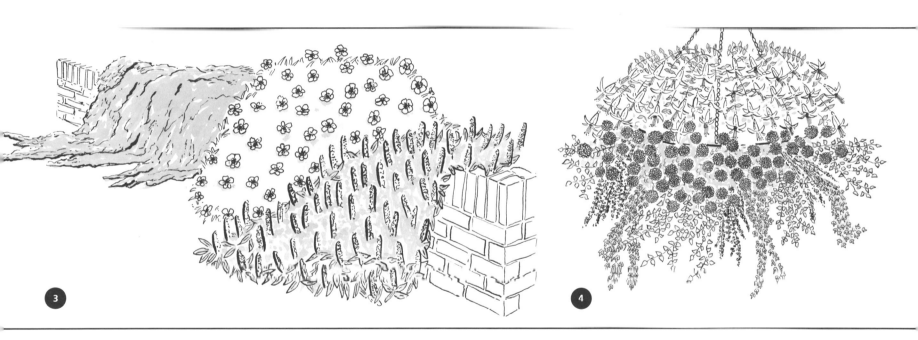

3

4

ground-hugging trailers (3)

If you have built some raised planters to make the most of a small site, they can be covered with a green blanket by using plants which follow the contours of the ground and continue over the "risers" of low walls. A rock rose (*Cistus*) will spread from the top bed to fall as a carpet over the edge of the retaining wall, its narrow evergreen leaves covered through summer with small white, crimson-centered flowers. The same effect can be achieved by planting with it a mat-like,

to make a fine formal arrangement in a traditional container. In this hanging basket a trailing fuchsia, with lax habit and pendulous flowers, is the centerpiece for a more informal combination. A purple/pink trailing verbena makes an attractive partner for the fuchsia, with gray-leaved helichrysum, ivy, and trailing lobelia spreading out to fill the basket below.

across

If an enclosed city garden is dominated by high-rise surroundings, one way of reducing the sense of oppression is to design and plant widthwise. Do not let the squareness of a site cramp your style: by stretching sideways, as opposed to upward, you will find that the courtyard appears more spacious. Horizontal forms are

Snowflake" with flattened, white, lacecap flowers carried in double rows along horizontal branches. The compact *Prunus laurocerasus* "Low 'n' Green" is a wide-spreading evergreen which will eventually grow to 6 feet (1.8 meters) diameter but is only 3 feet (1 meter) high; it will grow in semi-shade, where its glossy foliage and white "candle" flowers are welcome. In shade or full sun, the hardy, ground-covering evergreen shrub,

1. **Pyracantha coccinea *"Rutgers"* with Scabiosa columbaria *"Butterfly Blue"* behind a low hedge of Buxus sempervirens *"Suffruticosa."***

2. **Picea pungens *"Prostrata Glauca"* with Hydrangea macrophylla *"Geoffrey Chadbund"* and Cotoneaster congestus.**

3. **Juniperus horizontalis *"Bar Harbor"* with Phlox subulata *"Oakington Blue Eyes,"* Achillea x lewisii *"King Edward,"* and Sedum *"Herbstfreude."***

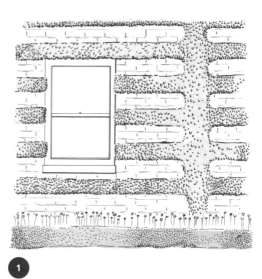

more relaxed and induce a feeling of tranquillity, just as the horizon or an expanse of calm sea soothes the spirit. In garden terms, there are planting patterns, some natural and some manipulated, which can achieve the same effect for you, making the garden feel comfortable and more spacious.

Some shrubs grow with a naturally tiered, spreading habit, like *Cornus controversa* "Variegata" which creates a light canopy or *Viburnum mariesii* "Summer

Lonicera pileata, layers itself naturally; as the horizontal bright green branches touch ground, they root. *Cotoneaster horizontalis* grows widely too, but with a more structured "fishbone" branching habit.

For ground level there are many carpeting plants, some of which provide ground cover, like *Cotoneaster microphyllus* var. *cochleatus* and *C. salicifolius* "Repens." Others can be trodden on, like the many forms of *Thymus serpyllum*, the felted *T. lanuginosus*,

and deep green *T. calspitosus*. Silvery gray *Raoulia australis*, aromatic *Chamomile* "Treneague," and pretty *Acaena* "Copper Carpet" are all fairly resistant to feet and grow in sun-filled yards among paving slabs.

plant murals (1)

Pyracantha can readily be trained in horizontal patterns and is here used to decorate a plain wall. Beneath it, in rich, well-worked soil, a mass of low-growing scabious, only 1 foot (30cm) tall, is covered with blue "pincushion" flowers all through summer. It grows behind a low hedge of dwarf box.

conifer associates (2)

The beautifully horizontal blue spruce, with its silver-blue, richly textured needle leaves and tiny, red flowers, looks wonderful spreading over red sandstone paving. It is good company, particularly in late summer, for the (Achillea) with flat-headed primrose-yellow flowers and feathery foliage will follow the contours and, later in the year, the sedum will lighten the color scheme with its jade-green foliage, and its flat heads of tiny, pink butterfly-seducing flowers will echo the horizontal line.

a woodland group for acid soil (4)

In moist, rich acid soils in a shady site, the low,

4 Cornus canadensis *with trilliums and* Gentiana asclepiadea.

5 Juniperus communis *"Depressa Aurea."*

compact hydrangea whose brick-red lacecap flowers appear as flattened corymbs; they darken as fall approaches. A mat of the tiny, ground-hugging cotoneaster will work its way around them.

a seasonal group (3)

In spring, this slow, rather than dwarf, dove-gray conifer with long whipcord-like branches will brighten up when the evergreen carpet of phlox is awash with bright blue flowers. For midsummer, a mass of the small yarrow spreading creeping dogwood (Cornus canadensis) will form attractive ground cover; its flattened, radiating ribbed leaves are covered in spring with four-petaled white bracts, which look beautiful with the deep pink trilliums. This shrub, native to North Anerica, needs constant checking to reduce its spreading ambitions. Later on, in late summer, the willow gentian (Gentiana asclepiadea) will arch widely, carrying spectacular deep blue, paired trumpet-flowers along the length of its stems.

horizontal container planting (5)

A wide, flattish dish planted with a specimen conifer is all that is needed for a stylish all-year-round look. Many conifers are wide spreading, particularly junipers, but they can stretch too far for a container, so check this when buying. The foliage of this juniper is bronzed in winter, but butter-yellow by the time summer comes. Another neat form, J. sabina "Tamariscifolia," is gray-blue and gradually develops concentric tiers of overlapping branches. It will need cutting back after about seven or eight years.

texture

Texture plays a large part in the effects that can be created with plants. Shape and form tend to dominate and color is a great draw, but textural differences are a joy in small gardens where they can be appreciated close to. Immaculate surfaces like those of hostas smooth the way for richer detail, as seen in astilbe

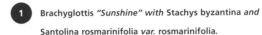
1 Brachyglottis *"Sunshine" with* Stachys byzantina *and* Santolina rosmarinifolia *var.* rosmarinifolia.

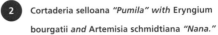
2 Cortaderia selloana *"Pumila" with* Eryngium bourgatii *and* Artemisia schmidtiana *"Nana."*

3 Dryopteris erythrosora *with* Brunnera macrophylla *"Variegata,"* Bergenia *"Baby Doll," and* Hakonechloa macra *"Aureola."*

1

2

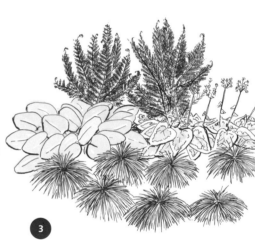
3

foliage, for example. Some textures are so fine that we can barely touch them, such as dandelion clocks, and others are almost entirely visual, like the tiny-leaved cotoneasters, thymes, or feathery ferns. While some leaves are actually tactile, others merely look textured.

Richly visual patterns can be created by associations of foliage. Detailed growth habits, such as the pinnate foliage of sorbaria or the heart-shaped epimediums, make their own statement in a group. Smooth, shiny

surfaces, like those of the like shiny aucubas, can be reflective in dark corners; spiky eryngiums add panache to a planting, and coarse, leathery textures, like that of *Rodgersia podophylla*, make impact among finer foliage.

Since hard surfaces tend to be dominant in small gardens, the challenge is to make them more inviting. Woolly *Thymus lanuginosus* will soften hard paving slabs, the rhythmical patterns made by *Hedera helix* "Sagittifolia Variegata" clinging to brick or concrete

walls adding textured charm, and hummocks of grassy thrift alleviate the gritty harshness of gravel.

a tactile group (1)

The smooth, kid-leather quality of senecio foliage makes this evergeen silver-gray shrub pleasing to the touch; sunshine-yellow daisies appear in summer among its downy and felted leaves. Lamb's ears (*Stachys byzantina*), also silvery and sun-loving, has thicker, furry leaves which are far less refined; woolly flower spikes appear in summer. The rounded shapes of santolina, with their soft green mounds and yellow button flowers, simply invite you to touch them.

a group for sun (2)
Reducing color contrast makes textural differences more noticeable. The small pampas grass (*Cortaderia selloana* "Pumila") produces fluffy white plumes in

large, heart-shaped leaves of brunnera, with its bright creamy-white variegation; this low, ground-covering plant has sprays of bright blue flowers in spring. The rounded, glossy leaves of bergenias are an excellent evergreen accompaniment. Fringing these plants, at the front, is a densely arching mass of narrow grassy-leaved hakonechloa, whose yellow-variegated blades gradually turn copper as the season moves into fall.

4 **Parthenocissus henryana** *with* **Anthemis punctata** *subsp.* **cupaniana.**

5 **Sempervivum** *species.*

summer from a tangle of foliage against which the blue thistle flowers of eryngium, their jagged basal leaves marked with white veining, look dramatic. They rise from a footing of silver, filigree-fine mounding artemisia.

a shade-loving group (3)
Ferns make ideal plants for shaded areas, providing bright green, richly pinnate foliage which has a lacy texture. The fronds of the buckler fern (*Dryopteris*) unfurl in spring, when it contrasts superbly with the

a wall group (4)
Any wall can be textured with the self-clinging hardy vine (*Parthenocissus*), which has velvety, deep green foliage marked with silver-white veining; in fall, the whole wall will turn crimson. Beneath this a fringe of silvery anthemis with its finely cut feathery foliage is the perfect complement. The picture will be enlivened by masses of white daisy flowers which cover the plant in early summer and again after clipping. Both plants like well-drained soil and an open position.

a container group (5)
There is nothing more textural than house leeks (*Sempervivum*) and there are so many to choose from that it is pointless to suggest one form. You may like species with a webbing of fine hairs, or large, reddish species, or compact green ones. All are hard to the touch and very prettily patterned. Some people collect them in all their variety and grow them in flat trays on poor, free-draining soil. Alternatively, they look very good in sink gardens.

bold accents

Some plants have an insistent presence and choosing plants for their sculptural or dramatic potential can make a small space memorable.

delicately veined petals. The leaves of the agapanthus are broad, strap-like, and fleshily green; its rounded flowerheads are carried on tall stems from mid- to late summer. All these plants like sunny conditions.

1 Macleaya cordata *"Flamingo"* with Geranium x magnificum *and* Agapanthus *Headbourne Hybrids.*

2 Acanthus spinosus *with* Penstemon *"Andenken an Friedrich Hahn" and* Liatris spicata *"Floristan White."*

3 Crocosmia *"Lucifer"* with Iris pallida *"Argenteovariegata."*

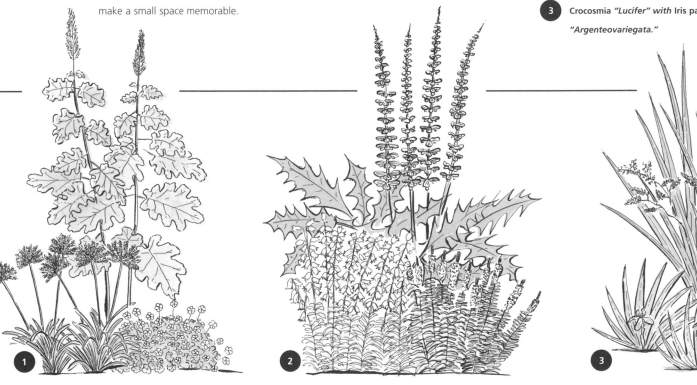

a bold, large-leaved group (1)

The plume poppy (*Macleaya cordata*) reaches 8 feet (2.5 meters) in a good year and its rounded pewter-gray leaves are sometimes 1 foot (30cm) long, so it cannot fail to dominate; its pinkish fluffy flower panicles are carried on leafy spikes in late summer. It rarely needs staking. With this group a soft green mound of *Geranium x magnificum*, about 2 feet (60cm) in diameter, has large leaves which redden in fall. It flowers earlier in summer, its blue blooms with

a vertical group (2)

The acanthus, an imposing plant whose prickly flower spikes need no support, grows about 5 feet (1.5 meters) high. With it a mass of tender penstemon blooms through the summer; the vertical flowers spikes, heavy with tubular bells. Liatris,another vertically formed perennial produces flowers which open from the tip down; they look like fluffy candles. Its slim foliage is willow-like. This mid- to late summer flowering group prefers a sunny, well-drained site.

spiky foliage group (3)

The effectiveness of this summer-flowering planting relies on just two plants. The sword-like crocosmia grows to a height of over 3 feet (1 meter), with no need of staking, except in heavy storms. In front is a group of iris, distinctive for their two-dimensional flat fans into which the leaves slot. The delicately variegated leaves are dove gray-green, with a thick white streak along one side which draws attention to their form.

exotic accents

The definition of "exotic" depends on where you are, but a general understanding is that it includes plants with a dramatic presence which originate in hot, dry areas of the world or those that are loosely described as subtropical. In temperate climates these plants will survive outdoors in the microclimates of tiny enclosed

yucca that carries fragrant panicles of white flowers in early summer. The ginger lily (*Alpinia*) has a clump of broad, lance-shaped, attractively ribbed leaves from which spikes of orange and yellow flowers emerge in late summer. All need sun and a well-drained soil.

1 **Chamaerops humilis** *with* **Yucca whipplei** *and* **Hedychium coccineum.**

2 **Eccremocarpus scaber** *with* **Lapageria rosea.**

3 **Begonia** *tuberosa* **"Fortune Peach Shades."**

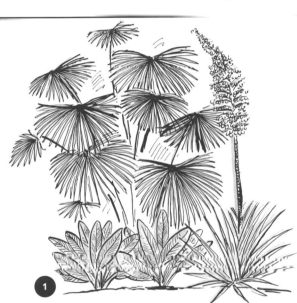

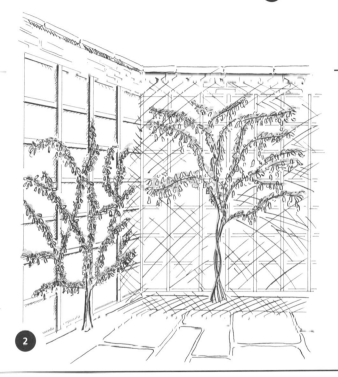

spaces or in areas small enough for each plant to be individually cared for by wrapping in winter and mulching the ground thickly to give protection.

a subtropical look (1)

These plants suggest the richness of exotic foliage without necessarily being subtropical. The dwarf half-hardy fan palm has leaves that can be 3 feet (1 meter) across which form rigidly concertina-ed fan patterns. Growing beside it, also 5 feet (1.5 meters) high, is a

exotic climbers (2)

The Chilean glory flower (*Eccremocarpus scaber*) is an evergreen, fast-growing climber which will thrive in any soil, but you may have to treat it as an annual; it will grow 6 feet (1.8 meters) in each season. Sprays of orange-red, narrowly tubular flowers are followed by inflated seedpods. Close by, on a lightly shaded wall, grows the Chilean bellflower (*Lapageria rosea*), a woody twining plant which grows to 15 feet (5 meters); it needs to be cut back in early spring. The

leaves are oblong and the flowers fleshy and pendent, over 3 inches (8cm) long. Well-drained but moisture-retaining soil is important for both plants.

Exotic containers (3)

There can be no more exotic plants for containers than tuberous begonias. The large-flowered *B. tuberosa* will flower throughout the summer, its flowers as big as 6 inches (15cm) across; depending on the form, they may be single or double and many are bi-colored.

mainstay (1)

This viburnum is a rounded shrub with simple, elliptical leaves with a distinctive pattern of veining. Behind it the tall, erect mahonia has prickly, pinnate foliage and fragrant yellow flower racemes in winter. When the plant is young, prune the terminal clusters after flowering to encourage branching. Beneath them grows the semi-evergreen lonicera, a low, wide

1. **Viburnum davidii** *with* **Mahonia "Winter Sun'"** *and* **Lonicera pileata.**

2. *The rich diversity of ivy foliage includes:* **a. Hedera helix** *"Oro di Bogliasco"* **b. H. helix** *"Pedata"* **c. H. colchica** *"Dentata"* **d. H. helix** *"Parsley Crested"* **e. H. helix** *"Merion Beauty."*

3. **Camellia x williamsii** *"Donation."*

evergreen

Invaluable evergreen forms are as steadfast as masonry. They can act as tapestries, like many wall shrubs, such as ceanothus or escallonia, they may blanket a wall, as do the invaluable self-clinging ivies, they can form the sculpture of a garden, like the dramatic fatsias, solid rounded hebes, or magnificent cultivars of mahonia, and they can even repel invaders—there is nothing so damaging as the spiked *Berberis julianae*.

spreader whose tiny, bright green leaves are refreshing against the dark greens of mahonia and viburnum.

climbing evergreens (2)

Few other self-clinging evergreen climbers are as compact and manageable as ivies. For full shade the small-leaved *Hedera helix* "Oro di Bogliasco" (syn. "Goldheart") cannot be surpassed. There are also large-leaved forms of the woody climbers *H. canariensis* and *H. colchica*, among which are some with variegated

and interestingly shaped leaves. In general, the smaller cultivars of *H. helix* are most suitable for small gardens.

container evergreen (3)

Using ericaceous compost means that acid-loving plants can be grown. This camellia is a dense evergreen shrub which will grow in shade or semi-shade. Camellias have both white-, pink- and red-flowered forms; this hardy cultivar has ice-cream pink blooms. Never place the shrub in a position where it receives morning sun.

plants for special purposes

These lists represent a personal choice of plants suitable for particular design purposes in small spaces. There will usually be many others to fulfill your requirements, however. Always check the ultimate dimensions of any plant and its needs as regards soil, light, and moisture to be sure it will suit your garden situation.

*   **acid soil**

c   **conifer**

h   **herbaceous**

sh **shrub**

g   **ornamental grasses**

cl **climber**

plants to create vertical form

Acanthus spinosus h

Asphodeline h

Bamboos (some)

Cimicifuga (some) h

Delphinium h

Digitalis h

Eremurus robustus h

Hedera helix "Erecta" sh

Juniperus communis "Hibernica" c

Juniperus scopulorum "Skyrocket" c

Kniphofia h

Lobelia (some) h

Lupinus h

Lythrum h

Rosmarinus officinalis "Miss
    Jessopp's Upright" sh

Sidalcea h

Taxus baccata "Fastigiata" c

Verbascum h

Veronica (some) h

plants with wide-spreading form or flat flowerheads

Abies procera "Glauca Prostrata" c

Acer (some) sh

Achillea h

Anaphalis margaritacea h

Cotoneaster horizontalis sh

Cornus controversa "Variegata" sh

Dianthus barbatus h

Hosta (layered foliage) h

Heuchera (layered foliage) h

Hydrangea macrophylla sh

Juniperus sabina "Tamariscifolia" c

Lonicera pileata sh

Prunus laurocerasus "Zabeliana" sh

Viburnum sargentii "Onondaga" sh

plants to create a rounded mass

Artemisia alba "Canescens" h

Anthemis punctata subsp.
    cupaniana h

Buxus microphylla "Green Pillow" sh

Cistus x hybridus sh

Choisya ternata sh

Hebe sh

Hypericum "Hidcote" sh

Pinus mugo "Winter Gold" c

Potentilla (some) sh

Santolina chamaecyparissus sh

Viburnum davidii sh

plants with a weeping form

Acer palmatum var. dissectum sh

Buddleja alternifolia (grown as a
    standard) sh

Cotoneaster salicifolius "Pendulus"
    (grafted as a standard) sh

Cedrus deodara "Aurea" c

Dicentra spectabilis h

Fuchsia h

Gentiana asclepiadea* h

Polygonatum x hybridum h

Tsuga canadensis "Bennett" c

Wisteria (grown as a
    standard) sh

spiked and grassy forms

Agapanthus h

Bamboos

Cordyline sh

Cortaderia selloana "Pumila" g

Crocosmia h

Gladiolus communis h

Grasses (ornamental) g

Hemerocallis h

Iris (some) h

Kniphofia h

Libertia h

Liriope h

Phormium sh

Sisyrinchium striatum h

Yucca sh

**plants with feathery
flowers or foliage**

Tamarix   sh
Artemisia   h
Astilbe   h
Cortaderia   g
Ferns
Foeniculum vulgare   h
Gypsophila   h
Grasses   g
Nepeta   h
Nigella damascena   h
Perovskia   h
Solidago   h
Thalictrum   h

large-leaved plants

Bergenia   h
Brunnera macrophylla   h
Canna   h
Ensete ventricosum   sh
Fatsia japonica
Ferns
Galax urceolata*   h
Hosta   h
Ligularia (some)   h
Macleaya cordata   h
Melianthus major   h
Phyllostachys bambusoides
Rheum palmatum   h
Ricinus communis   h
Rodgersia   h
Rumex sanguineus   h
Veratrum   h
Zantedeschia aethiopica
   "Crowborough"   h

**herbaceous plants with
an eye-catching habit**

Agapanthus
Allium (some)
Anthericum liliago
Camassia leichtlinii
Cleome hasslieriana
Crinum
Dicentra
Dierama pulcherrimum
Erythronium (some)
Fritillaria (some)
Galtonia viridiflora
Hedychium gardnerianum
Lilium (some)
Nectaroscordum siculum
Nicotiana langsdorfii
Schizostylis coccinea
Trillium*
Thalictrum delavayi
Grasses and ferns (some)

**plants for topiary
and hedging**

Artemisia abrotanum   sh
Azara microphylla   sh
Buxus (some)   sh
Carpinus   sh
Corylus   sh
Euonymus   sh
Fagus   sh
Hedera   sh
Ilex   sh
Juniperus   c
Laurus nobilis   sh
Lavandula   sh

Ligustrum   sh
Lonicera nitida   sh
Osmanthus x burkwoodii   sh
Pyracantha   sh
Santolina   sh
Taxus   c
Teucrium chamaedrys   sh
Thuja   c

wall shrubs and climbers

Campsis x tagliabuana "Madame
   Galen"   cl
Ceanothus (some)   sh
Chaenomeles (some)   sh
Clematis (some)   cl
Euonymus fortunei "Silver Queen"   sh
Escallonia (some)   sh
Hedera helix (some)   cl
Itea ilicifolia   sh
Jasminum officinale "Affine"   cl
Lapageria rosea   cl
Lonicera japonica "Aureoreticulata"   cl
Parthenocissus henryana   cl
Parthenocissus quinquefolia   cl
Passiflora (some)   cl
Pyracantha (some)   sh
Solanum crispum "Glasnevin"   cl
Solanum jasminoides   cl
Trachelospermum jasminoides   cl
Vitis vinifera "Purpurea"   cl
Wisteria (some)   cl

very small shrubs

Acer palmatum (slow-growing)
Berberis candidula
Cistus x dansereaui "Decumbens"

Conifers (slow growing)   c
Convolvulus cneorum
Cotoneaster (some)
Daphne (some)
Euonymus fortunei
Fuchsia (some)
Gaultheria shallon*
Genista lydia
x Halimiocistus sahucii
Hebe (some)
Helianthemum (some)
Hypericum x moserianum
Hyssopus officinalis
Lavandula (some)
Potentilla (some)
Rhododendron* (some)
Rosa (patio)
Rosmarinus officinalis Prostratus
   Group
Ruta graveolens
Salix (some)
Salvia officinalis
Santolina (some)
Sarcococca
Skimmia* (some)

index

Page numbers in *italic* refer to illustrations.
Plant hardiness zones are given in [ ]
after each entry; [A] indicates annual.

acknowledgments

The author and publishers would like to acknowledge the memory of John Kelly whose initial idea was the inspiration for this book.

author's acknowledgments

In gratefully acknowledging the team work behind this book, I must say that it puts a whole new light on "Ladies who Lunch." The group who worked so well together include Carole McGlynn, the editor, whose exceptional thoroughness, tact, and concern to retain my "voice" made her phone calls most welcome. I greatly appreciate the creative vision of Francoise Deitrich, the art editor, who set a style I felt completely at one with, and Nathalie Hennequin, her highly creative "trusty," who worked with the same patience. I also value the role of Nadine Bazar for her picture research as she persistently trawled for specials. Rachel Gibson turned the layout of the final part of the book into a masterly balance between visuals and text. Jane O'Shea, who commissioned the book, followed its progress with clear-sighted encouragement at all times. Altogether this team work has been a very happy experience.

Marianne Majerus took some remarkable photographs for this book and I am very appreciative of Alison Barratt's mood-setting abstract color illustrations. Julia Brett carried out thorough and imaginative research as well as supporting me throughout with her good-humored wit. Nancy Alderson undertook typing for me when the pressure grew and Freya Billington showed her aesthetic talents when I needed an ear. There are too many designer colleagues to mention here, but friends like Barbara Hunt, Cleve West, Johnny Woodford, George Carter, Paul Cooper, and Victor Shanley deserve an individual mention. And as regards my husband, who is so supportive both practically and creatively, I feel quite simply that without him there would be no book.

Art editor: Françoise Dietrich

Project editor: Carole McGlynn

Designers: Rachel Gibson, Nathalie Hennequin

Editorial assistant: Katherine Seely

Picture research: Nadine Bazar

Production manager: Candida Lane

Illustrations (Parts 1, 2 and 3) by Alison Barratt; (Part 5) by Michael Hill

The publisher thanks the photographers and organizations for their kind permission to reproduce the following photographs in this book:

2–3 Beatrice Pichon-Clarisse; 4 Guy Bouchet; 6 far left Jill Billington/designer Victor Shanley; 6 left designer Jill Billington; 6 center Marianne Majerus/Dominique Lubar, for IPL Interiors; 6 right Marianne Majerus/designer Johnathan Baillie; 6 far right Beatrice Pichon-Clarisse/designer Sylvie Devinat; 7 Marianne Majerus/designer Paul Cooper; 8 Marianne Majerus/Catherine Geraghty; 9 left Marie Claire Maison/Gilles de Chabaneix/Marie Kalt; 9 center Christian Sarramon/C Decarpenterie; 9 right Garden Picture Library/Gary Rogers; 10 left Marianne Majerus/Catherine Geraghty; 10 right Elizabeth Whiting & Associates/Jerry Harpur/Michael Love; 11 Agence Top/Pascal Chevallier/designer Jacques Grange; 12 Marianne Majerus/Architect Rick Mather; 13 left Christine Ternynck; 13 right Jerry Harpur/designer Stephen Brady, San Fransisco; 14 above Beatrice Pichon-Clarisse/designers Camille Muller and H Peuvergne; 14 below Marianne Majerus/Jane Short; 15 Garden Picture Library/Ron Sutherland/designer Anthony Paul; 16 left Marianne Majerus/designers Jill Billington with Anne and Roger Harrabin; 16 right MichÈle Lamontagne; 17 Inside/Claire De Virieu/designer Loup de Viane; 18 left Marianne Majerus/designer Lucy Gent/Bernadette & John Thompson; 18 right Jill Billington; 19 Beatrice Pichon-Clarisse/designer Sylvie Devinat; 20 left Clive Nichols/Christian Wright, San Francisco; 20 right Marianne Majerus/designer Christopher Masson; 21 Jerry Harpur/designer Robert Watson, Christchurch, New Zealand; 22 Jerry Harpur/designer Sonny Garcia, San Fransisco; 23 left John Glover/designer Barbara Hunt; 23 right Jerry Harpur/designer Jason Payne, London; 24 The Interior Archive/Peter Woloszynski; 25 left Marianne Majerus/designer Thomasina Tarling; 25 right Jerry Harpur/designer Andrew Weaving, London; 26 above Marianne Majerus/Dominique Lubar, for IPL Interiors; 26 below Camera Press; 27 Jerry Harpur/designer Tim Vaughan, London; 28 John Glover/designer Barbara Hunt; 29 left S&O Mathews/Beth Chatto Gardens; 29 right Inside/Jean-Pierre Godeaut; 30 Marianne Majerus/Carol Lee; 31 left Jill Billington; 31 right Marianne Majerus/David French; 32 Marianne Majerus/Rose Cooper; 33 above Marianne Majerus/designer Kim Whatmore/contractor Nick Ryan; 33 below S&O Mathews/Sir H Hillier Gardens; 34 S&O Mathews/Longhatch, Hampshire; 35 MichÈle Lamontagne; 36 Marianne Majerus/Architect Rick Mather; 37 above Marianne Majerus/Rose Cooper; 37 below Marianne Majerus/Leslie Sayers; 38 left Beatrice Pichon-Clarisse; 38 right Jerry Harpur/designer Patricia Dymond, London; 39 Marianne Majerus; 40 Jill Billington/designer Victor Shanley; 41 Marianne Majerus/Sandy and Fiona MacLennan; 42 Marianne Majerus/designer Lucy Gent/Bernadette & John Thompson; 43 left MichÈle Lamontagne; 43 right Marianne Majerus/Rose Cooper; 44 left Jerry Harpur/designer Keeyla Meadows, San Fransisco; 44 right Jerry Harpur/designer Gunilla Pickard, Fanners Green, Essex; 45 Derek St Romaine/designers Hiroshi Nanamori and Andrew Butcher; 46 left Jerry Harpur/designer Sonny Garcia, San Fransisco; 46 right Jerry Harpur/designers Peter Wooster and Gary Keim, Connecticut; 47 Marianne Majerus/designer Pamela Johnson; 48 Marianne Majerus/Mrs Adamsí garden designed by Anthony Noel; 49 left Noel Kavanagh; 49 right Marianne Majerus/Jane Short; 50 Clive Nichols; 51 above Inside/Jerome Darblay; 51 below MichÈle Lamontagne/designer Sonny Garcia; 52 above Garden Picture Library/Ron Sutherland/designer Anthony Paul; 52 below Marianne Majerus/Kathy Lynam; 53 Marianne Majerus/David French; 54 Marianne Majerus/designer Christopher Masson; 55 John Glover; 56 Jill Billington; 57 Noel Kavanagh; 58 S&O Mathews/Old Barn Close, Hampshire; 59 Marianne Majerus/David French; 60 Marianne Majerus; 61 Jerry Harpur/designer Robert Chittock, Seattle; 62 left Marianne Majerus; 62 right Marianne Majerus/designers Jill Billington with Anne and Roger Harrabin; 63 Marianne Majerus; 64 Beatrice Pichon-Clarisse; 65 Marianne Majerus/designer Johnathan Baillie; 66 left Christine Ternynck/Menken; 66 right Jerry Harpur/designer Jean Goldberry; 67 left Marianne Majerus/designer Christopher Masson/Professor Ian Macdonald and Stanley Hamilton; 67 right Marianne Majerus/Architect Rick Mather; 68 far left Marianne Majerus/designers Jill Billington with Anne and Roger Harrabin; 68 left Marianne Majerus/David Altaras; 68 center Beatrice Pichon-Clarisse/tromp l'oeuil by Christin Merle; 68 right Marianne Majerus/Rose Cooper; 68 far right Jerry Harpur/designer Raymond Hudson, Johannesburg; 69 Vogue Living/John Hollingshead; 70 Vogue Living/Chris Chen; 71 left Marianne Majerus/designers Jill Billington with Anne and Roger Harrabin; 71 right Inside/Claire de Virieu; 72 left Marianne Majerus/Mrs Adamsí garden designed by Anthony Noel; 72 right Christian Sarramon; 73 Marie Claire Maison/Laurent Teisseire/Catherine Ardouin; 74 Christine Ternynck/Menken; 75 left John Glover/designer Barbara Hunt; 75 right Christian Sarramon/Zoy di Lorenzo; 76 above Beatrice Pichon-Clarisse; 76 below Jerry Harpur/designer Sonny Garcia, San Fransisco; 77 Jerry Harpur/Martin Sacks, London; 78 above left Marianne Majerus/Architect Rick Mather; 78 below left Clive Nichols/Turn End Garden, Bucks; 78 below right Marianne Majerus/John Sarbutt; 79 Outdoor Lighting Company/Hugh Palmer; 80 Jill Billington; 81 above left MichÈle Lamontagne/designer Chris Rosmini; 81 above center Garden Picture Library/Ron Sutherland/design by Duane Paul Design Team; 81 right Garden Picture Library/Steven Wooster/designer Anthony Paul; 82 left Marianne Majerus/mural designed by Francis Hamel-Cooke; 82 right Marianne Majerus/David Altaras; 83 left Marianne Majerus/designer George Carter; 83 right Jerry Harpur/designer Raymond Hudson, Johannesburg; 84 left Jerry Harpur/designer Ron Simple, Philadelphia; 84 right Jerry Harpur/designer Patrick Presto, San Francisco; 85 Marianne Majerus/Rose Cooper; 86 left Beatrice Pichon-Clarisse/trompe l'oeil by Christian Merle; 86 right MichÈle Lamontagne; 87 © 1997 Harel; 88 far left Marianne Majerus/designer Patrick Rampton/contractor Nick Ryan; 88 left Derek St Romaine/designer Cleve West; 88 center Marianne Majerus/designer George Carter, Fulcher Tate; 88 right Marianne Majerus/John Sarbutt; 88 far right Derek St Romaine/Johnny Woodford; 89 Christian Sarramon; 91 above left Christine Ternynck/Menken; 91 above right Beatrice Pichon-Clarisse; 91 center Marianne Majerus/designer Patrick Rampton/contractor Nick Ryan; 91 below Jerry Harpur/designer Keeyla Meadows, San Fransisco; 92 above Marianne Majerus/Rose Cooper; 92 below Noel Kavanagh; 93 Inside/Claire de Virieu/designer Camille Muller; 94 Clive Nichols/designer Keeyla Meadows; 95 left Clive Nichols/designer Sonny Garcia; 95 right Marianne Majerus/David French; 96–97 Marianne Majerus/designer Patrick Rampton/contractor Nick Ryan; 99 above Undine Prohl/Enrique Albin, Albin Vasconce los Elizondo Architects; 99 center left Derek St Romaine/Johnny Woodford; 99 center S&O Mathews/Pashley Manor; 99 center right Marianne Majerus/designer Paul Cooper; 99 below Christine Ternynck/designer E d'Avdew; 100 above left Derek St Romaine/designers Hiroshi Nanamori and Andrew Butcher; 100 above right Beatrice Pichon-Clarisse/designer Sylvie Devinat; 100 below left Jill Billington; 101 Vogue Living/Trevor Fox; 102 above Garden Picture Library/Ron Sutherland; 102 below Camera Press; 103 MichÈle Lamontagne/designer Camille Muller; 104–105 Derek St Romaine/designer Cleve West; 107 above left Christine Ternynck; 107 above right Marianne Majerus/designer George Carter, Fulcher Tate; 107 center Marianne Majerus; 107 below Marianne Majerus/Mrs Adamsí garden designed by Anthony Noel; 108 Dennis Krukowski/designer Michael Formica Inc.; 109 above Christine Ternynck; 109 below Henk Dijkman; 110–111 above Marianne Majerus/designer George Carter, Fulcher Tate; 113 above Marianne Majerus/John Sarbutt; 113 center Christian Sarramon; 113 below Marianne Majerus/Carol Lee; 114 Marianne Majerus/designer Johnathan Baillie; 115 left Jerry Harpur/designer Jason Payne, London; 115 center Marianne Majerus/John Samuel; 115 right John Kelly; 116–117 Marianne Majerus/John Sarbutt; 119 above left Christian Sarramon; 119 above right Marianne Majerus/Architect Rick Mather; 119 center Marianne Majerus/designer Lucy Gent/Bernadette & John Thompson; 119 below Marianne Majerus/designer Jonathon Baillie; 120 left Marianne Majerus/designer Christopher Masson; 120 right Christian Sarramon; 121 left MichÈle Lamontagne/designer Harry Gullickson; 121 right Christian Sarramon; 122–123 Marianne Majerus/Architect Rick Mather; 125 above left Derek St Romaine/designer Johnny Woodford; 125 above right Marianne Majerus/designers Jill Billington with Anne and Roger Harrabin; 125 center Inside/Claire de Virieu/designer Madison Cox; 125 below Garden Picture Library/Ron Sutherland/Duane Paul Design Team; 126 Dennis Krukowski/designer Madison Cox/Lexington Gardens, New York City; 127 above Belle Magazine/Simon Kenny; 127 below Christian Sarramon; 128–129 Derek St Romaine/Johnny Woodford; 130 left S&O Mathews/Sir H Hillier Gardens; 130 center & far right John Glover; 130 right Andrew Lawson; 131 S&O Mathews/Morton Manor; 132 left & center S&O Mathews; 132 right John Glover; 133 left John Glover; 133 right Andrew Lawson; 134 left Clive Nichols; 134 right Garden Picture Library/John Glover; 135 left Andrew Lawson; 135 right Neil Campbell-Sharp; 136 left Clive Nichols; 136 right Neil Campbell-Sharp; 137 left A–Z Botanical/Geoff Kidd; 137 right John Glover; 138 left Garden Picture Library/Sunniva Harte; 138 center Andrew Lawson; 138 right S&O Mathews; 139 Andrew Lawson; 140 left A–Z Botanical/A Young; 140 right Andrew Lawson; 141 left John Glover; 141 right Andrew Lawson; 142 left John Glover; 142 right S&O Mathews; 143 John Glover; 144 left John Glover; 144 right S&O Mathews; 145 left Andrew Lawson; 145 center Clive Nichols; 145 right John Glover; 146 left Clive Nichols; 146 right Garden Picture Library/J S Sira; 147 left S&O Mathews; 147 right Andrew Lawson; 148–149 Andrew Lawson; 150 left S&O Mathews/53 Ladywood, Eastleigh; 150 right Andrew Lawson; 151 left A–Z Botanical; 151 center John Glover; 151 right Eric Crichton; 152 left Clive Nichols; 152 right John Glover.